New Perspectives on Racial
Identity Development

New Perspectives on Racial Identity Development

A Theoretical and Practical Anthology

EDITED BY

*Charmaine L. Wijeyesinghe and
Bailey W. Jackson III*

New York University Press

NEW YORK AND LONDON

NEW YORK UNIVERSITY PRESS
New York and London

Library of Congress Cataloging-in-Publication Data
New perspectives on racial identity development : a theoretical
and practical anthology / edited by Charmaine L. Wijeyesinghe
and Bailey W. Jackson III.
p. cm.
ISBN 0-8147-9342-8 (cloth : alk. paper) —
ISBN 0-8147-9343-6 (pbk. : alk. paper)
1. Ethnicity. 2. Race awareness. 3. Identity (Psychology) 4. Race
awareness—United States. I. Wijeyesinghe, Charmaine L.
II. Jackson, Bailey W. III. Title.
GN495.6 .N49 2001
305.8—dc21   00-011193

New York University Press books are printed on acid-free paper,
and their binding materials are chosen for strength and durability.

Manufactured in the United States of America
10 9 8 7 6 5 4 3 2 1

This book is dedicated to those theorists, researchers, and practitioners who provided the foundations for the modern study of racial identity development. We also recognize and appreciate the work of those who continue to deepen and broaden our understanding of racial identity development.

Contents

Acknowledgments

We wish to acknowledge the many people who have helped us develop, write, and edit this publication. First, we thank the contributors who have shared their time, knowledge, and inspiration with us. They were our partners in all the phases of this project from the development of the initial proposal to the submission of the final manuscript. We also thank the people whose support and encouragement allowed the authors to produce the chapters that appear in this volume.

During the early development of the prospectus and proposal for this book, we sought several consultations from our friend and colleague, Maurianne Adams. Her willingness to share her perspectives helped us to grow as editors. Niko Pfund of New York University Press provided much initial guidance and enthusiasm from a publisher's perspective on early drafts of the prospectus and proposal. In addition, Nancy Kaminski used her immense organizational skills to coordinate the final distribution of material with publishers.

As the manuscript developed and chapters came flooding in, we relied heavily on the professional skills and personal support of Mary McClintock. Her expertise in copy editing, proofreading, and formatting were invaluable. In addition, we thank Mary for coordinating communication between us and the contributors and managing the continuous flow of chapters to and from the editors and authors.

We are grateful to Jennifer Hammer, our editor at New York University Press. In addition to providing editorial guidance and expertise, her flexibility and commitment to this project gave us the time and support needed to develop this book to its fullest potential.

We wish to thank those people in our own lives who supported us throughout the duration of this project. For their support and encouragement, Bailey Jackson acknowledges Rita Hardiman-Jackson, Amber and Maya. Charmaine Wijeyesinghe acknowledges Christian

Lietzau, Diane Goodman, Mary Ellen Sailer, Katja Hahn D'Errico, James Bonilla, and Ann-Margaret Foley.

Lastly, we acknowledge our process and role as coeditors. Our relationship brought together a diversity of styles, backgrounds, and perspectives in what we hope is an important contribution to the field of racial identity theory. This diversity enriched both our discussions and the quality of the book.

Figures and Tables

New Perspectives on Racial Identity Development

Introduction

Charmaine L. Wijeyesinghe and
Bailey W. Jackson III

Racial identity development has become a central theme in the study of race and race relations. From initial theories inspired by the experience of African Americans during the most recent civil rights movement, the study of racial identity development has expanded to encompass the experiences of other racial groups, including Whites, Asian Americans, Native Americans, Latinos, and people with a multiple racial heritage.

The theoretical foundations of this volume stem from several works on racial identity development (Thomas 1971; Cross 1971; Jackson 1976; Hardiman 1982; Helms 1984) that emerged in the 1960s, 1970s, and 1980s. Inherent in these models were a number of assumptions. For example, the models indicate that an individual's identification with a larger racial group and aspects of that group's culture affected his or her racial identity development. Racism was presumed to influence the racial identity development of those targeted by racism (Blacks, Latinos, Native Americans, and Asians) as well as those who benefit from it (Whites). The development of racial identity has been described as a dynamic, developmental process that occurs over the lifetime of the individual.

A number of years have passed since the majority of these original theories appeared, during which we have seen profound changes in society, social movements, and our perspectives of race, racism, and racial groups. For example, the discussion of the validity of the socially constructed nature of race and racial groups has raised the question of what constitutes race and membership in racial groups. As a result, the language used to identify or describe groups of people has increasingly shifted from words based on racial group membership, such as Black and Latino, to words based on ethnic affiliation, such as African American, Cape Verdean, Chicano, and Mestizos.

This book updates foundational theories of Black, White, and Asian racial identity development. It also presents more recent models of racial identity development in Latinos, Native Americans, and Multiracial people that contribute to the emerging literature on these populations. Specific chapters discuss the use of racial identity development theory in the fields of counseling and conflict resolution and the implications of extrapolating principles drawn from specific racial and ethnic identity models to other racial and social groups. Taken as a whole, the volume identifies and discusses key issues that are likely to affect our understanding of racial identity in the twenty-first century.

This text reflects our belief that the understanding of racial identity development is constantly evolving in response to changing social dynamics, ongoing research, and the fluidity of our understanding of both race and the experience of racial groups in the United States. The process of writing and editing this book was like "taking a snapshot of a moving picture." In this sense, the book provides a view of the particular moment in the ever-changing social context related to race and racial identity in the United States. This book joins the works of Cross (1991), Helms (1993), Salett and Koslow (1994), Espiritu (1992), Root (1992), and others in the growing body of literature on racial identity and racial identity development. The analysis and debate this and other volumes evoke offer opportunities for ongoing refinement and expansion of racial identity development models, as well as assessment of beliefs that have been part of the field for decades.

The diversity of opinions and perspectives in this volume is one of its greatest strengths. For example, the first six chapters, which address racial identity development across various racial populations, do not represent a single approach to nor a unified definition of racial identity. Instead, the authors present context-specific models that acknowledge the history and experiences of different racial groups in the United States. The analysis and information presented in these chapters invite the reader to consider such core questions as:

- How are models of racial identity development influenced by the dominant social consciousness about race and racism at a given period of time?

- Do varying definitions of core concepts such as race enhance or confuse the elaboration of racial identity development theory? To what extent do we need commonly held definitions which are relevant from model to model, study to study?
- What are the ways in which we understand or define racial group membership? Does a person's racial group membership dictate their racial identity? How much is racial identity determined by lineage, by imposed social constructions of race at a given moment in time, or by a name assumed by individuals through their own process of selection?
- Can the field of racial identity development accommodate models that reflect diversity in underlying structure and assumptions? What are the strengths and limitations of each kind of paradigm? What are the boundaries of racial identity development theory? Where are the limits to what it can explain?
- How does racial identity development inform the process of identity development for other social groups, such as those based on gender, class, or sexual orientation?
- To what extent can the experiences of one racial group, such as Blacks, be used to shed light on those of other racial groups, such as Latinos or Asians?

Questions such as these are implicitly and explicitly posed and discussed throughout the book. Taken together, the authors' perspectives offer a rich dialogue about issues that have often been overlooked in previous discussions about racial identity development. In addition, by identifying future issues related to the topic, the book lays the foundation for an exciting research agenda.

While presenting diverse perspectives, the chapters in this book are bound together by similar goals. Contributors to each chapter build a context for the specific theories, models, or interventions that they propose. In some chapters, this context reflects a personal, introspective presentation. In others, the supporting framework is grounded in analysis of the literature or of survey research. Each author then presents a functional model or analysis, based on his or her understanding of the current state or application of racial identity development theory. Each chapter closes with a discussion of the issues, challenges, and possibilities that lie ahead.

The first six essays in the book address racial identity development in a range of racial populations: Black, Latino/a, Asian, American Indian, White, and Multiracial.

In chapter 1, Bailey W. Jackson III elaborates on the context and thinking that went into the development of his original Black Identity Development (BID) model. Specifically, he discusses how race and ethnicity affected the development of this theory, as well as how the current meaning and usage of these terms are influencing his ongoing thinking about Black identity development. He then presents an enhanced version of his model which incorporates social dynamics of the past two decades. Following the description of his updated model, Jackson suggests the changes we might see during its next major evolution.

In chapter 2, Bernardo M. Ferdman and Plácida Gallegos provide a detailed analysis of the ways in which the imposed racial system used in the United States results in racial categories and constructs that do not reflect or accommodate diverse Latino perspectives or experiences. Ferdman and Gallegos cite census data, survey research, and examples of personal narrative to create a context for a new paradigm for understanding Latino identity. This model is based on what they describe as "orientations" or responses that Latinos make in relation to the U.S. racial system. The chapter concludes with several suggestions for the further testing and development of this model.

Jean Kim presents her foundational model of Asian American identity development in chapter 3. In setting the context for this framework, she discusses the impact of Asian cultural traits, racial dynamics, and racism directed at Asians in the United States on Asian American racial identity formation. Kim's five-stage model of Asian American Identity Development (AAID) is outlined and illustrated through quotations from various Asian American individuals. Her chapter concludes with a discussion of how evolving social dynamics, such as an increasing emphasis on ethnic rather than racial identity among Asian Americans, create opportunities for future research and possible revision of her original model.

In the following chapter, Perry G. Horse examines the subject of racial identity in a population that has been largely overlooked in the literature: American Indians. He discusses the influence of language, culture, tribal perspectives and historical consciousness, and U.S. notions of race on American Indian identity, and the ability to conceive models of racial identity development for American Indians. Horse presents a paradigm of Indian individual and group consciousness based on five psychosocial influences. His chapter concludes with a discussion of the impact of issues such as Indian political resurgence and cultural transmission on Indian identity in the future.

In chapter 5, Rita Hardiman provides new insight into the background and assumptions that guided the development of her original model of White identity development, which was the first of its kind in the field of racial identity development. She compares her model with the subsequent work on White identity by Helms, and provides a critique of the strengths and weaknesses of both. The chapter includes an overview of some of the major perspectives that Hardiman believes are emerging from the area of White studies to shape our understanding of Whiteness and White identity. She considers the impact these perspectives might have on future White identity development models.

In chapter 6, Charmaine L. Wijeyesinghe explores how early research on Multiracial people as well as models of Black and White racial identity development shape current perspectives on Multiracial identity. She reviews and critiques two prominent models of Multiracial identity development, and then presents her Factor Model of Multiracial Identity. In discussing this model, Wijeyesinghe evaluates how factors such as physical appearance, family heritage, and a sense of cultural attachment can lead to different choices of racial identity by Multiracial people. In addition to the ways in which her model can be applied, she identifies several areas and questions for future research related to Multiracial identity.

The next four chapters focus on the application of racial identity development theories and their expansion beyond their original borders.

In chapter 7, Amy Reynolds and Suraiya Baluch consider the application of racial identity theory to both counseling relationships and the supervisory process. They highlight research findings and tools useful to understanding counselor/client and supervisor/supervisee dynamics, and apply some of this theoretical material to case study examples. Their chapter concludes with a discussion of emerging trends that may set the agenda for future research in this area.

Leah Wing and Janet Rifkin discuss the intersection between theories of racial identity development and oppression, and the conflict resolution process in chapter 8. They review perspectives related to social justice, oppression, and racial identity development that guide their unique approach to mediation. They then analyze how traditional approaches to conflict resolution and mediator training can be challenged and informed by racial identity development and oppression theory. Wing and Rifkin also provide insight into areas that might block and facilitate the use of racial identity development theory in conflict resolution.

In chapter 9, Maurianne Adams reviews several models of racial and ethnic identity development to discern generic processes of identity development that may be applied across racial and ethnic groups. Working with original theories of racial identity development, more recent works that expand on these earlier models, and models of ethnic identity development Adams identifies five such generic processes. She discusses how these processes may increase our understanding of identity development across and between different racial groups, and comments on the potential application of their core principles to other nonracial or ethnic social groups.

William E. Cross, Jr., and Peony Fhagen-Smith examine Black identity development across the human life span in chapter 10. They expand Nigrescence Theory to cover three growth patterns: that which occurs during infancy through adolescence, that which occurs through the process of identity conversion in adulthood, and that which represents an expansion and modification of an extant Black identity during different life periods. Cross and Fhagen-Smith also comment on both issues of identity variability and different kinds of growth trends.

By including both foundational and emerging racial identity models, examples of their application, and philosophical analysis this book contributes to the growing literature that will chronicle and influence the evolving field of racial identity development. This book is one frame in a much larger moving picture.

REFERENCES

Cross, William E., Jr. 1971. "The Negro-to-Black Conversion Experience: Towards a Psychology of Black Liberation." *Black World* 20(9):13–27.
———. 1991. *Shades of Black: Diversity in African-American Identity*. Philadelphia: Temple University Press.
Espiritu, Yen Le. 1992. *Asian American Pan Ethnicity: Bridging Institutions and Identities*. Philadelphia: Temple University Press.

Hardiman, Rita. 1982. "White Identity Development: A Process Oriented Model for Describing the Racial Consciousness of White Americans." Doctoral dissertation, University of Massachusetts, Amherst.

Helms, Janet E. 1984. "Toward a Theoretical Explanation of the Effects of Race on Counseling: A Black/White Model." *Counseling Psychologist* 12(4): 153–165.

———, ed. 1993. *Black and White Racial Identity: Theory Research and Practice.* Westport, Conn.: Praeger.

Jackson III, Bailey W. 1976. "Black Identity Development." Pp. 158–164 in *Urban, Social, and Educational Issues,* ed. L. H. Golubchick and B. Persky. Dubuque, Iowa: Kendall/Hunt.

Root, Maria P. P., ed. 1992. *Racially Mixed People in America.* Newbury Park. Calif.: Sage.

Salett, Elizabeth P., and Diane R. Koslow, eds. 1994. *Race, Ethnicity, and Self: Identity in Multicultural Perspective.* Washington, D.C.: National MultiCultural Institute.

Thomas, Charles W. 1971. *Boys No More: A Black Psychologist's View of Community.* Beverly Hills, Calif.: Glencoe.

Chapter 1

Black Identity Development
Further Analysis and Elaboration

Bailey W. Jackson III

The conception of a Black Identity Development (BID) theory was stimulated, in part, by the social transformation that occurred for Black people in the United States during the 1960s. It was during this period that the most recent exploration into what some referred to as the *"Negro to Black conversion experience"* (Cross 1971) was witnessed. While there have been other significant turning points in the development of the group self-concept of people of African heritage, the 1960s was the most recent point in the history of Black people in the United States when social scientists, psychologists, and other applied behavioral scientists[1] were prompted to advance theories that explain how the identity of Black people changes in relation to their sense of their social group membership and their experiences with Black culture and White racism.

Two of the major theorists to emerge from this period with theories focusing on the identity development of Black people were William Cross and me. William Cross first published his "Nigrescence Model" in 1971. Independent of Cross, I developed a "Black Identity Development" (BID) theory in the early 1970s but didn't publish it until 1976. Both Cross and I were influenced by Charles Thomas (1971), and Sherif and Sherif (1970) in developing paradigms to explain some of the dynamic transformations that were occurring in the Black community and with Black individuals during the 1960s. These theories described the nature of this lasting identity transformation, or conversion, experience for Black people in the 1960s, as well as the identity development of Black people from a broader psychosocial, political, and historical perspective. I hoped that the results of my work would lead to a tool that, when coupled with the work of Erik Erikson (1968) and Paulo Freire (1970), might assist other applied behavioral scientists and practitioners in their efforts to serve Black people and the Black community.

During the decades of the 1970s, 1980s, and 1990s Cross's Nigrescence model (Cross 1985, 1991; Cross and Fhagen-Smith 1996; Cross, Strauss, and Fhagen-Smith 1999) and my BID served as useful paradigms, or models, for understanding the so-called *Black experience* and the Black identity development process or "Nigrescence." As we enter the third decade of evolution of BID theory, it is time to take a retrospective look at the way these theories have evolved as the theorists continue to refine their work.[2] It is also time to rethink and recontextualize these theories and make appropriate adjustments and corrections in the BID.

In this chapter, I present more of the context and thinking that went into the development of the BID model than has been presented in my earlier writing. Specifically, I offer a look at how *race and ethnicity* were viewed when I initially developed this theory and how that view has changed over time. I also enhance my discussion of *BID stage transitions*. It has become increasingly clear that the transition from one stage of BID to another is as important to understanding the journey as is each individual stage of identity development.

Additionally, this chapter provides an updated review of the changes or enhancements to BID theory that, taken as a whole, reshape the theory in some significant ways. I start with the most recent publication of the BID (Hardiman and Jackson 1992). I have expanded the stage descriptions of BID so that they can be applied beyond the academic setting. I also offer updated descriptions and examples of stage descriptions and manifestations where appropriate. Many of these revisions come about as a result of both the profound and subtle societal changes as well as changes in the Black, especially African American, community. The chapter closes with my thoughts about the next evolutionary phase of both racial identity development theory and BID.

Black Identity Development Theory

The BID was conceived as a result of my search for a conceptual organizing tool that would account for and describe the range of views that Black people hold about their racial identity, or *Blackness*. It was meant to guide educators, behavioral scientists, and change agents like myself in the development of interventions and techniques that facilitate the process of individual, group, and systems development. Such tools assist in the contemplation of the myriad variables that determine the success or failure of an intervention.

In the 1960s I, like many of my colleagues, received many requests from community leaders and workers, campus administrators, public agency heads, and corporate CEOs and human resource professionals for help in explaining the social unrest in the United States. There was a particular need to understand what was going on in the streets of the Black community and in the minds and hearts of Black individuals. Considerable interest was expressed in gaining an understanding of why some Blacks seemed to be extremely angry at their life circumstances, while others, who seemed to live in the same circumstances, were not as angry or were even quite content. I was intrigued with what appeared to be a heightened concern of those I met in professional situations about what Black people should be called. Were we to be called *Negroes, people of color, Afro-Americans, Africans, or Black Americans*? And still others were more interested in the changing nature of the way that Black people thought and felt about ourselves. It was clear that the self-concept and the self-esteem of Black people had changed, but how could we make sense of these dynamics?

As William Cross was trained as a psychologist, his approach to the challenge of making sense of what he called the *"Negro to Black conversion experience"* was to first observe the changes that appeared to be taking place in the self-concept and self-esteem of Black individuals. He also paused to reflect on the observations that others had made in these areas of the Black experience. These observations led him to the identification of his stages of *Nigrescence*. The Cross model is one of the seminal works in the field of Black identity development and has been replicated and expanded upon by many others, primarily in the fields of counseling and psychology, most notably the work of Janet Helms (Helms 1990, 1994, 1995).

My approach to the challenge of trying to understanding the social transformations of the 1960s and what they were signaling for Black people was consistent with my training as well. Being grounded in the fields of laboratory training, education pedagogy, organizational development and organizational behavior, as well as what was then called race relations training, my interest in the questions about the nature of the *Black experience* and the dynamic changes that we were witnessing in that experience was more practical than existential or theoretical. I wanted to understand how this *transformation or "conversion" experience* was affecting the way Black people saw themselves and responded to their world and with each other and how it affected the motives and behavior patterns of Black people, particularly in organizational contexts. It was my hope that once I understood these things, I could design and deliver group and organizational interventions that were more relevant to the experiences and needs of the broadest segment of the Black community.

My initial investigations started not with the study of individual Black people, but with the community or race of Black people in the United States.[3] I started with a very select study of the consciousness of Black people since Reconstruction or postslavery. Through historical accounts, biographies, and autobiographies I was able to identify what I called the consciousness of Black people as it developed or emerged from Reconstruction through the 1960s. While my review was not a definitive historical study, it provided a basis for the identification of specific sequences or patterns in the views of the world, or levels of consciousness, among Black people. I also noted as a result of this historical review that the sequence or pattern observable in the history or collective consciousness of Black people in the United States could also be observed in the identity development sequence for a particular Black person. And finally, I believed that this identity development sequence could help explain or contextualize the transformation or Negro to Black conversion experience that we were experiencing.

During this period, I was also influenced by the work of Erik H. Erikson. In his book *Identity: Youth and Crisis* (1968), Erikson made a case for his "eight stages in the development of the personality." His stages included: *(1) Trust versus Mistrust; (2) Autonomy versus Shame, Doubt; (3) Initiative versus Guilt; (4) Industry versus Inferiority; (5) Identity versus Identity Confusion; (6) Intimacy versus Isolation; (7) Generativity versus Stagnation; and (8) Integrity versus Despair.* His presentation of each stage was consistent with his sense that each point in the sequence was a crisis point that had to be dealt with and learned from. Erikson indicated that "each stage becomes a crisis because incipient growth and awareness in a new part function go together with a shift in instinctual energy and yet also cause a specific vulnerability in that part" (1968:95). While Erikson was interested in the development of individual personality, many of his foundational concepts proved useful in considering BID theory.

Erikson wrote that "Personality . . . can be said to develop according to steps predetermined in the human organism's readiness to be driven toward, to be aware of, and to interact with a widening radius of significant individuals and situations" (1968:93). He described these "steps" as personal crises that individuals experienced over a life span. It was Erikson's description of stages that first attracted me to this sequenced or patterned way of thinking about individual development. I was also intrigued by the notion that these stages or developmental crisis points were significant in the way that individuals experienced themselves, others that they interacted with, and social "situations." Erikson's views on "proper development" also influenced my thinking as I considered what I called stage movement. Erikson states that:

> each item of the vital personality to be discussed is systematically related to all others, and . . . they all depend on the proper development in the proper sequence of each item; and . . . each item exists in some form before its decisive and critical time arrives. (1968:93)

This perspective led me to develop, and later confirm, the hypothesis that an individual Black person will move through stages in a developmental sequence. I further hypothesized that one cannot effectively skip a stage and that healthy individuals do not regress in their BID stage development. However, it is possible for a person to get stuck in a BID stage. These last two hypotheses have only been anecdotally confirmed to date.

Although I was impressed with Erickson's work on stages of personality or identity development, I was disappointed that he was unable to carry some of this thinking forward in his consideration of "Negro identity" in the same book (Erikson 1968). I was intrigued and challenged by his admission at the end of his book that there was a need to bring the clinical, historical, developmental, and social domains closer together. In retrospect, I believe that it was admissions or observations of this type that led me to see the significance of an individual's racial group membership in the development of their identity.

When I first developed the BID theory, I was interested in understanding the nature of the different worldviews that Black people held, and the impact that those world views had on individual attitudes and behavior. I did not attend to the events or "crises" or "encounters" that were responsible for the formation of a particular worldview. My interest and understanding of what I now call stage transitions came later.

Initially, it seemed to me that there was more than one worldview or consciousness in the Black community. I further thought that a sequence or pattern of different levels of social consciousness could be described as stages of identity development. It also seemed that these stages of identity development functioned like lenses in a pair of eyeglasses. Each set of lenses had a different prescription, shaped by the experience of growing up as a member of the Black community in a racist society and influenced by the many aspects of Black culture. I thought that while a person was wearing a pair of these metaphorical glasses, his or her view of the world and world events would be shaped by the prescription of the glasses. I further thought that the person's view of him or herself would be significantly shaped by these glasses, just as one's view of oneself is influenced when wearing glasses and then looking in a mirror.

Informed by my historical review, and influenced by the work of Erikson and others such as Albert Memmi (1965, 1968), Frantz Fanon (1967), and Paulo Freire (1970) I set out to describe the stages of consciousness and the sequence of Black Identity Development. I hoped that this theory would enable educators and applied behavioral scientists to more accurately determine the issues and/or needs of Black clients and/or the dynamics in situations involving Black people. I also hoped that it would be useful to Black people engaged in their own identity development (personal growth), by providing a kind of road map for their Black identity development or Negro to Black conversion experience.

Since the initial study (Jackson 1976), the BID theory has proven to be useful for educators and applied behavioral scientists. One of its unexpected consequences has been the extent to which it has been used as a model or point of departure for like theories of racial identity development and Black identity development. BID has had a significant influence on the development of the White Identity Development Theory (Hardiman 1982), the Asian Identity Development Theory (Kim 1981), the Jewish Identity Development Theory (Kandel 1986), the conceptualization of Multiracial identity (Wijeyesinghe 1992), Oppression/Liberation Identity Development (Hardiman and Jackson 1997), and the Minority Identity Development Model (Atkinson, Morten, and Sue 1979).

The presentation of the stages of the Black Identity Development theory in this chapter is an updated review of previous stage descriptions, reflecting a number of enhancements and refinements of those descriptions.

BID's View of Race and Ethnicity

The BID is a model of racial identity development (RID). It was developed during a period in U.S. history when ethnicity was used primarily to distinguish between White groups and ethnic groups. When Blacks were discussed, the two words race and ethnicity were often used synonymously. Black people were often described as a race and in other places described as an ethnic group. In BID, I took the position that Black people were members of a racial group. From my point of view, a racial group is made up of people from compatible ethnic groups. That is, they have shared or similar physical and cultural attributes. In fact, in an unpublished paper, "Perspectives on Race" (Hardiman and Jackson 1980), drawing on the works of Ashley Montagu (1972) and Pierre L. Van den Berghe (1967), Hardiman and I used the term "pan-ethnic" to refer to race.

With the introduction of the term "African American" in the 1970s—a term that had emerged during the 1960s but was not fully embraced by the Black community until almost a decade later—one's ethnic identity became a point of attention. Initially, the term African American was used synonymously with Black. In fact one might hear them used interchangeably in the same sentence. Today, there is still some confusion about these terms and what they are meant to describe. For some, the term African American implies people of African heritage born in the United States who are also the descendants of slaves. This would mean that not all Blacks in America are African Americans. For others, the term describes people of African heritage with U.S. citizenship, thus including individuals who were recent immigrants from Africa or the Carribean. This would also suggest that not all Blacks are African Americans. But in both cases African Americans are part of the Black group or race. Therefore,

Blacks or people of African heritage can have subgroups or ethnic groups that would include Nigerians, Jamaicans, South Africans, and African Americans, just to name a few. If one follows this line of thinking, which I do, while Black and people of African heritage are synonymous, Black and African American are not.

The BID theory was conceptualized at a time when these terms and their meanings were in transition. During the 1960s, the term Black served not only as the name for the Black racial group, but also as the name for those we now refer to as African Americans. As I consider the data used to support my research on BID in the early 1970s, the sample was largely made up of African Americans and not the full range of Black ethnic groups. Therefore, while I still believe that the model can be applied to all Black people, it would probably be more accurate to refer to it as the African American Identity Development Theory (AAID).

Stages of Black Identity Development (BID)

In the BID theory, there are fives stages of development or consciousness. They are: (1) *Naive*, the absence of a social consciousness or identity; (2) *Acceptance*, suggesting the acceptance of the prevailing White/majority description and perceived worth of Black people, Black culture, or experience; (3) *Resistance*, the rejection of the prevailing majority culture's definition and valuing of Black people

FIGURE 1.1
Five Stages of Jackson's Black Identity Development Model

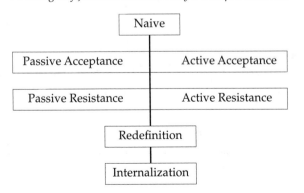

and culture; (4) *Redefinition,* the renaming, reaffirming, and reclaiming of one's sense of Blackness, Black culture, and racial identity; and (5) *Internalization,* the integration of a *redefined* racial identity into all aspects of one's self-concept or identity. The stages of *Acceptance* and *Resistance* can manifest themselves in one of two ways, as *passive* (unconscious) or *active* (conscious). The stages of *Redefinition* and *Internalization* involve conscious, active choices by their very nature, and therefore have no passive manifestations. The *Naive* stage is by definition not conscious.

Stage Transition

In the original version of the BID (Jackson 1976) there was scant mention of the transitions between stages. There was a suggestion that an individual might move from one stage to another as a result of some internally or externally motivated contradiction to the world-view that he or she subscribed to at a previous stage. For example, if a Black person whose views were consistent with either the *passive* or *active Acceptance* stage of consciousness became aware that these held views were in fact causing him or her, in Paulo Freire's (1970) words, to play "host" to his or her oppressor, that person might experience enough cognitive or emotional dissonance to stimulate the beginning of a stage transition to the *Resistance* stage. In his "Nigrescence" model Cross (1971) he presents "*Encounter*" as the second stage in his process. In the BID, Cross's "encounter" would best be described as a transition between stage two, *Acceptance,* and stage three, *Resistance,* not as a separate stage of identity.

Transitions also occur between each of the other stages in BID. The transition from one stage to another usually occurs when an individual recognizes that his or her current worldview is either illogical or contradicted by new experiences and/or information. A transition may also be prompted by an awareness that one's current worldview or stage of consciousness is detrimental to a healthy self-concept or no longer serves some important self-interest. During these transition periods, a person may appear to him or herself and to others to be in two stages simultaneously. This seeming two-stage consciousness results from that phase in the stage transition process when one is leaving, or *exiting,* one stage of consciousness and trying on, or *entering,* the next stage.

It is important to understand that the transition from one stage of consciousness to another can be, and often is, a challenging, even a traumatic process. When a Black person is making this transition, usually unconsciously at first, it can be extremely disorienting. One can be filled with strong emotions such as anger, even rage, or sadness and grief over the loss of one's former consciousness. When attempting to describe this transition experience, some have used Kubler-Ross's (1975) stages of *death and dying* to describe their feelings. My observations of the stage transition experience in a number of Black individuals have led me to expand my view of each stage so that it incorporates the transformation process.

Since each stage of the BID represented a fully *"adopted"* consciousness or identity, what needed to be added was a representation of the *entry* phase which comes before one has *"adopted"* each stage of consciousness as well as the *exit* phase or the exiting of a stage of consciousness. Consequently the presentation of the BID stages was expanded from a simple five-stage model (Figure 1.1) to the current model (Figure 1.2).

FIGURE 1.2
Five Stages of Jackson's Black Identity Development with Transitions

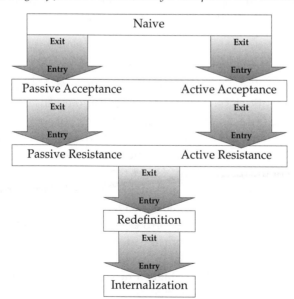

With this expanded perspective of the BID process of fully *adopted* stages and *exit/entry* transitions between them, it is easier to consider, at least visually, what happens when one is changing stages. The overlap of the *exiting* phase of one stage, filled with sadness, anxiety, and reluctance to leave the comfort of a worldview that one has become used to, and the *entry* phase, filled with expectation and fear of the unknown, can be extremely disconcerting for the individual and those interacting with that person. While there is still much to be learned about the transition points from one stage to the next in BID, it seems clear that if the stages are the *snapshots* of a *moving picture*, it is the stage transitions that provide the *action*. While the stages and the stage transitions are experienced very differently and have a different effect on the individual who is experiencing them, we must understand that we need them both to make this Black identity development process come alive.

Description of the Black Identity Development Model

As mentioned earlier in this chapter, much of the description of the BID that follows was excerpted from my most recent publication of the model (Hardiman and Jackson 1992). In the current presentation, I have recontextualized, updated, and enhanced the model and the examples that illustrate the stages and stage transitions.

STAGE ONE—NAIVE

The Naive stage of BID was not in the original conceptualization of BID (Jackson 1976). The influence of Erikson's model, which suggests that social identity issues do not occur until adolescence, had resulted in my giving little consideration to preadolescent identity development. Somewhat later, as a result of work with elementary and junior high school students, I began to notice that at best there was only a mimicking of the racial identity issues that could be observed in those who were in their late teens and older. Some scholars (for example, Tatum 1997) believe that the racist incidents that children experience in school coupled with the positive experiences that their parents often provide at home can shape the identity experience of Black children. While identity shaping or socializing may be happening, I would not suggest that it is a stage of racial identity or consciousness.

In BID, the *Naive* stage is that point in our development, early childhood, in which there is little or no conscious social awareness of race per se (Derman-Sparks, Higa, and Sparks 1980). During this period, children are vulnerable to the logic system and worldview of their socializing agents (such as parents, teachers, the media, and significant others). Children at this stage become aware of the physical differences and some of the obvious cultural differences between themselves and others, and while they may not feel completely comfortable with people who are different, they generally do not feel fearful or hostile, inferior or superior. They may display a curiosity about or an interest in understanding the differences between people, but they have not yet learned to value some differences over others in the social world. This stage generally covers the development period between birth and about four years of age.

In the *transition* from the *Naive* to the *Acceptance* stage of consciousness, two related changes take place. One is that children begin to learn and adopt an ideology about their own racial group as well as other racial groups. For most Blacks in the United States, this involves internalizing many covert and some overt messages that being Black means being less than, and that Whiteness equals superiority, or *normalcy*, beauty, importance, and power. The second change is that children learn that formal and informal rules, institutions, and authority figures do not treat everyone the same way. They learn that people face negative consequences if they violate the rules regarding the way the races relate to one another.

STAGE TWO — ACCEPTANCE

The *Naive* stage of consciousness is followed by a stage of *Acceptance*. This stage represents the internalization, conscious or unconscious, of an ideology of racial dominance and subordination which touches all facets of one's private and public life. A person at this stage has internalized many of the messages about what it means to be Black in the United States.

The core premise that undergirds the *Acceptance* stage has remained essentially unchanged since BID was developed. The Black person in the *Acceptance* stage of consciousness follows the prevailing notion that "White is right." This person attempts to gain resources—such as approval, sense of worth, goods, power, and money—by accepting and conforming to White social, cultural, and institutional standards. His or her response to the dominant social mode is an unexamined rather than an explicitly examined pattern of behavior consciously adopted for personal survival. The internal acceptance of these standards as a worldview requires the rejection and devaluation of all that is Black. A Black person who consciously (*active acceptance*) adopts the prevailing White view of the world weakens his or her positive self-concept or positive view of Black people. This consciousness typically causes a Black person to avoid interactions with other Blacks and to desire interactions with Whites, a behavioral pattern which may at first seem to conform to the dominant mode in most social situations.

Black people in this stage may continue to manifest long-held beliefs in new ways. For example, the belief that *People are people, and if Blacks just work hard they will be judged by their merits* is one of the prevailing views held by Black people at this stage. With the media attention being given to "right-wing" or conservative views expressed by a few Black Americans (Masci 1998), it might appear that beliefs of this type, typical of this stage, are gaining popularity. Studies have shown, however, that the opposite is true (Bositis 1996). It seems that the increased conservatism of the media has put the spotlight on those Black people who support that political agenda and the social consciousness that goes with that worldview.

Another such belief is: *There is no race problem. The problem is with those Blacks who don't want to work hard and better themselves. They are messing it up for the rest of us.* This can be seen as an extension of the thinking exemplified above. It is not the predominate opinion in the Black community (Roach 1997), but it does exist. I have heard such sentiments expressed by younger Black people for whom the 1960s and 1970s are a part of American history. These Black people may have been raised and socialized in that small part of the Black community that has done better economically than their parents and grandparents, and been exposed to the logic of the dominant social class in the United States.

As Black people have moved up the socioeconomic ranks in the 1980s and 1990s, they have had more professional and social contact with White people. Blacks in this stage of consciousness believe it is necessary to be able to look the other way or explain away certain attitudes and behaviors held by White people in order to "get along in this world."

The *transition* from the stage of *Acceptance* to *Resistance* can be confusing and often painful. The transition generally occurs over time and is usually stimulated by a number of events that have a cumulative effect. Black people in an *Acceptance* consciousness begin to be aware of experiences that contradict the *Acceptance* worldview, experiences they had earlier ignored or passed off as isolated exceptional events. But gradually as a person begins to encounter greater dissonance the isolated incidents form a discernible pattern. The contradictions that initiate the transition period can occur in the form of interactions with people, social events, the media, or as a result of so-called "racial incidents." Many who saw racism as a "60's issue" often reevaluate their thinking in light of events such as the numerous acts of open hostility and unconscionable violence against Black people in the workplace, on the college campus, and in the community, such as the dragging death of James Byrd in Texas in 1999.

Black people who begin to exit from the stage of *Acceptance* reluctantly acknowledge their own collusion in their victimization and develop an emerging understanding of the harmful effects of holding on to the *Acceptance* consciousness. In Freireian terms, the members of these target groups begin to become aware of the many ways they have played "host" to their oppressors (Freire 1970).

STAGE THREE—RESISTANCE

The initial questioning that begins during the exit phase of *Acceptance* continues with greater intensity during the third stage, *Resistance*. The worldview that people adopt during *Resistance* is dramatically different from *Acceptance*. At this third stage, one begins to understand and recognize racism in its complex and multiple manifestations—at the individual and institutional, conscious and unconscious, intentional and unintentional, attitudinal, behavioral, and policy levels. Individuals in *Resistance* become painfully aware of the numerous ways in which covert as well as overt racism impacts them daily as Black people.

The acknowledgment of the pervasive existence of racism and its negative effects is typical of one who is exiting the *Acceptance* stage. The first manifestation of the *Resistance* stage—active, often vehement, questioning—usually follows. Once a Black person has acknowledged the existence of racism, he or she wants to find out more about it. A Black individual generally begins by questioning the truths about the way things are. The values, moral codes, and codes of personal and professional development handed down by the majority White culture and those who collude in their victimization are the first things to be scrutinized through the lenses of this new and more critical consciousness. These values and codes are reexamined for their role in the perpetuation of racism. Gradually, the Black person becomes more skilled at identifying racist premises that have been woven into the fabric of all aspects of social experience. This person experiences a growing hostility toward White people, as well as toward fellow Blacks or other people of color, who collude with White people.

The often overt expression of hostility to the existence and effects of racism marks the transition from the *entry* to the *adoption* phase of the *Resistance* stage. It is at this point of the *Resistance* stage that the Black individual fully internalizes the antithesis of the *Acceptance* stage of development. The person experiences anger, pain, hurt, and rage. The effects of racism may appear to be all-consuming. In extreme cases, some people may become so consumed by these emotions that they remain at this stage of consciousness for some time. In other instances, the Black persons may find that by fully embracing the *Resistance* stage they stand to lose the "benefits" they enjoyed when they were in *Acceptance*. They may choose the path of *passive Resistance*, in the hope that they will be able to stay in favor with White society while rejecting racism. This strategy usually proves too frustrating and contradictory to be sustained. For most Blacks at this stage the primary task is to stop colluding in their own victimization. It is time to cleanse their consciousness of those internalized racist notions that have served to stifle their own personal development and to stop *passively accepting* the racism of their environment.

During the course of the *Resistance* stage, the Black person is energized and experiences a sense of personal power. At this stage, individuals who rail against the *system* discover that they can make that system respond. They can get the attention of those in authority. They can get people to the table even if it takes acts of civil disobedience to do it. While the power they gain at this stage is not of the same type and quantity as that available to the White majority, it is power nonetheless. The Black person at *Resistance* recognizes that to varying degrees and in a variety of situations, she or he can stop things from happening. For many this is the first lesson in personal and social power. The person also begins to recognize that a considerable amount of energy must go into unlearning as well as undoing considerable earlier programming about his or her identity as a Black person. The primary focus at this stage is the exact reverse of *Acceptance*: it is directed toward being clear about *who I am not.* This person is now ready to put energy into the question, *"Who am I, who are we?"*

The *transition* from *Resistance* to *Redefinition* occurs when the Black person realizes that she or he is not clear about who she or he is racially speaking, or what her or his racial group membership means to her or him personally. At the stage of *Resistance*, he or she recognizes that the sense of self as a Black person had been defined for him or her in a White racist environment and then actively seeks to question it and reject aspects of it. Now they are no longer actively consumed by rejection or the need to reject, but experience a new sense of void from a lack of positive self-definition of Blackness. Attempts to grapple with the question of what it means to be Black lead to the *Redefinition* stage.

REDEFINITION STAGE

The *Redefinition* stage is that point in the developmental process in which the Black person is concerned with defining her or himself in terms that are independent of the perceived strengths and/or weaknesses of White people and the dominant White culture. At this juncture the Black person focuses his or her attention and energy on developing primary contact and interacting with other Blacks at the same stage of consciousness. Unlike the Black person at the *Acceptance* and *Resistance* stages, the Black person with a *Redefinition* consciousness is not concerned either with emulating or rejecting Whites and White culture. The *Redefining* person does not see interaction with Whites as necessary and useful in the quest for a positive or nurturing sense of self and racial identity. Because renaming is the primary concern in this person's life, he or she begins a search for paradigms that will facilitate the accomplishment of this task.

While this search can begin in a number of places, for most Black people it seems to begin with the conscious or unconscious formation of a new referent group. As mentioned above, it is critical that this new referent group consist of other Blacks with a *Redefinition* perspective. Black people at this stage are particularly concerned with the perspective of other Black people and as a consequence tend to limit their interactions to Blacks (where this is an option). But this type of behavior tends to be viewed negatively by both White and Black people at earlier stages of consciousness. Whereas Black people who are in the *Resistance* stage are generally viewed as troublemakers or "militants," those in the *Redefinition* stage may be seen as "separatist" or "self-segregating," especially by liberal Whites who view themselves as kind and benevolent, and for whom this behavior appears counterproductive.

While some Black people in *Redefinition* may begin to see connections between the racism that Blacks experience and that experienced by other people of color (such as Native Americans, Latino/as, and Asians), they may not be invested in forming an alliance or a coalition with these groups. The psychological tasks at this stage are very ingroup or Black-centered. Adopting a multicultural worldview, rather than a Black worldview, may be premature from this point of view.

It may be difficult for those who are not Black to interact with Blacks who are preoccupied with *Redefinition* issues. What they may fail to understand is these issues involve new and different ways of redefining one's self and one's social group membership. Old allegiances are being reevaluated. Many relationships that appeared essential in the past tend not to be as important at this stage.

The search for a new understanding of Blackness often begins by reclaiming one's group heritage. Blacks often find values, traditions, customs, philosophical assumptions, and concepts of time, work, and family that are appealing and nurturing by revisiting or uncovering their heritage and culture. They discover that many aspects of their heritage that have been handed down through the generations still affect their life today and they become clear about the uniqueness of their group identity. They come to understand that they are more than the victims of racism, more than just people who are different from Whites. Their sense of self is no longer determined by how well they can assimilate into the majority White culture. Black people at *Redefinition* come to experience their sense of Blackness in a way that engenders pride.

INTERNALIZATION STAGE

The *transition* from *Redefinition* to *Internalization* occurs when an individual begins to apply or to integrate some of the newly defined sense of values, beliefs, and behaviors into all aspects of his or her life. This transition is somewhat different from the transition process between the earlier stages. The transition to *Internalization* brings the growth and development from all previous stages forward into this final stage. The learning and awareness derived from living in the *Acceptance, Resistance,* and *Redefinition* stages of consciousness, as well as some of the pain and frustration experienced during that developmental process, is critical to the realization of this stage. To demonstrate this point, I will highlight some of the experiences that are typically carried forward into the *Internalization stage.*

In the *Acceptance* stage, Black people employed many techniques to survive and maintain our humanity in a hostile and inhumane environment. The capacity to survive under these conditions, while not without its costs, has resulted in a resolve not only to survive but to do so without lowering ourselves to the level of our oppressors. The development of an acute sensitivity to the likes and dislikes of the dominant White society was one of the many qualities necessary to survive in a hostile environment. While this sensitivity was useful as an aid to assimilation into White society, it also allowed us to detect subtle forms of racism in the environment. The *Resistance stage* can be credited with helping Black people understand power and power politics.

While the application of this learning took place predominately in a White-dominated power structure, nonetheless Black people did learn how power works and how to use it. This understanding becomes extremely important in the *Internalization* stage where power is needed not to react but to be proactive in pursuit of self-defined goals. The *Redefinition* stage can be described as the place where self-defined goals and identity are developed. Thus, the sensitivity from *Acceptance,* the lessons about power from *Resistance,* and the self-definition from *Redefinition* carry the Black person into the stage of *Internalization.*

Black people at the *Internalization* stage no longer feel a need to explain, defend, or protect their Black identity, although they may recognize that it is important to nurture this sense of self. Nurturing is seen as particularly important when the environment continues to ignore, degrade, or attack all that is Black. For example, Blacks who have decided to organize their lives and sense of Blackness around an Afrocentric perspective and the lifestyle that goes with that perspective, may find that it takes some special attention to keep that focus healthy and alive as long as they are living in a society dominated by Eurocentrism or some other worldview.

Some Blacks have or will adopt a multicultural perspective, which brings together worldviews from as many compatible cultural perspectives as possible. This might mean integrating two or more racial/panethnic cultural perspectives (such as Asian/Asian American, Pacific Islander, Native American, Latino, or White/Euro-American). And there are those who follow the thinking of W. E. B. Du Bois ([1903] 1961), who prescribed a bicultural perspective for Black people in America, one that integrates the cultures of people of African and European heritage. Some have suggested that Dr. Martin Luther King manifests this stage, while others add Malcolm X to the list of those who should be considered. Clearly, the BID stages of development are evident in their autobiographies (Haley 1965). Although there don't appear to be many Black people who can be held up as role models or exemplars of the *Internalized stage* of consciousness or identity, these Black men notwithstanding, we can point to specific attitudes and behaviors in specific situations as evidence that many of us can and do operate from this stage of consciousness to varying degrees.

Social Dynamics of the 1980s and 1990s and Their Impact on BID Theory

There have been at least three social phenomena in the 1980s and 1990s that I believe have significantly affected the original BID theory. The first is the emergence of ethnicity as a prominent social organizer. For some, ethnicity can and should replace race as a social organizer. Many of those who believe that race is a failed, flawed, or negative term have embraced ethnicity as an alternative (Phinney 1989). I believe ethnicity has always been there but has not been given the attention it deserves. We have both an ethnic and a racial identity and should pay attention to both and the effect they have on our self-concept and social interactions.

Regardless of the prominence that ethnicity ultimately attains, it seems clear that identity theoreticians and applied social/behavioral scientists who may not have given it much attention will not be able to continue to treat ethnicity so lightly. However, as long as race is an operational social organizer, there will be those who identify themselves and others in those terms as well. In the future, the development of an African American Identity Development Theory that recognizes and complements Black identity development theories would not only make a useful contribution to African American people, but would also serve as a model or point of departure for other ethnic and racial groups grappling with similar issues.

The second phenomenon that will continue to grow and have a dramatic impact on the thinking about BID and the "Nigrescence" models is Afrocentricity. Afrocentricity (Asante 1988, 1998), a philosophical underpinning for people and ethnic groups of African heritage, has in a relatively short time had a profound effect on the way Black people think about themselves. No longer being limited to philosophical assumptions of European derivation, Afrocentric thinking offers a depth to the *Redefinition stage* similar to the impact that the phrase "Black Power" had on those in the *Resistance stage*.

The Afrocentric perspective will deepen and broaden our way of thinking about Blackness and the Black experience at the *Redefinition* and *Internalization* stages. No longer will our understanding of these stages be defined by the Aristotelian logic system (that is, either/or thinking) embedded in Eurocentric thinking. True Afrocentric thinking (that is, both/and thinking) will undoubtedly be influenced to some degree by the oppression that Black people have suffered for generations, but it will not be defined by that oppression. Afrocentricity promises to reclaim the philosophical and spiritual core of the experience of people of African heritage. This will make a qualitative difference to the way we understand our social identity as African Americans and as Black people.

The third social phenomenon that must be recognized as having a significant impact on the evolution of the BID model is the economy of the United States. While the economy always has an impact on the lives of the members of a society, its repercussions are felt in other parts of the social structure when dramatic shifts occur in the strength or health of the economy and those shifts last for an extended period of time. This is particularly true when this occurs in a class-based society like the one in the United States.

Many in the United States have benefitted from a strong economy in the 1990s. Unlike in the past, Black Americans have also benefitted, although less so than others. One of the effects of the strong economy has been the rise of a larger percentage of Black people—though still small compared to White Americans—to the middle and upper-middle classes (Cose et al. 1999). With the rise of the few and the lack of substantial change in the economic condition of the vast majority of Black Americans, the gap between the "haves" and the "have nots" is being felt not just between Blacks and Whites, but also between classes of Blacks (Cose et al. 1999; Prosperity Gap 1999). Some suggest that one's socioeconomic class identity is as significant as, if not more significant than, one's racial identity in determining how we think and feel about ourselves (Wilson 1980, 1987; Marable 1983; Rothman 1999; Oliver and Shapiro 1997). I think it would be wrong to try to decide which is more or less important. In the future, we must learn more about how they interact and influence each other.

Conclusion

This chapter has covered much of the past, present, and future of the foundation theory, Black Identity Development. It was also intended to upgrade the presentation of this theory. While these are worthy tasks in and of themselves, this chapter's contribution to the chronicling of the evolution of BID theory is its greatest value. Racial identity development theory can be an extremely powerful tool for understanding the identity development process of members of different racial groups. And BID, like other racial and ethnic identity development models, will always be a work in progress.

NOTES

1. The term *Applied Behavioral Scientist* is used herein to include counselors, psychologists, organizational development specialists, and organizational behaviorists, and may also include some diversity consultants.

2. The next major evolution of Cross's work can be found in this volume (Cross and Fhagen-Smith).

3. What I did not consider well enough at the time was that what I was in fact studying was the experience of the group now called *African Americans*, not Blacks.

REFERENCES

Asante, Molefi Kete. 1988. *Afrocentricity.* Trenton, N.J.: Africa World Press.
———. 1998. *The Afrocentric Idea.* Philadelphia: Temple University Press.

Atkinson, Donald, George Morten, and Derald W. Sue. 1979. *Counseling American Minorities: A Cross-Cultural Perspective.* Dubuque, Iowa: W. C. Brown.

Bositis, David A. 1996. *African Americans and the Republican Party.* Washington, D.C.: Joint Center for Political and Economic Studies.

Cose, Ellis, Ana Figueroa, John McCormick, Vern Smith, and Pat Wingert. 1999. "The Good News about Black America." *Newsweek* (7 June):28.

Cross, William E., Jr. 1971. "The Negro-to-Black Conversion Experience: Towards a Psychology of Black Liberation." *Black World* 20(9):13–27.

———. 1985. "Black Identity: Rediscovering the Distinction between Personal Identity and Reference Group Orientation." Pp. 155–171 in *Beginnings: The Social and Affective Development of Black Children,* ed. M. B. Spencer, G. K. Brookins, and W. R. Allen. Hillsdale, N.J.: Lawrence Erlbaum.

———. 1991. *Shades of Black: Diversity in African-American Identity.* Philadelphia: Temple University Press.

Cross, William E., Jr., and Peony Fhagen-Smith. 1996. "Nigrescence and Ego Identity Development: Accounting for Differential Black Identity Patterns." Pp. 108–123 in *Counseling across Cultures,* ed. P. B. Pedersen, J. G. Draguns, W. J. Lonner, and J. E. Trimble. Thousand Oaks, Calif.: Sage.

Cross, William E., Jr., Linda Strauss, and Peony Fhagen-Smith. 1999. "African American Identity Development across the Life Span: Educational Implications." Pp. 29–47 in *Racial and Ethnic Identity in School Practices: Aspects of Human Development,* ed. R. H. Sheets and E. R. Hollins. Hillsdale, N.J.: Lawrence Erlbaum.

Derman-Sparks, Louise, Carol T. Higa, and Bill Sparks. 1980. "Children, Race, and Racism: How Race Awareness Develops." *Interracial Books for Children Bulletin* 11(3–4):3–9.

Du Bois, William E. B. [1903] 1961. *The Souls of Black Folk: Essays and Sketches.* Greenwich, Conn.: Fawcett.

Erikson, Erik H. 1968. *Identity: Youth and Crisis.* New York: W. W. Norton.

Fanon, Frantz. 1967. *Black Skin, White Masks.* New York: Grove Press.

Freire, Paulo. 1970. *Pedagogy of the Oppressed.* New York: Continuum.

Haley, Alex. 1965. *The Autobiography of Malcolm X.* New York: Grove Press.

Hardiman, Rita. 1982. "White Identity Development: A Process Oriented Model for Describing the Racial Consciousness of White Americans. Doctoral Dissertation," University of Massachusetts, Amherst.

Hardiman, Rita, and Bailey W. Jackson. 1980. "Perspectives on Race." Unpublished manuscript.

———. 1992. "Racial Identity Development: Understanding Racial Dynamics in College Classrooms and on Campus." Pp. 21–37 in *Promoting Diversity in College Classrooms: Innovative Responses for the Curriculum, Faculty, and Institutions,* ed. M. Adams. San Francisco: Jossey-Bass.

Hardiman, Rita, and Bailey W. Jackson. 1997. "Conceptual Foundations for Social Justice Courses." Pp. 16–29 in *Teaching for Diversity and Social Justice: A Sourcebook*, ed. M. Adams, L. A. Bell, and P. Griffin. New York: Routledge.

Helms, Janet E. 1990. *Black and White Racial Identity: Theory, Research, and Practice*. New York: Greenwood Press.

———. 1994. "The Conceptualization of Racial Identity and Other 'Racial' Constructs." Pp. 285–311 in *Human Diversity: Perspectives on People in Context*, ed. E. J. Trickett, R. J. Watts, and D. Birman. San Francisco: Jossey-Bass.

———. 1995. "An Update of Helms's White and People of Color Racial Identity Models." Pp. 181–198 in *Handbook of Multicultural Counseling*, ed. J. G. Ponterotto, J. M. Casas, L. A. Suzuki, and C. M. Alexander. Thousand Oaks, Calif.: Sage.

Jackson, Bailey W. 1976. "Black Identity Development." Pp. 158-164 in *Urban, Social, and Educational Issues*, ed. L. H. Golubchick and B. Persky. Dubuque, Iowa: Kendall/Hunt.

Kandel, Andrea C. 1986. "Processes of Jewish American Identity Development: Perceptions of Conservative Jewish Women." Doctoral dissertation, School of Education, University of Massachusetts, Amherst.

Kim, Jean. 1981. "Processes of Asian American Identity Development: A Study of Japanese American Women's Perceptions of Their Struggle to Achieve Positive Identities." Doctoral dissertation, School of Education, University of Massachusetts, Amherst.

Kubler-Ross, Elisabeth. 1975. *Death: The Final Stage of Growth*. Englewood Cliffs, N.J.: Prentice-Hall.

Marable, Manning. 1983. *How Capitalism Underdeveloped Black America: Problems in Race, Political Economy, and Society*. Boston: South End Press.

Masci, David. 1998. "More Black Conservatives Enter the Limelight." *Plain Dealer* (17 February):6A.

Memmi, Albert. 1965. *The Colonizer and the Colonized*. Boston: Beacon Press.

———. 1968. *Dominated Man*. Boston: Beacon Press.

Montagu, Ashley. 1972. *Statement on Race: An Annotated Elaboration and Exposition of the Four Statements on Race Issued by the United Nations Educational, Scientific, and Cultural Organizations*. 3d ed. New York: Oxford University Press.

Oliver, Melvin L., and Thomas M. Shapiro. 1997. *Black Wealth/White Wealth: A New Perspective on Black Inequality*. New York: Routledge.

Phinney, Jean S. 1989. "Stages of Ethnic Identity Development in Minority Group Adolescents." *Journal of Early Adolescence* 9:34–49.

Prosperity Gap. 1999. *Business Week*, 27 September.

Roach, Ronald. 1997. "Racial Attitudes: Gaps Narrow for Young People." Black Issues in Higher Education 14(10):12–13.

Rothman, Robert A. 1999. *Inequality and Stratification: Race, Class, and Gender*. Upper Saddle River, N.J.: Prentice Hall.

Sherif, Muzafer, and Carolyn W. Sherif. 1970. "Black Unrest as a Social Movement toward an Emerging Self-Identity." *Journal of Social and Behavioral Sciences* 15(3):41–52.

Tatum, Beverly Daniel. 1997. *"Why Are All the Black Kids Sitting Together in the Cafeteria?" And Other Conversations about Race.* New York: Basic Books.

Thomas, Charles W. 1971. *Boys No More: A Black Psychologist's View of Community.* Beverly Hills, Calif.: Glencoe.

Van den Berghe, Pierre L. 1967. *Race and Racism: A Comparative Perspective.* New York: Wesley.

Wijeyesinghe, Charmaine. 1992. "Towards an Understanding of the Racial Identity of Bi-Racial People: The Experience of Racial Self-Identification of African-American/Euro-American Adults and the Factors Affecting Their Choices of Racial Identity." Doctoral dissertation, School of Education, University of Massachusetts, Amherst.

Wilson, William J. 1980. *The Declining Significance of Race: Blacks and Changing American Institutions.* 2d ed. Chicago: University of Chicago Press.

———. 1987. *The Truly Disadvantaged: The Inner City, the Underclass, and Public Policy.* Chicago: University of Chicago Press.

Chapter 2

Racial Identity Development and Latinos in the United States

Bernardo M. Ferdman and Plácida I. Gallegos

As their numbers have grown, Latinos[1] in the United States have been the focus of increasing attention by the media (Larmer 1999) and by scholars. Latino identity and its many manifestations constitute a key theme for social scientists and others interested in better understanding this population. Given the intense spotlight on race in the United States, an understanding of Latino identity development must necessarily address the relationship of members of this group to a racial system of categorization.

A focus on racial identity and its development should essentially consider how individuals and groups deal with the surrounding racial order and its constructs (Helms 1996). Both individually and collectively, people can accept and internalize the racial order, resist it, or transform it. These reactions should be viewed in the context of the relationship of individuals and groups to intergroup structures of dominance and oppression. In this chapter, we consider these issues specifically with regard to Latinos and Latinas in the United States. Because Latinos do not fit easily into the prevailing system of racial categories in the United States, understanding Latino racial identity presents special challenges and challenges the prevailing racial order itself. This lack of fit often creates dilemmas for individuals, organizations, or institutions that must figure out what to do with us. As a recent *Newsweek* cover (Larmer 1999) attested, "Young Hispanics Are Changing America." The accompanying magazine articles, implying that most people have not yet paid sufficient attention to these changes and their implications, call attention to the growth of the

Latino population in the United States, its internal diversity, and its impact on the country.

Our goal in this chapter is both to clarify and to amplify the dilemmas inherent in understanding Latinos and Latinas as a group, focusing in particular on how our identities relate (or do not relate) to racial constructs. In our own personal experience as a Latino and Latina, we find that many non-Latinos often prefer simple answers to questions about our group. We frequently encounter questions about our racial identity, countries of origin, or native language, as well as requests to provide simple "rules" for dealing with Latinos in general. Our answers are not always satisfactory because they may not fit an expected form. We have found this challenging, because our experience of Latinos as a group is of a multifaceted, dynamic, complex, and very heterogeneous people for whom simple answers are never sufficient. The difficulty we often face is that to facilitate comprehension we must gloss over the more complex aspects of our understanding or describe the Latino experience in the context of constructs and frameworks that do not necessarily fit and that were generated by the experience and perspective of other groups.

In preparing this chapter, we had a similar experience, because so much of the thinking on race in the United States stems from the history of Blacks and Whites and their relationship. We found ourselves required to be somewhat reactive to models that were constructed without Latinos in mind.[2] Our task became more than simply to attempt to make a cogent statement about Latino identity; we were faced with the need to explain it to others who are relatively unfamiliar not only with what it is about, but also with the appropriate constructs or reference points with which we would prefer to talk about it. One of the challenges Latinos have faced in the United States has often been the need to manage the comfort level of others. Thus we were caught in something of a bind in explaining Latino identity, especially from a racial perspective. If we uncritically focused on predominant constructs of race in the United States, this would not fully reflect or capture the Latino experience. On the other hand, if we simply used Latino-based constructs, we would risk not being understood, and so would continue to reframe our experience in terms other than our own. When we think about Latino identity, a first step for us is usually to see race as secondary at best. It is one of many factors constituting identity for Latinos, but certainly not the most prominent. Writing about Latino "racial" identity has therefore been a challenge for us.

Individual identity is developed in the context of group and inter-group realities. Given the complexity and heterogeneity of Latino experience, it is important to frame theoretical statements about individual identity in the context of group experiences and patterns. Thus, in this chapter we discuss Latinos and Latinas as a group before presenting our perspectives on racial identity development at the individual level. First, we describe the diversity and unity among Latinos, and then we consider the applicability of racial constructs to Latinos, including a brief review of Latino experiences of and perspectives on race. We conclude the chapter with our own model of Latino orientations to racial identity in the context of Latino diversity.[3]

Latinos and Latinas in the United States: One Group or Many?

Latinos (often also referred to as "Hispanics" or "Hispanic-Americans")[4] are the fastest growing "minority group" in the United States, and will soon exceed African Americans in number. In August 1999, there were 31.5 million persons of Hispanic[5] origin in the United States, or 11.5 percent of the total population (U.S. Bureau of the Census 1999). This represented an increase of 41 percent since 1990, when there were 22.4 million Hispanics (9 percent of the U.S. population) counted by the Census. This estimate did not include the 3.8 million residents of Puerto Rico, the vast majority of whom are citizens of the United States and would be categorized as Hispanics on the mainland. By 2040, according to U.S. Census estimates, Hispanics will comprise over 18 percent (or almost 1 in 5) of the U.S. population.

Latinos are quite diverse. A range of factors—including cultural, historical, sociological, political, and others—both contribute to this diversity and point to the development and existence in the United States of an overarching Latino identity. Thus, in many contexts, it can make sense to study Latinos/as as one group. Some (such as Quiñones-Rosado 1998) argue, for example, that it is the experience of colonialism that unites Latinos. Moreover, Latinos and Latinas can be strongly identified as such, especially in relation to non-Latinos. However, Latino/a as a category is best seen as panethnic and certainly very heterogeneous, in the sense that it encompasses a range of cultures, racial backgrounds, national origins, and other important dimensions of diversity (Delgado and Stefancic 1998).

Latino Diversity

Latino and Latina heterogeneity is often ignored in much of the social science literature, which often does not distinguish between the many national-origin groups included under the broad "Latino/a" umbrella. Glossing over identifications based on national origin can be problematic, both because Latino experiences and social processes differ systematically across subgroups and because Latinos themselves have not adopted the Latino label as a primary identity without also making reference to their specific national origin or subgroup. As Romero (1997) points out:

> The reduction of Mexicans, Chicanos, Puerto Ricans, Cubans, Dominicans, Salvadorans, Nicaraguans, Costa Ricans, and other groups to the single category of "Hispanic" has met with resistance. There are two main objections: one is the depoliticization of each group's distinct history with the U.S. (colonized, conquered, exploited, etc.); the other is the emphasis upon Hispanic (European) culture and ancestry, rather than African and indigenous cultures. (1997: xv).

The larger category of Latinos and Latinas is actually comprised of many subgroups, typically identified in terms of national origin. The largest of these subgroups—those explicitly mentioned on the Hispanic question on the 1980 and 1990 U.S. Census forms—are of Mexican, Puerto Rican, and Cuban origin. Table 2.1 shows the number and proportion of each group in 1997. The largest subgroup, comprising over two-thirds of all Latinos, is of Mexican origin. Mexican Americans can include those whose families have resided in the United States for two or more generations and often identify as Chicanos, as well as recent immigrants or their children, who tend to identify as Mexican or Mexican American (Gurin, Hurtado, and Peng, 1994; Flores Niemann et al. 1999). Mexican Americans are concentrated in California, Texas, New Mexico, and Arizona, with sizable populations in Illinois and New York.

Puerto Ricans, comprising over a tenth of Latinos (not including those residing in Puerto Rico), are concentrated in New York and Florida, with sizable numbers in New Jersey, Illinois, and New

TABLE 2.1
U.S. Latinos by National Origin or Ancestry, 1997

Group	Number (in thousands)	Proportion
Mexican Americans	18,795	63.3%
Puerto Ricans	3,152	10.6%
Cubans	1,258	4.2%
Central and South Americans	4,292	14.4%
Other Hispanics	2,206	7.4%
Total	29,703	100.0%

SOURCE: U.S. Bureau of the Census 1998.

England. The largest numbers of Cuban Americans are in Florida and New Jersey. Central and South Americans comprise about 1 in 7 Latinos and are concentrated in California (especially Los Angeles), Florida, and New York. The largest groups in this subcategory are Dominican, Salvadorian, and Colombian. Finally, other Hispanics include those who trace their ancestry to the original Spanish settlers of what is now the southwestern United States, as well as others who come from mixed families or did not otherwise identify a specific national origin. Many in this group live in New Mexico.

These national origin subgroups are diverse in a variety of ways, including geographic distribution, political affiliation, socioeconomic status, language use, and many cultural features. They also vary in terms of their relationship to U.S. racial constructs. Therefore, some groups are more likely to identify as White, while others more typically see themselves as neither White nor Black, but as comprising a distinct racial category. Both between and within these subgroups, there are variations in gender, nativity, immigration status, generation in the United States, acculturation status, social class, education, sexual orientation, and other variables that have an impact on intergroup relations, both among Latinos/as and between Latinos/as and other groups.

For example, for Latinas, *both* gender and ethnicity/race are significant and salient elements of their identity (see, for example, Ferdman and Gallegos 1996; Holvino 1996; Hurtado 1997; Moraga and Anzaldúa 1983). Within the family structure and in society at large, Latinas are seen as representing both women and Latinos rather than one or the other. When Latinas have negative experiences or encounter systemic barriers, it is often difficult or impossible for them to identify which part of their identity is being targeted or the extent to which their individual performance or personality is responsible for the situation. The resulting disorientation and uncertainty create fertile ground for Latinas to define themselves situationally and become astute at attending to the perceptions and expectations of others. This example illustrates how important it is to view identity as comprised of the interaction and combination of many elements, each of which gives meaning to the others (Ferdman 1995, 1999a, 1999b; Holvino 1997).

Latino "Groupness"

Given the great heterogeneity among Latinos and Latinas, what constitutes the group? Social science, literature, popular culture, and politics all support the idea of Latino unity in the context of Latino diversity. The unique historical and sociological context of the United States creates the backdrop for Latino identity.

Quiñones-Rosado (1998) argues that what unites and distinguishes the broad diversity of groups that constitute Latinos is a combination of geographical, cultural, and racial factors, together with the collective and overarching experience of colonialism. Both newcomers to the United States and those born here are defined and see themselves as different. At the same time, the racial thinking in the United States—which involves fairly rigid categories and views Latinos as distinct from Whites—has led to an inability to distinguish between Latinos of varying national origins. Thus, a new immigrant from Peru soon finds herself grouped together with a fourth-generation Chicano and the New York-born son of a Puertorriqueño.

Moore and Pachon (1985) argue that what makes Latinos a group is a combination of converging life situations, such as urban residency, disproportional poverty, and the experience of prejudice and discrimination, together with their treatment by the larger society and the large increase in their total number. Additionally, as Latinos have dispersed outside traditional geographic areas such as New York, Miami, and the southwestern United States, the similarities across subgroups become more salient than the differences. For example, in Vermont, where there are few Latinos, fewer distinctions are made on the basis of national origin, even within the group, than in Los Angeles, where communities are distinguished not only by nation but also by towns of origin. Overall, Latino identity has become defined as such in interactions with others. As Alejandro Portes (1990) puts it:

The emergence of a Hispanic "minority" has depended more on the actions of government and the collective perceptions of Anglo-American society than on the initiative of the individuals so designated. (1990:160)

We do not see it as an either/or question. In our view, Latino groupness emerges both from external factors, as Portes suggests, and from within-group factors, including common experiences and features among Latinos. For many Latinos these commonalities include Spanish language use, the valuing of cultural maintenance, a cultural focus on family, and religious traditions.[6] Yet, even by these criteria it is impossible to make sweeping generalizations that apply to all or even most Latinos.

A third element leading to Latino groupness, perhaps combining the external and internal factors, has been sociopolitical. A unified Latino identity has brought increased visibility, potency, and even political power to a large proportion of those so identified. Thus, both individual and group interests pull people together. Once that happens, Latinos feel connected and are effectively connected across subgroups. In sum, this sense of identification as a group is based on commonalities, treatment by others, and utilitarian reasons.[7]

Latinos and Racial Constructs

Latinos have had an uneasy relationship with prevailing racial constructs in the United States. These "either/or" notions, typically Black/White or White/not White, have not easily incorporated or allowed for the polychromatic (that is, multicolored) reality of Latinos. Latinos generally trace their heritage to the indigenous peoples of the Americas, to Africa, and to Europe, in varying combinations, and there are some with Asian roots as well. This means that, in terms of color and other markers used to categorize race in the United States, Latinos can span the complete range.

For example, Clara Rodríguez (1991) uses the term "rainbow people" to describe how confusing Puerto Ricans were to North Americans, because they were both White and Black, but they were also neither White nor Black. This was problematic on the mainland where race, rather than ethnicity or culture, was viewed as the primary marker. Based on her research, Rodríguez argues that for Puerto Ricans cultural identification comes first, before racial identification;

this is the opposite pattern to that common in the United States. Thus, even though Puerto Ricans can be quite sensitive to color (for example, Betances 1992; Rivera 1982), they identify culturally and ethnically across lines that seem, to Anglo eyes, to be uncrossable. Indeed, Puerto Ricans vary in their racial identification depending on context, including class, education, language, and birthplace (Rodríguez 1992; Rodríguez and Cordero-Guzman 1992).

Puerto Ricans and other Latinos who trace their origins to the Caribbean do not follow the binary system of racial classification that is common in the United States. For them, "race is perceived as a spectrum running from White to Black, with many people falling in between" (Denton and Massey 1989:791; see also Duany 1998; Rodríguez and Cordero-Guzman 1992). Similarly, for Mexicans and Mexican Americans the racial spectrum ranges from White to Indian; those who identify as representing a combination of Indian and European ancestries are typically referred to as "mestizo."[8] The continuous systems of color classification used by Latinos do not fit well with the dichotomous system predominant in the United States. Non-Hispanic Americans are much more accustomed to assuming that being of different racial categories implies a different ethnicity, while Latinos do not necessarily make this assumption. Thus, for example, when a dark-skinned Puerto Rican—who may be classified as Black on the U.S. mainland—looks at a person with light skin—classified as White—he does not necessarily assume a different ethnicity solely on that basis.

The bipolar system of racial categorization that predominates in the United States has a great impact on Latinos, however. Denton and Massey (1989) have shown, for example, that Caribbean Hispanics who identified racially as Black in the 1980 Census are highly segregated from non-Hispanic Whites, but only somewhat segregated from U.S. Blacks. Those Hispanics who classified themselves racially as White, in contrast, were highly segregated from U.S. Blacks, but only somewhat segregated from Anglos. The two groups of Hispanics were also somewhat segregated from each other. Finally, those Hispanics who identified as neither White nor Black were also highly segregated from both Black Hispanics and U.S. Blacks but quite integrated with White Hispanics.

In his memoirs of growing up in Manhattan, Edward Rivera (1982), a light-skinned Puerto Rican, gives an example of internalizing anti-Black prejudice and the divisions this sometimes caused with his darker-skinned friends. In his autobiography, *Down These Mean Streets*, Piri

Thomas (1967), who migrated from Puerto Rico to the mainland with his family, provides a particularly poignant and well-known account of the experience of being confronted with the dichotomous notions of Black and White that operated in the New York of the 1950s. As Haney López (1998) puts it, Thomas "describes his transformation, which is both willed and yet not willed, from a Puerto Rican into someone Black" (1998:161). Interestingly, dark-skinned Piri had a very different experience in the Long Island schools than his light-skinned siblings. Piri's classmates refused to see him as anything but Black. This impacted his family, who wanted to choose to be White as the key to social mobility and the American dream. Also, the family's experience and treatment, as well as the way they were viewed racially, were very different in Puerto Rico, where the range of skin color in the family was typical, and in New York, where they were forced to choose between Black and White. This contrast eventually split the family (Haney López 1998). Haney López further explains that Thomas's "dislocations suggest a spatial component to racial identities, an implication confirmed in Thomas's travel from Spanish Harlem, where he was Puerto Rican, to Long Island, where he was accused of trying to pass, to the South, where he was black" (1998:165). Duany (1998) cites the case of a "mulatto Dominican colleague . . . [who] 'discovered' that she was Black only when she first came to the United States; until then she had thought of herself as an *india clara* (literally, a light Indian) in a country whose aboriginal population was practically exterminated in the 16th century" (1998:147).

A common response to this situation has been the tendency to treat Latino identity as one more racial category and to attempt to force it to fit into the U.S. racial system.[9] Many surveys or forms inquiring about race, for example, include Latino or Hispanic as one of the categories from which to choose. The U.S. government, however, including the Bureau of the Census, classifies Hispanic identity as an ethnic—not a racial—classification. Hispanic or Latino is not an option on the Census race question, and the U.S. Office of Management and Budget (1998) in its official definition describes "Hispanic" as a "person of Mexican, Puerto Rican, Cuban, Central or South American or other Spanish culture or origin, regardless of race."[10] This directive goes on to make the following suggestion:

> To provide flexibility, it is preferable to collect data on race and ethnicity separately. If separate race and ethnic categories are used, the mini-

mum designations are: a. Race: American Indian or Alaskan Native, Asian or Pacific Islander, Black, White; b. Ethnicity: Hispanic origin, Not of Hispanic origin. When race and ethnicity are collected separately, the number of white and black persons who are Hispanic must be identified, and capable of being reported in that category. (U.S. Office of Management and Budget 1998:158)

Within this system, Latinos are asked to identify themselves (or are identified by others) in terms of one of the four racial categories listed. In practice, this would mean classifying Latinos as either Black or White. Nevertheless, in 1990 a large proportion of Latinos (43 percent) classified themselves as being of "Other" race on the U.S. Census race question. Fifty-two percent of Latinos identified themselves as White on the 1990 Census, and 3 percent identified racially as Black. These percentages varied depending on the state, indicating both subgroup and regional differences in the degree to which being Hispanic was viewed as a racial construct. For example, in California, 50 percent of those responding "yes" to the Hispanic question said they were of "other" race, suggesting that they viewed Latino identity as a racial category. In contrast, in Florida only 15 percent of Hispanics said that they were of "other" race, while 80 percent said they were White. These percentages also vary as a function of the Hispanic subgroup. In the 1980 U.S. Census, for example, 37.5 percent of those of Mexican origin and 43.1 percent of Puerto Ricans said they were neither White nor Black, while only 10.5 percent of Cubans did so (Denton and Massey 1989). The proportion claiming White race in each of these groups was 55.4 percent, 48.3 percent, and 83.8 percent, respectively.[11] Massey and Denton (1992) have shown that people of Mexican origin with higher socioeconomic status—both native- and foreign-born—were much more likely to self-identify as White than as mestizo (that is, of mixed European and Indian background). Also, Mexican immigrants who had greater English language ability and were older (and thus had more experience in the United States) were also more likely to identify as White. Mestizos, in contrast to White Mexicans, were also less likely to live in suburban areas and thus were less likely to come into contact with non-Hispanic Whites.

Rodríguez (1992; Rodríguez and Cordero-Guzman 1992) interprets the high number of Latinos who identify as "other" as indicating a rejection of U.S. concepts of race as well as the fluidity of Latino racial constructs. Indeed, in her research she found that among Puerto Ricans who were asked about their race in an open-ended format ("How would you describe yourself racially?"), only 11.1 percent said they were "White" and 1.6 percent said they were "Black," (compared to 44.2 percent and 3.9 percent, respectively, on the 1980 Census). Instead, they used a variety of terms, mostly referring to sociocultural characteristics rather than physical attributes. Interestingly, a substantial number of individuals labeled themselves as "other" in response to a closed question, but were seen as White by the interviewers (16.2 percent), or labeled themselves as White but were considered to be "Other" by the interviewers (23.3 percent). Finally, while 5.1 percent of the sample labeled themselves as "Black," 11.9 percent thought that North Americans would see them as Black. Rodríguez and Cordero-Guzman conclude:

> The findings indicate that we cannot automatically assume that because Puerto Ricans choose to identify as "Other" they are placing themselves in a racially intermediate situation. For some Puerto Ricans, a cultural response also carries a racial implication, that is, they see race and culture as being fused. They emphasize the greater validity of ethnic or cultural identity. Culture is race, regardless of the physical types within the culture. Others see their culture as representing a "mixed" people. Still others view these concepts as independent, and a cultural response does not imply a racial designation for them. In this latter case, a respondent may identify as "Other-Puerto Rican" because he or she is not culturally or politically like white Americans or black Americans, regardless of his or her particular race. In essence, the United States of America may choose to divide its culture into White and Black races, but a Puerto Rican will not. (1992:539)

Thus, the variation in their relationship to predominant racial constructs in the United States makes it difficult to try to describe the racial identity of Latinos in conventional ways. Latinos both transcend and challenge the predominant categories. At the same time, Latinos have been molded and impacted by those very categories.

Luis Angel Toro (1998), reacting to the implications of OMB Directive No. 15 for Latinos, writes that "for most Chicanos, Directive No. 15 presents no right answer. Instead, Chicanos must choose some formula that misstates their identity or be forced into the statistical limbo of the 'Other' classification" (1998:211). He then goes on to give examples of the difficulties that some individuals may encounter when they try to answer questions based on the Directive. This includes a Chicano family in which the parents classify themselves differently from their children, and a fourth-generation Chicano who identifies with the American Indian category, based on his mestizo identity, rather than with the term Hispanic.

Similarly, Weinstein (1998) found in her study of ethnic identity among the children of one Mexican or Mexican American and one European American parent that self-assessed phenotype was not related to strength of ethnic identity. However, there was a negative correlation between respondents' assessment of how much they looked like a "typical Mexican" and how much they looked like a typical "White." This suggested a racialized[12] concept of Mexicanness among this group of individuals, in the sense that looking Mexican was generally seen as distinct from and incompatible with looking White. This is consistent with common usage in California, where newspapers and other media typically use "Latino" as a racial label, similar to the use of "Caucasian," "Black," or "Asian."

In her assessment of the operation of race and racial constructs among Puerto Ricans, Clara Rodríguez (1991) noted five key trends. First, she described Puerto Ricans as tending to see "White" and "Black" as cultural terms. While (at least initially) both Black and White Americans tend to assign these categories on the basis of phenotypes, and so would put Puerto Ricans in one or the other group depending on their physical appearance, Puerto Ricans themselves assign these categories on the basis of ethnic affiliation. Thus, Puerto Ricans generally do not see themselves as White or Black or as belonging to either group. Second, Puerto Ricans tend to use non-White as the default category for themselves. In other words, if forced to think in racial terms, they will not classify themselves as White. Third, Puerto Ricans use contextual racial definitions, often using different terms to self-identify racially at different times or in different situations, depending on the context. Fourth, Puerto Ricans apply a concept of deflected race, in the sense that the racial categorization of those in an individual's social surroundings can "rub off" on that person. When someone is accepted into a Whiter environment, for example through marriage or occupation, she can in a sense blend in and be considered White, regardless of phenotype or prior racial categorization. Fifth and finally, Puerto Ricans can appear to others as racial chameleons, switching racial identities from one situation and from one time period to another.

These dynamics are not limited to Puerto Ricans. Certainly, they are present in varying degrees in all the Latino subgroups. More recent immigrants from Mexico, for example, sometimes refer to Whites on the basis of national origin as "Americanos" (Americans). In this context, Whiteness and U.S. citizenship are considered synonymous. This label may also be a reflection of the dominance of the United States in the Mexican psyche without reference to race or color as distinguishing factors. Also, this nomenclature suggests implicitly that while there are "Americans" throughout the continent, those who count most are citizens of the United States.

In sum, the racial constructs that have predominated in the United States do not easily apply to Latinos, and when they are forced to fit, they truncate and distort Latino realities. We shall now briefly discuss a few themes key to understanding Latino experiences of and reactions to race and racism.

Race and Color Are Important, but Secondary to Culture

As discussed earlier, Latinos identify with each other across lines that would be seen as racial in the United States (and therefore indicative of different groups). This is because "Latino" is experienced and treated as an ethnic and cultural category more than a racial one. This also means that someone claiming Latino identity solely on the basis of ancestry, with no ethnic or cultural markers attached, is less likely to be accepted as a genuine member of the group.[13]

Nevertheless, color is a large issue in the Latino community, and racism, in the sense of a preference for and valuing of Whiteness and denial of African and indigenous heritage, remains common. A reaction to this can be seen in much Latino poetry (for example, Lorna Dee Cervantes, Tato Laviera, Aurora Levins Morales) and music (for example, Rubén Blades; see also Flores and Yúdice 1990; Padilla 1989) as well as in the Chicano rights movement that sought in part to instill pride in the mestizo heritage (see Klor de Alva 1999).

"Rainbow" Identities: Racial Fluidity and Mestizaje

Because they span the color spectrum, Latinos cannot be racially categorized in a simple manner. One result of this is that the categories used constantly shift from one individual to another and from one situation to another. In Mexico, "Indians" are considered to be those living in their villages and maintaining Indian cultural traditions. Once the same individuals move to the city and assimilate into the dominant Mexican culture, they are no longer classified as "Indians" but become "Mexicans."

Historically Latinos have been the product of the blending of many cultures and ancestors. When Spain's dominance was at its peak, Spanish explorers covered the globe, gaining resources and territories for their native country. In the process, they conquered, colonized, and intermarried with native, indigenous people in most of the regions in which they established themselves. The intermingling process often included native "indios," Africans, Asians, and many other subgroups. The generations resulting from this blending of groups cannot be considered to belong to any one race but rather to many races. Thus the terms "mestizaje" or "mestizo" are meant to represent the current group—including many elements but none to the exclusion of others. Furthermore, it goes beyond a concept of biological blending to include cultural unity as well.[14]

Diverse Reactions to the U.S. Racial Order

Reactions to the imposed and self-imposed racial categories in the United States range from denial and shame to pride and acceptance. As described earlier, many Latinos choose to see themselves as White, while others place themselves in a distinct Latino racial category. Choosing to self-label as White could simply be a way of coping with the Census and describing one's perceived skin color. Or it could indicate a preference for one's European ancestry over one's African and/or Native American background. While some Latinos reject the label "person of color," because they see it as lumping them together with other groups that they would rather not compare themselves to, others are very proud of this denomination, and use it for precisely the same reason that others reject it. This theme is developed in later sections.

Variables in Individual Identity Development

Certainly, life experiences have a strong impact on the way individuals view themselves ethnically and racially. The familial and cultural context one is born into sets the initial parameters for one's identity.

Parents and extended family members instruct and inform children about the boundaries of "groupness," defining "our people" and distinguishing them from the "others" to be avoided, feared, respected, or emulated. The messages and attitudes about one's group conveyed by significant caregivers set the stage for understanding who one is in relation to other groups. Many Latinos are raised in relatively homogeneous environments where most significant contacts are primarily with other Latinos. Only upon entry into educational institutions do they begin to encounter people unlike themselves and get messages from others about how their group is seen. What they learned at home about themselves (for example, "we are better than others," "we are less than others," "we are no different than others," and so on) begins the process of orientation to the group. Later, in school, new messages about the group impact them and further shape their identity (see, for example, Zanger 1994). Again, these messages can be positive or negative depending on the environment and demographics of the region and teachers' attitudes to Latinos.

While the messages individual Latinos receive about the group may be positive, negative, or neutral, they have choices about how to respond to those messages. For example, if, as is all too common, teachers send the message that speaking Spanish is a barrier to the child's success, the child and the family can respond by accepting the teacher's viewpoint and work to eliminate Spanish from the child's communication, or they can resist the teacher's influence and strive to retain the child's bilingualism, or they can go underground and teach the child to speak Spanish only at home and avoid speaking it at school. They can accept the systemic push toward assimilation into the mainstream or they can find other ways of managing the tension of bilingualism. In this and other situations, individuals and families constantly make choices about how they see their difference and how they accommodate societal messages about themselves.

Early experiences with other ethnic and racial groups also have a strong influence on one's identity. Whether the exposure is to highly segregated or integrated environments influences how a particular Latino sees him/herself in relation to others. For example, being one of only a few Latinos in a predominantly White school would have very different consequences for the individual than being exposed to a highly diverse, multiethnic environment or a primarily Latino environment. This exposure, especially to Whites and other ethnic groups, influences whether these groups are seen as allies or potential enemies, as competitors or colleagues.

While early experiences lay the foundation for group identification, adult life experiences also influence the way people identify their group and other groups. For example, individuals raised in fairly homogeneous, primarily Latino environments can be significantly affected by later exposure to more heterogeneous situations. Whether adult experiences with other groups are positive or negative can profoundly impact and modify early messages about one's identity in relation to other groups. Limited exposure to other ethnic and racial groups during their formative years of development may not adequately prepare people to deal with the diverse reality they encounter in adult life. If their messages about other groups were fairly positive, it may be unsettling and confusing to encounter racism and intergroup conflict. On the other hand, if there was a lack of exposure to other groups, or early messages about them were primarily negative, the reality of individual variation and group differences can challenge preexisting paradigms about others and the "racial order" they learned in their youth.

How one navigates one's way through various life experiences and the meanings attributed to these experiences shapes the ongoing sense of self in relation to other Latinos and other groups. Thus identity development needs to be seen as an ongoing, dynamic process rather than a static event, fluid rather than immutable once established. Additional factors that influence identity have been mentioned in prior sections of this chapter. National origin, generational status, early socialization, socioeconomic status, language patterns, levels of acculturation, physical appearance, color, gender, and geographical location are some of the major determinants of how an individual comes to see her- or himself in the racial order of U.S. society. In the next section, we present an initial framework for conceptualizing varying orientations to racial identity among Latinos and Latinas.

Reflections on Latino Diversity and Identity Development: Toward a Model?

Latino realities and perceptions, as described in prior sections, are complex and multifaceted. Ilan Stavans (1995), describing Latino

identity, refers to it as a "labyrinth" and discusses its mazelike qualities. Those just entering the maze and trying to make their way
through it can find it quite confusing and exasperating, especially if
they are accustomed to simple and linear paths. However, even
mazes have some logic and certainly beauty to them, especially when
examined from above. Stavans describes the labyrinth as follows:

> Linear and circuitous, inextricable and impenetrable, the maze—com-
> plex, curved, distorted, wandering, winding, with constant double
> tracks—is a map of the Latino psyche. The apparent confusion it pro-
> jects is only an illusion, a mask that is designed to entrap the mind, a
> concealment ready to catch you, to fool your senses in spite of your
> most purified awareness. A metaphor of metaphysical ambiguity, a fig-
> ure that changes according to perspective, it confuses, infuriates, and
> disorganizes, but in its lack of organization, in its chaos, it is an exam-
> ple of perfected craftiness. . . . We simultaneously incorporate clarity
> and confusion, unity and multiplicity. (1995:93)

The reality of Latino identity, then, is precisely its labyrinthine nature. The difficulty in understanding Latinos is caused primarily by
attempts to impose models from other racial groups onto Latinos,
who defy easy categorization.[15] Here, we try to provide a guide
through this meandering path with some thoughts about the types
of identities Latinos may display, with particular reference to race
and the racial order. We do not, however, intend this to be a model
based on stages of development, but rather as a description of patterns we have observed. Stage models often imply that people
move in a fairly sequential way through the various stages and
build from one developmental step to the next (for example, Cross
1995; Helms 1995; Thompson and Carter 1997). Although some of
the models acknowledge that racial identity development can be
cyclical and is not necessarily linear, the stages are usually presented
in the order that most people are thought to progress through them.
Our thinking about Latino development at this point certainly suggests more patterns and orientations than clear-cut, predictable
steps. In the context of our initial model, there may be movement
from one orientation to another depending on a number of factors. It is also possible and feasible for some individuals to maintain
one orientation throughout their lives with little or no movement
or change.

A Model of Latino Identity Development

As we have stressed throughout this chapter, many factors influence the way individual Latinos identify with their group. We present the following model as a way of describing various possible orientations. Each of the patterns identified can be a valid response to the myriad pressures Latinos face in coming to define themselves in a society that often disparages their identity and seeks to impose definitions rather than allow self-identification.

The most important dimensions in defining one's orientation toward one's identity as Latino/a, according to this model, include one's "lens" toward identity, how individuals prefer to identify themselves, how Latinos as a group are seen, how Whites are seen, and how "race" fits into the equation (see Table 2.2; it is important to stress again that the graphic representation of the orientations in the table is not meant to imply a linear stage model of development.)

TABLE 2.2
Latino and Latina Racial Identity Orientations

Orientation	Lens	Identify as/ prefer	Latinos are seen	Whites are seen	Framing of Race
Latino-integrated	Wide	Individuals in a group context	Positively	Complex	Dynamic, contextual, socially constructed
Latino-identified (Racial/Raza)	Broad	Latinos	Very positively	Distinct; could be barriers or allies	Latino/not Latino
Subgroup-identified	Narrow	Own subgroup	My group OK, others maybe	Not central (could be barriers or blockers)	Not clear or central; secondary to to nationality, ethnicity, culture
Latino as Other	External	Not White	Generically, fuzzily	Negatively	White/not White
Undifferentiated/ Denial	Closed	People	"Who are Latinos?"	Supposed color-blind (accept dominant norms)	Denial, irrelevant invisible
White-identified	Tinted	Whites	Negatively	Very positively	White/Black, either/or, one-drop or "mejorar la raza" (i.e., improve the race)

The metaphor of a "lens" fits well into our model, as it summarizes the way individuals view their ethnicity, how they "see" the wider issues and context of racial groups in the United States, and how much they take in versus how much they keep out. Our lenses for race limit the data we take in and support our frameworks for making sense of the environment.

Orientations toward Latino Identity

In this section we present the types of orientations that we see among Latinos and Latinas. These do not exhaust the possibilities, nor do they address the complex issues involved in ethnic and cultural identity (see, for example, Ferdman 1990; Ferdman and Cortes 1992; Ferdman 2000; Ferdman and Horenczyk, in press).

ORIENTATION: LATINO-INTEGRATED

Latino-integrated individuals understand and are able to deal with the full complexity of Latino identity. They are aware of their own subgroup background and culture as well as how these relate to those of other Latino subgroups. Their Latino identity is fully integrated with their other social identities—for example, those based on gender, class, professional, and other dimensions. They are able to understand, explain, and use the interconnections, and understand and identify with many parts of themselves. Latinos with this type of racial identity orientation have a sense of themselves based on a philosophy of "both/and" rather than "either/or." Their identification with Latinos as a group encompasses both positive and negative attributions; they are able to appreciate the beauty and resilience of Latinos together with negative aspects of the group. They take into account the importance of their group membership without making this the only part of themselves they are aware of. For example, Latinas with an integrated orientation can identify fully with their culture and appreciate many of its aspects, while still being able to criticize other features and advocate for equality as women within the group. Identifying with their gender identity as women does not preclude their identification with Latinos as a group.

A Latino-integrated individual is quite comfortable with and inclusive of all types of Latinos. He or she is able to educate other Latinos about race and racial identity, and is quite likely to challenge prevailing constructions of race. Of all the orientations in this model, this one utilizes the widest lens possible in viewing Latinos and the social context of the United States. Latino-integrated individuals see themselves and other Latinos as one of many groups coexisting in the multicultural fabric of the United States. Whites and members of other groups are seen broadly as well, and the complexity of their cultural and individual orientations is recognized and accepted. Individuals are seen as distinct from one another and as members of various groups.

ORIENTATION: LATINO-IDENTIFIED

Latinos with what we call a "Latino-identified" orientation maintain a pan-Latino identity but in a relatively nonrigid fashion that places culture, history, and other ethnic markers in a relatively prominent place. Compared to the orientations described later, they also have a less rigid view of other groups, which increases the possibilities and skills for networking and coalition building. Their notion of race is a uniquely Latino one, which means they do not accept the either/or nature of U.S. racial constructs. Theirs is a much more fluid, inclusive, and dynamic orientation than the others.

Many Latinos of this orientation define themselves as *La Raza*, a complex term that defies easy translation. As Oquendo describes it:

> [T]he word "race"—or rather the Spanish equivalent *raza*—has special significance for Latino/as in the United States, particularly for Chicanos. *Raza* evokes a primeval and mythical union with the indigenous people that populated the North American expanse of Aztlan. The natives of Aztlan spread south and eventually formed the Nahuatl tribes living in Mexico as the European conquest began. The concept of race also has political connotations. "Raza" is the name taken by the organizations that initiated and have continued the struggle for political, social, and economic empowerment of the Chicano community. (1998:69)

Latino-identified persons view Latinos as a whole as constituting a distinct racial category across all Latino subgroups, and they identify with the entire group broadly defined, which they see very positively. They view Whites as constituting a distinctly different racial group, whose members can be potential barriers or allies, depending on their behavior. They see systemic factors and institutional racism as quite real and therefore actively value the fight against discrimination. For Latino-identified persons, culture is typically secondary to *raza*, which they see as transcending cultural markers. They may see Whites, Blacks, and other groups in categorical and relatively rigid, unshifting terms.

ORIENTATION: SUBGROUP IDENTIFIED

Subgroup identified Latinos think of themselves primarily in terms of their own ethnic or national-origin subgroup, which is the focus of their identification. They view themselves as distinct from Whites but do not necessarily identify with other Latinos or people of color. Although aware of discrimination against themselves and other Latinos, they do not easily connect or identify with other Latino groups. They may join coalitions across subgroups, not so much from a sense of shared history or culture but more from necessity and the practical reality of greater numbers leading to increased societal power. Also, such individuals may vary in the degree to which their subgroup is a source of positive versus negative social identity, but in general they will prefer strategies for collective social change over the strategies for individual social mobility preferred by those who are White-identified.

At the same time, subgroup identified Latinos do not have the broad pan-Latino perspective of Latino-identified or Latino-integrated persons. In terms of our model, individuals with this orientation employ a more narrow and exclusive view of their groupness. They prefer to identify almost exclusively with their own particular subgroup, which they view positively, and they may view other groups, including other Latino subgroups, as deficient or inferior. Whites are not central to their thinking though they are conscious that Whites can be barriers to their full inclusion. Subgroup-identified Latinos do not view race as a central or clear organizing concept; instead nationality, ethnicity, and culture are seen as primary.

ORIENTATION: LATINO AS "OTHER"

Individuals with the orientation of Latino as "Other" are not very aware of their specific Latino background, history, and culture, but because of mixed background, phenotype, prevailing racial constructions, and other factors simply see themselves in a generic fashion as "persons of color" without distinguishing themselves from other subgroups. Thus, an individual with this orientation may describe him- or herself in some situations as a "minority." He or she may also resist such categorization and unite with others to eliminate such terminology.

In terms of our model, the lens primarily utilized by people with this orientation is an external one focused on the way the group is viewed by those outside the group. Such individuals see themselves as "not White" and do not have a clear view or much knowledge of their own group. They do not adhere to Latino cultural values or norms but do not identify with White cultural values or norms either. They see Whites as distinct and frame race as White or not White. The difference between a "White-identified" orientation (below) and Latino as "other" is that those with the latter orientation identify themselves as being on the other end of the continuum and see their color as a major unifying factor that connects them to other people of color rather than to the dominant group.

ORIENTATION: UNDIFFERENTIATED

Latinos with an undifferentiated orientation use a lens that is relatively closed in comparison to the other patterns. They prefer to identify themselves and others as "just people," often claiming to be color-blind and promoting this orientation to others of all groups. "Why can't we all just get along?" might be the motto for this group. They do not share the focus on racial categorization that many people have in the United States and they live their lives relatively oblivious to differences in general. They accept the dominant norms of our society without question and when they encounter barriers to their inclusion, they attribute these setbacks to individual behavior rather than intergroup dynamics. They do not seek any particular association with other Latinos, since they prefer to view each person as distinct from his or her racial or ethnic identity.

ORIENTATION: WHITE-IDENTIFIED

White-identified Latinos are those who are likely to see themselves racially as White, and as distinct from, and generally superior to, people of color. This orientation includes individuals who value and prefer "Whiteness" and all that it connotes. Such persons can be assimilated to White culture and society and quite disconnected from other Latinos, or alternately can be connected to a particular Latino subgroup (for example, Cuban refugees) while denying or not seeing any connection to other subgroups. This orientation is also reflected in people who recognize, either consciously or unconsciously, that they are different in some way from Whites as defined in the U.S., but they continue to prefer all that is connected to Whiteness, and to empha-size that for themselves and/or their children. Essentially, this means that they are generally accepting and unquestioning of the U.S. racial order. Although people in this orientation may be bicultural, they value Whiteness as an essential and primary element of their identity.

Latinos who are White-identified see the world through a White-tinted lens, preferring Whites and White culture over Latinos and Latino culture. They generally view Latinos as less than Whites, whom they view very positively when making cross-group compar-isons. White-identified Latinos view race in bifurcated terms—White or Black—with clear-cut distinctions. Such individuals may ascribe to the "one-drop rule," seeing people clearly on one side or the other of the racial divide. They view intermarriage with Whites positively while viewing marriage to darker groups negatively. A term often heard among Latinos with this orientation is *mejorar la raza*, which in-dicates that they see marrying Whites as a way of improving Latinos, while marrying Blacks or Browns diminishes the group.

Extending the Model

What we have presented so far is an initial framework that can and should be extended and further developed. Areas that we believe it would be most fruitful to pursue include the following:

- To what extent does each orientation capture the range of an in-dividual's experience? Can someone incorporate elements of more than one orientation at once? Under what conditions will this be the case?
- What factors lead to each orientation? How are the specific so-cialization contexts or life experiences related to individual ori-entations? What is the role of variables such as external stres-sors, perceived threats from others to oneself or to one's group, relationships with other people, language use and ability, phe-notype, and family composition? How do life circumstances and their meanings relate to individual orientations, both as an-tecedents and as consequences?
- How fluid are individuals' orientations? When and how do peo-ple transition between different orientations? What life events or other factors trigger or facilitate such transitions? Are there

typical transition sequences that can be observed or are transitions relatively idiosyncratic? What is the experience of such movement like for the person?

- What are the unique strengths associated with each orientation? How do individuals with the various orientations fit into varying roles in organizations or other societal institutions?
- What are the consequences of individuals' orientations for life choices and other outcomes? Are there systematic differences between people with different orientations?
- What is the best way to assess where an individual is in terms of the model? What are the types of manifestations or indicators best suited to measuring racial identity orientations?

The question of transitions between orientations is a particularly important one. As individuals change their social circumstances or their ecological conditions—for example, by moving from one neighborhood or city to another, going to college or the military, encountering discrimination, or living through social change processes such as the civil rights movement of the 1960s—their racial identity orientation is likely to be challenged and in many cases modified. An example of this process is provided by Joseph Tovares (1998), a college-educated Chicano from Texas reporting on farm workers for a television news program, who in the process of engaging with the subjects of his story reconnected with other Latinos across class lines. In summarizing his experience, he stated that it "made me confront ugly realities about how this society treats a hidden underclass. Most important, it made me realize how easy it is for many of us who have escaped to simply forget" (98).

Implications of the Model for Research and Practice

The model we have presented is not intended to pigeonhole individuals, but to be a descriptive approach to capturing some of the richness and variety inherent in the Latino experience in the United States. By acknowledging the diversity among Latinos in orientations toward race and racial identity, we hope to help foster a societal environment in which Latinos and Latinas are more fully included and understood. Thus we must caution against overgeneralizations about individuals on the basis of this model. Nevertheless, it can provide a basis for research and practice with Latinos that is especially cognizant of the range of orientations toward race in this population.

This model represents an initial attempt to describe the various orientations that Latinos and Latinas may have regarding their own racial identity. We believe that it can be useful to someone seeking to understand or work with Latinos and Latinas in a way that more broadly recognizes and accepts the breadth of their experience. By cutting across traditional demographic markers such as national origin, the model provides a way of describing many of the psychological commonalities among Latinos without force-fitting them into one mold. In this sense, the model is useful not only as an account of Latino and Latina identity, but also as a reminder of broader lessons regarding the complexity of identity among all groups.

The model may have specific applications in research, education, the workplace, or other contexts. For example, researchers interested in Latinos can use it to consider more carefully the characteristics of the specific subgroups on which they focus. It may be insufficient to describe the demographic composition of a research sample when variations in results may be related to the different racial identity orientations represented. Those interested in more fully including Latinos in educational or work contexts will need to consider how an initiative may be interpreted by those holding different orientations. For example, individuals who are White-identified may react quite differently to opportunities targeted specifically to Latinos than those who are Latino-identified. Dynamics that may be puzzling to non-Latinos—for example, apparent in-group conflicts—may become more comprehensible when seen through the prism of the model we have presented.

As the Latino population in the United States grows, it will be incumbent on everyone to learn more about this group. As Latinos play an increasing role in the future of the United States, perspectives and information that deepen our knowledge about how best to include this group will be especially important. The model we have presented may be useful in increasing our collective capacity to deal with the complexity of Latino diversity specifically and racial constructs more generally. Rather than force-fitting Latinos into categories that do not fit, we may need to create larger or different categories. This will involve shifting frameworks for individuals and groups, and can provide valuable insight not only into Latinos but into other groups as well. For example, the U.S. Census is now dealing with the growth of "Multiracial" as a category. From all indications, this will be the wave of the future. Latinos have a long history of dealing with mixture, from which much can be learned.

The broadening of racial thinking in the United States to include groups other than Blacks and Whites will expand our collective understanding, and will help us address the complexities and realities of race relations in this country.

NOTES

We are grateful to Evangelina Holvino and the editors of this volume for their thoughtful and very helpful comments on earlier drafts of the chapter.

1. When we refer to Latinos, we mean the term to include both men and women. We have chosen this usage to avoid the cumbersome "Latino/a" or "Latinos and Latinas" in every case, although we often do use the longer terms to highlight our discomfort with using the male-gendered noun or adjective "Latino" exclusively.

2. For elaborated accounts of similar experiences and discussion of the implications for Latinos of the bipolar Black/White paradigm for racial classification prevalent in the United States, see Delgado 1998; E. Martínez 1998; Perea 1998. In a related vein, Evangelina Holvino (personal communication, November 20, 1999) reminded us that while identity is complex for anyone, Latinos are unique in the United States in that we have tried to maintain this complexity in the foreground.

3. It is important to point out that we do not address Latino ethnic identity in this chapter. This has been the subject of much theoretical and empirical work (e.g., Bernal and Knight 1993; Padilla 1995) which focuses on the cultural aspects of Latino identity (see also Ferdman 1992 for a discussion of the components of ethnicity). Helms (1996) distinguishes racial and ethnic identity models, suggesting that those primarily related to intergroup relations of domination and oppression should be considered "racial," while those focused on the acquisition and maintenance of cultural characteristics should be considered "ethnic." This chapter addresses primarily the former and not the latter.

4. We believe that there is a shift going on at present toward a growing usage and preference for the term "Latino" as the denominator for the group. However, a significant segment of the population, including many members of the group, prefers and continues to use the term "Hispanic." Thus, while

our own preference is for "Latino" and "Latina," we also use "Hispanic," in particular when this is how the authors or sources that we cite used it. (See note 5 for further discussion of this issue.)

5. The Census uses the term "Hispanic" and includes people from Spain in this category. Most social scientists using the term Latino, however, focus on people from the Americas. Quiñones-Rosado provides a useful discussion of the debate on the use of these terms and the reasons why he prefers "Latino" to "Hispanic." As he puts it:

> In contrast with the term "Hispanic," the primary point of reference of the term "Latino" is not Spain, but rather Spain's former colonies in Latin America. Therefore, "Latinos/as" are people of Latin-American origin, with ties to the region that encompasses virtually all of South America, much of the Caribbean, and Central America, and Mexico, *including* those parts of the national territory of the United States which were appropriated from Mexico not all that long ago: Texas, New Mexico, Colorado, Nevada, California, Arizona. (1998:21, italics in original)

He goes on to argue:

> So it is the combined forces of geography, culture, race, nationality and colonialism that define the Latin-American experience. And it is this gestalt, this dynamic interaction of elements, that provides the basic framework for a definition of U.S. "Latinos,"—not merely the Spanish language or other cultural ties to Spain. (1998:22)

6. In 1990, over three-fourths of Latinos over the age of five spoke at least some Spanish at home (U.S. Bureau of the Census 1993). The growth of the Latino population has allowed and fostered the maintenance of cultural values and traditions. In contrast to the one-way assimilation predicted by sociologists in the past (Frederickson 1999), Latinos as a group value cultural preservation a great deal. Even though assimilation continues to take place for many individuals, the dominant patterns are often absorbed and converted to Latino realities, and bicultural patterns are quite prevalent (Bernal and Knight 1993; Birman 1998; Cuellar et al. 1997; Phinney and Devich-Navarro 1997). Latinos who leave ethnic enclaves for more mixed neighborhoods, rather than assimilating, often show increases in ethnic pride (Safa 1988). Further, a focus and valuing of family continues to be a common denominator in Latino communities. Finally, the vast majority of Latinos are Roman Catholic in practice or background (although this is rapidly changing with the influx of many Latinos into fundamentalist Protestant denominations and other religions).

7. For additional discussion of these issues, see Jones-Correa and Leal (1996). These authors review and critique the competing positions regarding the degree to which Latino identity reflects shared cultural features across the various national- origin groups versus simply an instrumental way to facili-

tate collective action. Using data from the Latino National Political Survey, they find that neither the cultural nor the instrumental model is sufficient to explain Latino identification with panethnic categories. Distinguishing between *constructed* and *instrumental* identities, these researchers conclude:

What the data suggest is that Latino identity is (as many have suggested) largely constructed in the United States, rather than being brought wholesale to the United States by immigrants from Latin America. However, the data also suggest that this identity, once constructed, is not being used simply instrumentally. People who choose a panethnic identifier seem to do so in general, regardless of the specific circumstances and apart from any strategic consideration . . . . The fact that people's identities may be constructed does not argue against the suggestion that they may have real attachments to these constructed identities. (1996:239–240)

8. Klor de Alva analyzes the development and use of the construct of "mestizo" over the centuries, as well as the associated "ideology of mestizaje" (1999:175), which he describes as being—in its Mexican form in the early part of the twentieth century—"the powerful nation-building myth that was to help link dark-skinned castas, Euro-Americans, and Indians into one nation-state" (1999:175). Klor de Alva refers to mestizaje as "cipher-like." According to him, a "cipher is a place holder denoting neither quantity nor magnitude" and also "stands both for a coded method of inscription and for the key that unlocks the coded meaning" (1999:175). Thus, he chooses the metaphor of "'cipherspace'—a space that can hide the secrets of identity while simultaneously providing the clues to its discovery" to describe "the conceptual and social space of mestizaje" (1999:175).

9. George Martinez (1998) discusses the contrasts and tensions between the frequent legal constructions of Mexican Americans as White and their construction as a racial "Other" by Anglo writers, opinion makers, and the general public.

10. In October 1997, the U.S. Office of Management and Budget (OMB) published revised standards for collecting data on race and ethnicity as Appendix A in U.S. Office of Management and Budget 1999. In this new document, Hispanic or Latino continues to be defined the same way as before. However, the standards provide that, with respect to the available categories on data-gathering forms, "respondents shall be offered the option of selecting one or more racial designations" (1999:75). Moreover, in a section of the implementation guide, the OMB writes: "Under the new standards, 'Hispanic or Latino' is clearly designated as an ethnicity and not as a race. Whether or not an individual is Hispanic, every effort should be made to ascertain the race or races with which an individual identifies" (1999:10). This could be interpreted in at least two ways. On the one hand, the OMB may be

acknowledging that Latinos conceptualize race differently from others in the United States. On the other hand, and more likely, this may be interpreted as reinforcing the racial categorization system that has predominated over the course of U.S. history (the only change being the recognition of the increasing Multiracial component of the population).

11. In 1996, the U.S. Census conducted studies to assess the impact of various potential changes for the 2000 Census, including (a) adding a Multiracial category to the race question, (b) permitting respondents to pick more than one category on the race question, and (c) placing the question about Hispanic origin before the race question, rather than after it as in the 1990 Census (see U.S. Bureau of the Census 1996, 1997). Some of the results of these studies were quite interesting from the perspective of understanding the racial identity of Latinos. First, over 25 percent of Hispanics did not respond at all to the question asking about race (which did not include a choice of *Hispanic*). Second, and most interesting in terms of the present chapter, when respondents were asked whether or not they were of "Hispanic/Spanish origin" before they were asked their racial category, those responding "Yes" to the Hispanic question were much less likely to indicate their race as "other." Only 24.9 percent of Hispanics in the sample said they were of "other race," compared to 42.9 percent in the group responding to the Hispanic question after the race question. Moreover, asking the Hispanic question first increased the self-identification of Hispanics on the race question as White from 52.5 percent to 72.1 percent. This and other related studies show that when Hispanics were given the opportunity to self-identify as Hispanic *before* being asked about their racial identification, a larger proportion was likely to see themselves as White, and a smaller proportion as of "other race" or of multiple races.

12. By "racialized," we mean a view that divides people into mutually exclusive categories that are primarily based on physical features (phenotype) and the meaning ascribed to those features. In this regard, see Torres, Mirón, and Inda (1999). These authors, citing Robert Miles, discuss racialization as a process by which biological features are given social meaning so as to construct social groups and structure their social relations. See also Small (1999), who explores the implications of racialization processes for individual and group experience.

13. See Corlett (1999) for a related philosophical discussion of the criteria of Latino identity. He outlines what he calls a "moderate conception of Latino identity" in which genealogical ties to a Latino group are a necessary and sufficient condition for Latino identity, yet the degree of Latino identity is established through a combination of other criteria, including knowledge of and interest in the Spanish language, a Latino name, engagement in Latino culture, self-perception and perception by others—both Latino and non-Latino—as Latino.

14. Klor de Alva describes the shifts over time in the conceptualization of mestizaje. In contrast to an earlier focus on "the collapse of distinct cultures into a Mexican way of being Spanish" (1999:176), later constructions reemphasized indigenous roots:

> Creative Chicanos, searching for common roots to unite the disparate communities, identified Aztlán, the mythical homeland of the Aztecs, with the US Southwest and consequently—in the imagination of many—symbolically transformed all Chicanos (despite their differences) into the most authentic of Mexicans: the direct descendants of the Aztecs! By leaping over the Europeanizing version of mestizaje all Mexican-Americans were thus linked to the *colonized* descendants of the pre-contact Aztecs. (1999:176, italics in original)

15. One example is Helms's (1995) People of Color racial identity development model (see also Thompson and Carter 1997), which takes a framework developed initially with reference to Blacks (Helms 1990), and essentially extends it to all people of color without much modification or consideration of the specific experience of the various groups.

REFERENCES

Bernal, Martha E., and George P. Knight. 1993. *Ethnic Identity: Formation and Transmission among Hispanics and Other Minorities*. Albany: State University of New York Press.

Betances, Samuel. 1992. "Race and the Search for Identity." Pp. 277–286 in *Race, Class, and Gender: An Anthology*, ed. M. L. Andersen and P. H. Collins. Belmont, Calif.: Wadsworth.

Birman, Dina. 1998. "Biculturalism and Perceived Competence of Latino Immigrant Adolescents." *American Journal of Community Psychology* 26:335–354.

Corlett, J. Angelo. 1999. "Latino Identity." *Public Affairs Quarterly* 13:273–295.

Cross, William E., Jr. 1995. "The Psychology of Nigrescence: Revising the Cross Model." Pp. 93–122 in *Handbook of Multicultural Counseling*, ed. J. G. Ponterotto, J. M. Casas, L. A. Suzuki, and C. M. Alexander. Thousand Oaks, Calif.: Sage.

Cuellar, Israel, Bill Nyberg, Roberto E. Maldonado, and Robert E. Roberts. 1997. "Ethnic Identity and Acculturation in a Young Adult Mexican-Origin Population." *American Journal of Community Psychology* 25:535–549.

Delgado, Richard. 1998. "The Black/White Binary Paradigm of Race." Pp. 359–368 in *The Latino/a Condition: A Critical Reader*, ed. R. Delgado and J. Stefancic. New York: New York University Press.

Delgado, Richard, and Jean Stefancic, eds. 1998. *The Latino/a Condition: A Critical Reader*. New York: New York University Press.

Denton, Nancy A., and Douglas S. Massey. 1989. "Racial Identity among Caribbean Hispanics: The Effect of Double Minority Status on Residential Segregation." *American Sociological Review* 54:790–808.

Duany, Jorge. 1998. "Reconstructing Racial Identity: Ethnicity, Color, and Class among Dominicans in the United States and Puerto Rico." *Latin American Perspectives* 25:147–172.

Ferdman, Bernardo M. 1990. "Literacy and Cultural Identity." *Harvard Educational Review* 60:181–204.

———. 1992. "The Dynamics of Ethnic Diversity in Organizations: Toward Integrative Models." Pp. 339–384 in *Issues, Theory, and Research in Industrial/Organizational Psychology*, ed. K. Kelley. Amsterdam: North Holland.

———. 1995. "Cultural Identity and Diversity in Organizations: Bridging the Gap between Group Differences and Individual Uniqueness." Pp. 37–61 in *Diversity in Organizations: New Perspectives for a Changing Workplace*, ed. M. Chemers, S. Oskamp, and M. A. Costanzo. Thousand Oaks, Calif.: Sage.

———. 1999a. June 12. "Learning about Our and Others' Selves: An Exercise to Provoke Thinking about Multiple Identities." In N. Boyacigiller and M. Phillips (Chairs), "Organizational Implications of Simultaneous Membership in Multiple Cultures." Symposium presented at Master Teachers' Workshop on Crossing Cultures, UCLA CIBER Cross-Cultural Collegium, University of California at Los Angeles.

———. 1999b. "The Color and Culture of Gender in Organizations: Attending to Race and Ethnicity." Pp. 17–34 in *Handbook of Gender and Work*, ed. G. N. Powell. Thousand Oaks, Calif.: Sage.

———. 2000. "'Why Am I Who I Am?' Constructing the Cultural Self in Multicultural Perspective." *Human Development*. 43(1):19–23.

Ferdman, Bernardo M., and Angelica Cortes. 1992. "Culture and Identity among Hispanic Managers in an Anglo Business." Pp. 246–277 in *Hispanics in the Workplace*, ed. S. B. Knouse, P. Rosenfeld and A. Culbertson. Newbury Park, CA: Sage.

Ferdman, Bernardo M., and Plácida I. Gallegos. 1996. "Crossing Borders: The Experience of a Mexican American HR Manager in a Maquiladora." Pp. 1–23 in *Managing Diversity: Human Resource Strategies for Transforming the Workplace. A Field Guide*, ed. E. E. Kossek, S. A. Lobel, and R. Oh. Cambridge, Mass: Blackwell.

Ferdman, Bernardo M., and Gabriel Horenczyk. In press. "Cultural Identity and Immigration: Reconstructing the Group during Cultural Transitions." In *Language, Identity, and Immigration*, ed. E. Olshtain and G. Horenczyk. Jerusalem: Magnes Press.

Flores, Juan, and George Yúdice. 1990. "Living Borders/Buscando America: Languages of Latino Self-Formation." *Social Text* 24:57–84.

Flores Niemann, Yolanda, Andrea J. Romero, Jorge Arredondo, and Victor

Rodríguez. 1999. "What Does It Mean to Be 'Mexican'? Social Construction of an Ethnic Identity." *Hispanic Journal of Behavioral Sciences* 21:47–60.
Frederickson, George M. 1999. "Models of American Ethnic Relations: A His-
torical Perspective." Pp. 23–34 in *Cultural Divides: Understanding and Over-
coming Group Conflict*, ed. D. A. Prentice and D. T. Miller et al. New York:
Russell Sage Foundation.
Gurin, Patricia, Aida Hurtado, and Timothy Peng. 1994. "Group Contacts and
Ethnicity in the Social Identities of Mexicanos and Chicanos." *Personality
and Social Psychology Bulletin* 20:521–532.
Haney López, Ian F. 1998. "The Mean Streets of Social Race." Pp. 161–176 in
The Social Construction of Race and Ethnicity in the United States, ed. J. Fer-
rante and P. Brown, Jr. New York: Longman.
Helms, Janet E., ed. 1990. *Black and White Racial Identity: Theory, Research, and
Practice*. Westport, Conn.: Greenwood.
———. 1995. "An Update of Helms's White and People of Color Racial Iden-
tity Models." Pp. 181–198 in *Handbook of Multicultural Counseling*, ed. J. G.
Ponterotto, J. M. Casas, L. A. Suzuki, and C. M. Alexander. Thousand
Oaks, Calif.: Sage.
———. 1996. "Toward a Methodology for Measuring and Assessing Racial as
Distinguished from Ethnic Identity." Pp. 143–192 in *Multicultural Assess-
ment in Counseling and Clinical Psychology*, ed. G. Sodowsky and J. Impara.
Lincoln, Nebr.: Buros Institute.
Holvino, Evangelina. Winter 1996. "Latinas and Latinos in the Workplace:
Barriers to Employment and Advancement." *Diversity Factor*: 35–39.
———. 1997. "Women of Color in Organizations: Revising Our Models of
Gender at Work." Pp. 52–59 in *The Promise of Diversity: Over Forty Voices
Discuss Strategies for Eliminating Discrimination in Organizations*, ed. E. Y.
Cross, J. H. Katz, F. A. Miller, and E. W. Seashore. Burr Ridge, Ill.: Irwin.
Hurtado, Aida. 1997. "Understanding Multiple Group Identities: Inserting
Women into Cultural Transformations." *Journal of Social Issues* 53:299–328.
Jones-Correa, Michael, and David L. Leal. 1996. "Becoming 'Hispanic': Sec-
ondary Panethnic Identification among Latin American-Origin Popula-
tions in the United States." *Hispanic Journal of the Behavioral Sciences*
18:214–254.
Klor de Alva, Jorge. 1999. "Cipherspace: Latino Identity Past and Present."
Pp. 169–180 in *Race, Identity, and Citizenship: A Reader*, ed. R. D. Torres, L. F.
Mirón, and J. X. Inda. Oxford: Blackwell.
Larmer, Brook. 1999. "Latin U.S.A." *Newsweek* (12 July).
Martínez, Elizabeth. 1998. "Beyond Black/White: The Racisms of Our Time."
Pp. 466–477 in *The Latino/a Condition: A Critical Reader*, ed. R. Delgado and
J. Stefancic. New York: New York University Press.
Martinez, George A. 1998. "Mexican Americans and Whiteness." Pp. 175–179

in *The Latino/a Condition: A Critical Reader*, ed. R. Delgado and J. Stefancic. New York: New York University Press.

Massey, Douglas S., and Nancy A. Denton. 1992. "Racial Identity and the Spatial Assimilation of Mexicans in the United States." *Social Science Research* 21:235–260.

Moore, Joan, and Harry Pachon. 1985. *Hispanics in the United States*. Englewood Cliffs, N.J.: Prentice-Hall.

Moraga, Cherrie, and Gloria Anzaldúa, eds. 1983. *This Bridge Called My Back: Writings by Radical Women of Color*. New York: Kitchen Table.

Oquendo, Angel R. 1998. "Re-Imagining the Latino/a Race." Pp. 60–71 in *The Latino/a Condition: A Critical Reader*, ed. R. Delgado and J. Stefancic. New York: New York University Press.

Padilla, Amado M., ed. 1995. *Hispanic Psychology: Critical Issues in Theory and Research*. Thousand Oaks, Calif.: Sage.

Padilla, Félix M. 1989. "Salsa Music as a Cultural Expression of Latino Consciousness and Unity." Pp. 347–358 in *Race, Class, and Gender: An Anthology*, ed. M. L. Andersen and P. H. Collins. Belmont, Calif: Wadsworth.

Perea, Juan F. 1998. "The Black/White Binary: How Does It Work?" Pp. 369–375 in *The Latino/a Condition: A Critical Reader*, ed. R. Delgado and J. Stefancic. New York: New York University Press.

Phinney, Jean S., and Mona Devich-Navarro. 1997. "Variations in Bicultural Identification among African American and Mexican American Adolescents." *Journal of Research in Adolescence* 7:3–32.

Portes, Alejandro E. 1990. "From South of the Border: Hispanic Minorities in the United States." Pp. 160–184 in *Immigration Reconsidered: History, Sociology, and Politics*, ed. V. Yans-McLaughlin. New York: Oxford University Press.

Quiñones-Rosado, Raúl. Summer 1998. "Hispanic or Latino? The Struggle for Identity in a Race-Based Society." *Diversity Factor*:20–24.

Rivera, Edward. 1982. *Family Installments: Memories of Growing Up Hispanic*. New York: Penguin.

Rodríguez, Clara E. 1991. *Puerto Ricans: Born in the U.S.A.* Boulder, Colo.: Westview.

———. 1992. "Race, Culture, and Latino Otherness in the 1980 Census." *Social Science Quarterly* 73:930–937.

Rodríguez, Clara E., and Hector Cordero-Guzman. 1992. "Placing Race in Context." *Ethnic and Racial Studies* 15:523–542.

Romero, Mary. 1997. "Introduction." Pp. xiii–xvi in *Challenging Fronteras: Structuring Latina and Latino Lives in the U.S.*, ed. M. Romero, P. Hondagneu-Sotelo, and V. Ortiz. New York: Routledge.

Safa, Helen I. 1988. "Migration and Identity: A Comparison of Puerto Rican and Cuban Migrants in the United States." Pp. 137–150 in *The Hispanic Ex-*

perience in the United States: Contemporary Issues and Perspectives, ed. E. Acosta-Belén and B. Sjostrom. New York: Praeger.

Small, Stephen. 1999. "The Contours of Racialization: Structures, Representations, and Resistance the United States." Pp. 47–64 in *Race, Identity, and Citizenship: A Reader,* ed. R. Torres, L. F. Mirón, and J. X. Inda. Malden, Mass: Blackwell.

Stavans, Ilan. 1995. *The Hispanic Condition: Reflections on Culture and Identity in America.* New York: HarperCollins.

Thomas, Piri. 1967. *Down These Mean Streets.* New York: Knopf.

Thompson, Chalmer E., and Robert T. Carter. 1997. "An Overview and Elaboration of Helms' Racial Identity Development Theory." Pp. 15–32 in *Racial Identity Theory: Applications to Individual, Group, and Organizational Interventions,* ed. C. E. Thompson and R. T. Carter. Mahwah, N.J.: Lawrence Erlbaum.

Toro, Luis A. 1998. "Directive No. 15 and Self-Identification." Pp. 211–215 in *The Social Construction of Race and Ethnicity in the United States,* ed. J. Ferrante and P. Brown, Jr. New York: Longman.

Torres, Rodolfo D., Louis F. Mirón, and Jonathan X. Inda. 1999. "Introduction." Pp. 1–16 in *Race, Identity, and Citizenship: A Reader,* ed. R. D. Torres, L. F. Mirón, and J. X. Inda. Malden, Mass.: Blackwell.

Tovares, Joseph. 1998. "Mojado Like Me." Pp. 93–98 in *The Social Construction of Race and Ethnicity in the United States,* ed. J. Ferrante and P. Brown, Jr. New York: Longman.

U.S. Bureau of the Census. 1993. "We the American Hispanics." Washington, D.C.: author. Retrieved October 16, 1999 from the World Wide Web: http://www.census.gov/apsd/wepeople/we-2r.pdf

———. December 1996. "Findings on Questions on Race and Hispanic Origin Tested in the 1996 National Content Survey." Population Division Working Paper No. 16. Retrieved October 16, 1999, from the World Wide Web: http://www.census.gov/population/www/documentation/twps0016/t wps0016.html

———. May 1997. "Results of the 1996 Race and Ethnic Targeted Test." Population Division Working Paper No. 18. Retrieved October 16, 1999, from the World Wide Web: http://www.census.gov/population/www/documentation/twps0018/twps0018.html

———. August 1998. "Nativity by Race-Ethnicity: Both Sexes." Table 10.1 in *Current Population Survey, March 1997.* Retrieved October 16, 1999, from the World Wide Web: http://www.census.gov/population/socdemo/hispanic/cps97/tab10-01.txt

———. 1999. "Resident Population Estimates of the United States by Sex, Race, and Hispanic Origin: April 1, 1990 to August 1, 1999." Retrieved October 16, 1999, from the World Wide Web: http://www.census.gov/population/estimates/nation/intfile3-1.txt

U.S. Office of Management and Budget (OMB). 1998. "Federal Statistical Directive No. 15: Race and Ethnic Standards for Federal Statistics and Administrative Reporting" (as adopted on May 12, 1977). Pp. 157–160 in *The Social Construction of Race and Ethnicity in the United States,* ed. J. Ferrante and P. Brown, Jr. New York: Longman.

———. 1999. February 17. "Draft Provisional Guidance on the Implementation of the 1997 Standards for the Collection of Federal Data on Race and Ethnicity." Retrieved on October 16, 1999, from the World Wide Web: http://www.whitehouse.gov/omb/inforeg/race.pdf

Weinstein, Roxana. 1998. "Mexican American Ethnic Identity among Monoethnic and Biethnic Individuals: Personal and Environmental Antecedents." Doctoral dissertation, California School of Professional Psychology, San Diego.

Zanger, Virginia V. 1994. "'Not Joined In': The Social Context of English Literacy Development for Hispanic Youth." Pp. 171–198 in *Literacy across Languages and Cultures,* ed. B. M. Ferdman, R.-M. Weber, and A. G. Ramírez. Albany, N.Y.: State University of New York Press.

Chapter 3

Asian American Identity Development Theory

Jean Kim

The primary purpose of this chapter is to share the Asian American Identity Development (AAID) Model.[1] This model provides insight into how Asian Americans resolve the racial identity conflicts they face as Americans of Asian ancestry in a predominantly White society. The chapter begins with a discussion of White racism and the way it impacts the experience of Asian Americans. This material provides a societal context for examining the racial identity conflicts of Americans of Asian heritage. The next section presents the AAID theory and discusses the assumptions underlying the model and the model's five conceptually distinct, sequential, and progressive[2] stages. These stages are *Ethnic Awareness, White Identification, Awakening to Social Political Consciousness, Redirection to Asian American Consciousness,* and *Incorporation.* The review of the AAID is followed by a section that reflects on the relevance of the AAID theory to Asian Americans today, and an outline of current issues for future research in the area of racial identity development for Asian Americans.

Social Context and Asian Americans

One cultural trait that Americans of Asian heritage share and that distinguishes them from the majority White population is the group orientation through which they learn to be sensitive to the expectations of the group and their social environment.[3] For example, Asian people's view of themselves (the private self) is primarily influenced by what other people (the public), and particularly what a specific group of people (the collective) think of them. Consequently, the development of the self is largely influenced by messages that are external to Asian Americans in both the collective and public environments. Given Asian Americans' tendency to be externally rather than internally focused, their racial identity development is especially affected by the social environment. In particular, the impact of White racism and the attendant oppression of Asian Americans by European Americans are critical factors in Asian American identity development (Kim 1981; Moritsugu and Sue 1983; Smith 1991; Chan and Hune 1995). However, before we can discuss the impact of racism on Asian Americans, it may be helpful to clarify how race is conceptualized in the United States and how racism is defined.

Discussions about race tend to be very emotional, and it is difficult to have a common understanding of what race is and why it matters. But many scholars, especially those associated with the Critical Race Theory movement (Crenshaw 1995; Delgado 1995; Begley 1995) have argued persuasively that the phenomenon of race is a social and legal construct.[4] A growing number of Asian American legal scholars also support this view, arguing that race is not simply an immutable biological attribute (as in skin color) but represents a complex set of social meanings which are affected by political struggle (Omi and Winant 1994). Understanding that race is socially and politically, rather than biologically, determined may help us to understand how racial prejudice and racial dominance operate in U.S. society.

Racial prejudice is created by inaccurate and/or negative beliefs that rationalize the *superiority* or *normalcy* of one race, (in this case Whites over people of color). Racial dominance, on the other hand, describes the control of societal structures by a single racial group which enforces that group's racial prejudice and maintains its privileges. Racism occurs when racial prejudice and racial dominance occur simultaneously (Wijeyesinghe, Griffin, and Love 1997). In the United States the White race is racially dominant and racial prejudice is taught to everyone, including members of racially oppressed groups. In addition, race tends to be seen in Black and White terms, and we are most familiar with racial prejudices directed against Black Americans. We are less aware of the experiences of other groups of color (Asian, Latino, and American Indian). We also assign a specific set of stereotypes to each racial group (Wijeyesinghe, Griffin, and Love 1997).

Since the mid-1960s, when the Black civil rights movement was gaining momentum, the media began depicting Asian Americans as the "model minority." Articles appeared in popular magazines portraying Asian Americans as one minority group who had made it in this country through hard effort (Kasindorf 1982; Chan and Hune 1995). These works cited higher academic attainments and combined family earnings of Asian Americans as indicators that Asians are a model minority. Therefore, several positive generalizations—such as, Asians work hard, are technological nerds, are good at math, focus on education, and the like—were added to the negative stereotypes of Asians—such as, Asians are sly, ruthless, untrustworthy, submissive, quiet, foreigners, and lack communication skills and leadership potential. Given this "model minority" myth and the so-called "positive" stereotypes of Asian Americans, some people are unaware of the fact that White racism is also directed against Asian Americans. In fact, the history of racism against Asians began with the first wave of Asian immigrants from China almost one hundred fifty years ago. Subsequent to this early period, Asians have been subjected to massive and intense discrimination, including the denial of citizenship, the segregation of schools and housing, lynching, massacres, internment in concentration camps, random acts of violence, and subtle forms of unfair treatment in employment.[5]

In spite of this history, there is a pervasive myth accepted by many, including Asian Americans themselves, that Asian Americans have overcome all these obstacles and succeeded in finding a place for themselves in the American dream through hard work, perseverance, and quiet suffering. It is true that many Asian Americans have obtained higher levels of education than the general population and have achieved middle-class status (Carnevale and Stone 1995). However, the model minority myth[6] ignores both the significant psychological cost of acculturation into a White racist society and the reality of continuing discrimination against Asian Americans. One such psychological cost is racial identity conflict.

Racism and Identity Conflict

Of the many problems faced by Asian Americans in the psychological arena, racial identity conflict is the most critical and severe (Sue and

Sue 1971; Suzuki 1975; Sue and Sue 1990). Conflict about one's identity can be said to exist when individuals perceive certain aspects or attributes of themselves which they simultaneously reject. In the case of Asian Americans, awareness of one's self as an Asian person is rejected in favor of the White models that are so pervasive in our society. The issue here is not the lack of awareness of one's racial self but rather how one feels about and values that part of oneself.[7]

This phenomenon of identity conflict is manifested in a number of ways, with varying degrees of severity (Kohatsu 1993; Huang 1994). An Asian American may experience identity conflict as a belief in his or her own inferiority (as well as the inferiority of other Asian Americans) perhaps coupled with deep-seated feelings of self-hatred and alienation. At some point in their lives, many Asian Americans have either consciously or unconsciously expressed the desire to become White, and tried to reject their identity as Asians (Kim 1981; Suzuki 1975; Huang 1994). A painful expression of this identity conflict among Asian American women is the practice of creating double-folded eyelids (many Asians have single-folded eyelids) either through surgery or by using scotch tape in a vain attempt to meet the beauty standards of White society. This practice of "Americanizing" Asian eyes is reminiscent of the practice among Blacks of straightening their hair and bleaching their skin to look Whiter in appearance (Suzuki 1975). Such experiences of denial and/or rejection of their Asian heritage contribute toward Asian Americans' negative self-concept and low self-esteem, both hallmarks of negative racial identity (Sue and Sue 1990).

The experience of identity conflict among Asian Americans is a direct result of living in a society that has institutionalized racism throughout its major structures, cultures, and value systems (Knowles and Prewitt 1969). An example of institutional racism are stereotypes of Asians evident in film and television. The history of the U.S. legal and political system also contains voluminous pages of violence and discrimination directed at Asian Americans (Takaki 1989; Chan and Hune 1995). Although the racism experienced by Asian Americans today may be more subtle than in prior decades, its effects have been shown to have a negative impact on Asian Americans' psychological well-being (Chin 1970; Sue and Kitano 1973; Sue and Sue 1971, 1990). Various manifestations of identity conflict can be seen as the result of Asian Americans' attempts to make it in a White society, which, for the most part, devalues racial minorities and considers people of color to be aliens and foreigners even though many have been here for generations. Identity conflict as experienced by Asian Americans seems inevitable in a society where being different is synonymous with being inferior.

Asian American Identity Development (AAID) Theory: Assumptions

Before we begin to discuss the actual AAID model, it is important to discuss some of its underlying assumptions. These assumptions stem from the fact that racial minorities in our society have to deal with the daily realities of White racism, whether or not they are managing this challenge consciously. The first assumption states that White racism cannot be separated from Asian American identity development due to racism's pervasive nature and the fact that the social environment (the public and collective self) has such a huge impact on the way Asian Americans determine who they are (the private selves).

The second assumption is that Asian Americans cannot shed their negative racial identity automatically. It involves a conscious decision to unlearn what Asian Americans have learned about themselves. This unlearning process requires that Asian Americans become conscious of the stereotypes about themselves that they have internalized, and get rid of perceptions that they accepted unconditionally in the past.

The third assumption is that the psychological well-being of Asian Americans is dependent on their ability to transform the negative racial identity they experience as a result of identity conflict and to acquire a positive racial identity.

These assumptions about AAID are similar to the general principles found in the racial identity development theories of other racial minorities (Helms 1990; Bernal and Knight 1993). This is not surprising, as all racial minorities experience White racism in this country. As Gay notes:

> Positive ethnic identification for most American racial minorities does not happen automatically nor does it happen for all individuals. When it does happen, it is learned . . . Second, the psychological well-being of ethnic minorities [is] contingent upon this rebirth or resynthesization

of ethnic identity. Part of this rebirth is the replacement of feelings of ethnic shame and denigration with self ethnic pride and acceptance. . . . Third, the reformation of ethnic identity is a progressional process. . . . Fourth, a dialectical interaction exists between the personal processes of ethnic identity development and the sociocultural contexts in which they occur. (1985:49–50)

Asian American Identity Development Theory: The Model

Within the AAID, the process of acquiring a positive Asian American racial identity occurs through five stages.[8] Each stage is characterized by the basic components of an identity, that is, a self-concept that includes evaluation and meaning attribution (ego identity). Experiencing the various stages lead in turn to specific behaviors and a social consciousness about being an Asian American. The five stages are sequential in nature, although the process is not linear or automatic. For example, it is possible for an Asian American to get stuck in a certain stage and never move to the next stage. Whether Asian Americans move on to the next stage in their racial identity development is dependent primarily on their social environment, and various factors in this environment determine both the length and the quality of experience in a given stage.

Stage One: Ethnic Awareness

Ethnic Awareness is the first stage of AAID, and represents the period prior to Asian Americans entering the school system. Awareness of their ethnicity comes primarily from interactions with family members and relatives. Asian Americans who live in predominantly Asian or mixed neighborhoods have greater exposure to ethnic activities and experience more ethnic pride and knowledge of their cultural heritage. One benefit of membership in a larger Asian community is that Asian Americans experience what it is like to be in the majority and have a sense of security and positive ethnic awareness. Asian Americans who live in predominately White neighborhoods and have less exposure to ethnic activities are not sure what it means to be a member of an Asian ethnic group and feel neutral about their ethnic membership. Furthermore, greater exposure to Asian ethnic experiences at this stage leads to a positive self-concept and clearer ego identity while less exposure is related to a neutral self-concept and confused ego identity (Kim 1981). For most Asian Americans, this stage lasts until they enter the school system. By the time they begin school, Asian Americans' social environment changes from a protective secure home and family setting to a more public arena. More significantly, this change in social environment heralds a period of increased contact between Asian Americans with the dominant White society. This is a key factor that moves individuals to the next stage.

Key features of the Ethnic Awareness Stage include:

Social environment: mostly at home with family.
Critical factor: extent of participation in Asian ethnic activities.
Self-concept: greater participation leads to positive self-concept; less participation leads to neutral self-concept.
Ego identity: greater participation leads to clear sense as a person of Asian heritage, less participation leads to less clear meaning about being a person of Asian heritage.
Primary reference group: family.
Hallmark of the stage: discovery of ethnic heritage.

Stage Two: White Identification

The beginning of the White Identification stage is marked by Asian Americans' strong sense of being different from their peers. They acquire this sense mostly through painful encounters, for example, being made fun of, being the object of name-calling, and the like. At this stage, Asian Americans are not sure what makes them different from their peers, and they are not prepared to handle these negative reactions. The following words by a second-generation Chinese American woman illustrates this phase.

> When I was younger I was always obsessed with my shadow. I used to look at it and then at my other school peers' shadows and realize that there was no differences from that perspective. Unfortunately, as soon as I heard the name "eggroll," or "gook," I was reminded all over again of my racial differences and set back in a state of self-consciousness.

Such experiences tell Asian Americans that being different is bad. Given the Asian cultural values of quiet suffering and avoiding public shame, most Asian parents are not able to help their children other than telling them to ignore these slights and hurts. The children, however, find this difficult to do. The Asian cultural tendency toward group or collective orientation has taught them to attend to the reactions of others in their social circle and to try to fit in rather than stick out.

In addition to group orientation, the significance of shame in Asian cultures may influence Asian Americans to try at all costs to fit into White society in order to avoid publicly embarrassing themselves. All these influences cause Asian Americans to gradually internalize White societal values and standards and see themselves through the eyes of White society, especially regarding standards of physical beauty and attractiveness. The following statement by a second-generation Korean American college student is illustrative of this stage.

> Junior high was a time in my life where image was everything and I didn't fit into that image. To me, the blonde-haired, blue-eyed girls were the lucky ones. I believed that I wouldn't have a boyfriend because I was Korean. Everyone assumed I was super smart, especially in math. But the only thing I really wanted to be was "the image." I was as White as a sheet. All of my friends were White. I had such a difficult time dealing with my different appearance. I would just freak out when someone would point out that I was Korean.

The hallmark of the White Identification stage are experiences of alienation from self and other Asian Americans. Although their reference group is White, Asian Americans in this stage often feel socially isolated from their White peers and enjoy little closeness or meaningful friendships with them. Many Asian Americans compensate for this by becoming involved in formal organizational roles and responsibilities within school such as becoming class presidents, class officers, club leaders, and by excelling academically.

This is a very painful time, a period when Asian Americans' self-concept begins to change from positive or neutral to negative. Consequently, Asian Americans' ego identity is centered on being inferior and being at fault and responsible for things that happen to them.

ACTIVE WHITE IDENTIFICATION

There is some variation as to how the White Identification stage is experienced, depending on the degree to which Asian Americans identify with White people. Asian Americans who grow up in predominantly White environments are more likely to experience what is called Active White Identification, and repress negative feelings and experiences associated with their Asianness. In actively identifying with White people, such Asian Americans consider themselves to be very similar to their White peers and do not consciously acknowledge any differences between themselves and Whites. They do not want to be seen as an Asian person and do all they can to minimize and eliminate their Asian selves. The following statement by a first-generation Korean American man is a good example of a person in Active White Identification:

> In time I learned to speak and write just like a White person, leaving no traces that my mouth had ever formed the words of another language. I was so proficient that oftentimes people who I had only spoken to on the phone were shocked when they met me, and discovered me to be something other than White.

PASSIVE WHITE IDENTIFICATION

Asian Americans who experience a positive self-concept during the first stage of Ethnic Awareness and who grow up in predominantly Asian or mixed neighborhoods are more likely to experience Passive White Identification. They also enter the White Identification stage later on in life, in junior high rather than in elementary school, for example. In Passive White Identification, Asian Americans do not consider themselves to be White and do not distance themselves from other Asians. However, they do experience periods of wishful thinking and fantasizing about being White. Like Asian Americans in Active White Identification, Asian Americans in Passive White Identification also accept White values, beliefs, and standards, and use Whites as a reference group.

The White Identification stage is most likely to be experienced in a passive way by first-generation Asian Americans who arrive in the United States as adults with a developed sense of themselves from their mother country, even when they reside in predominantly White neighborhoods. However, the neighborhood environment will influence how children who emigrated to the United States prior to their teens (also known as the 1.5 generation) (Harklau, Losey, and Siegal 1999) experience this stage. Although these Asian Americans were born elsewhere, their primary reference growing up is the United States. Thus, they resemble second-generation Asian Americans. If these 1.5 generation folks grow up in predominantly White neighborhoods, they will likely experience the White Identification stage actively. However, if they grow up in predominantly mixed or Asian neighborhoods, they will experience this stage more passively.

Whether experienced actively or passively, White Identification is a stage marked by negative attitudes and evaluations of self as Americans of Asian ancestry and includes behaviors that reflect turning one's back on other Asian Americans and on other minorities. These behaviors and attitudes are accompanied by a lack of political understanding, or a context that could enable them to make sense of their experiences. At this stage, Asian Americans personalize their experiences and are not conscious of social injustice or racism. They are likely to say that there is no racism and that they have not encountered any discrimination. The goal of Asian Americans at this stage is to fit in, to be treated like White people, and to pass for a White person. As long as Asian Americans believe they can be fully assimilated into White society, they remain in this stage of White Identification.

Key features of the White Identification Stage include:

Social environment: public arenas such as school systems.
Critical factor: increased contact with White society which leads to acceptance of White values and standards.
Self-concept: negative self-image, especially body image.
Ego identity: being different, not fitting in, inferior to White peers, feel isolated and personally responsible for any negative treatment.
Primary reference group: White people and dominant society.
Hallmark of the stage: feelings of being different, alienation from self and other Asian Americans, and inability to make connections between personal experience and racism.

Stage Three: Awakening to Social Political Consciousness

It is during the stage of Awakening to Social and Political Consciousness that some Asian Americans are able to shift their worldview and realize that they are not personally responsible for their situation and experiences with racism. In moving their paradigm from personal responsibility to social responsibility, Asian Americans acquire social and political understanding that transforms their self-image. While there is some variation as to how these shifts occur, they are a critical factor in changing Asian Americans' self-concept from negative to positive. It is also apparent that Asian Americans must acquire an awareness of White racism and develop a resistance to being subordinated if they are to move out of the White Identification stage.

How then, does the awareness of White racism bring about change? First, the new awareness leads to a realistic assessment of Asian Americans' social position, that is, a clear realization of the existence of societal blocks and the futility of trying to "pass" or to strive for acceptance within the White world. Second, the political awareness of White racism provides alternative perspectives, a new paradigm for Asian Americans. This new worldview allows people to reinterpret their lives and lets them know that things could be different. Prior to the Awakening to Social Political Consciousness stage, Asian Americans blamed themselves for their negative experiences and believed these were the result of personal failings. An alternative perspective in Stage Three is that these negative encounters have societal rather than personal roots. This understanding releases the individual from unnecessary guilt and feelings of inferiority. Similarly, having a different analysis of the past and present facilitates the generation of new solutions, which lead to a belief that change is possible.

In my original study underlying the AAID (Kim 1981), this paradigm shift occurred through participants' involvement in the political movements of the 1960s and 1970s.[9] A family member's or a close friend's interest in a sociopolitical issue initiated the political involvement of some participants. Others were influenced by the campus politics of the late 1960s and early 1970s when student activism was high and centered around the issues of war, Black studies, and women's rights. A significant theme among Asian Americans' experience in the original study (Kim 1981) was that their political consciousness was initially centered on being a minority and they became politically conscious about being Asian Americans later. Asian Americans often enjoyed greater support for their fledgling political consciousness from other minority groups than from White Americans.

Another major change that occurs during Stage Three is a reaction against White people. For Asian Americans at this stage, White people are no longer the reference group to which they aspire. Rather, White people become the antireferent group, people they don't want to be like. For example, one Asian American at the stage of Awakening to Social and Political Consciousness noted that:

> Most of our friends were Black, so there were a lot of antiWhite feel-
> ings. It was the political atmosphere that made us feel alienated from
> Whites. We would say anti-White things because we were looking at
> White people in terms of the society. They were responsible for the
> things that were happening in the world. I put Whites in a general
> grouping and they were more the "enemy." Of course, we always had a
> number of White friends. I guess I saw them as exceptions.

In summary, through political involvement, Asian Americans at Stage
Three find meaningful support systems and a new paradigm, which enables them to reinterpret their past negative experiences of personal
shame and take ownership of their identities in light of the societal illness called racism. Asian Americans also realize that regardless of what
they achieve, they will never be fully accepted into the dominant society as long as White racism exists. They no longer blame themselves for
the discrimination and racial prejudice they have encountered. Ego
identity at this stage is centered on being a minority and being oppressed. Asian Americans no longer feel inferior to Whites, and they relate to the experiences of other racial minorities. A third-generation
Japanese American woman recalled her feelings at the time as follows:

> I had a context for the first time to think about it. In racism and stereo-
> types, I had a whole context. It was a really nice opening time for me in
> a lot of ways. I had friends. I felt like I had friends for the first time in
> ages. I felt safer to deal with things like racism.

Key features of the Awakening to Social Political Consciousness
Stage include:

Social environment: social political movements and/or campus
  politics.
Critical factor: gaining political consciousness related to being a
  racial/political minority and awareness of White racism.
Self-concept: positive self-concept, identification as a minority
  in the United States.
Ego identity: accepts being a minority but resists White values and
  White domination, feels oppressed but not inferior to Whites.
Primary reference group: individuals with similar social politi-
  cal philosophy and antiestablishment perspective.
Hallmark of the stage: gaining new political perspective and so-
  ciological imagination, political alienation from Whites.

Stage Four: Redirection to an Asian American Consciousness

Although in the preceding stage Asian Americans changed their affiliation from Whites to minorities, they had not yet identified with Asian Americans. This change occurs at the fourth stage of AAID, *Redirection to an Asian American Consciousness*. With support and encouragement from friends, Asian Americans begin to feel secure enough in themselves to look at their own experiences. Some Asian Americans are motivated to develop this orientation by observing and learning from other political movements. This point is aptly illustrated by the words of a fourth-generation Japanese American woman:

> The civil rights movement was the vehicle to express our concern. That's when I became concerned with Asian identity. We were involved in the Black Nationalist movement and people would talk a lot about Africa, or about culture, and returning to your tradition. Because most of our friends were Black and changing their names to African names, at that point everyone in our family started to think more about being Asian and what that meant. I started to feel for the first time proud to be an Asian. That was because of the civil rights movement.

A critical step taken by Asian Americans during this stage is an immersion in the Asian American experience. Through related activities, Asian Americans discover that while they had some knowledge of their Asian cultural heritage, they don't really know very much about the Asian American experience. As they learn more about the real experience of Asian Americans, they feel anger and outrage toward the dominant White system for the acts of racism directed toward Asians. Eventually Asian Americans are able to move out of this reactionary state into a more realistic appraisal of both themselves and other Asian Americans and to figure out what parts of themselves are Asian and what parts are American.

The ego identity of Asian Americans at this stage is centered on being an Asian American, which entails knowing they belong here, having a clear political understanding of what it means to be Asian American in this society, and no longer seeing themselves as misfits. They finally acquire racial pride and a positive self-concept as Americans with Asian heritage. The following statement by a third-generation Japanese American woman is a good illustration of this outcome.

In the context of America, it's a good feeling to have an Asian American identity finally. Until we got to that point, we didn't know where we fit. We weren't Black, we weren't White, and we weren't Japanese. Having an Asian American identity means that you share an experience that other Asians experience. It's a positive side to your makeup.

Key features of the Redirection to an Asian American Consciousness Stage include:

Social environment: Asian American community.
Critical factor: immersion in Asian American experience.
Self-concept: positive self-concept, and identification as Asian American.
Ego identity: proud of being Asian American, experience a sense of belonging.
Primary reference group: Asian Americans, especially those at similar stage of identity development.
Hallmark of the stage: focus on personal and Asian American experience, feel anger against Whites about treatment of Asian Americans.

Stage Five: Incorporation

The key factor in Stage Five, *Incorporation*, is confidence in one's own Asian American identity. This confidence allows Asian Americans to relate to many different groups of people without losing their own identity as Asian Americans. Having been immersed in an Asian American experience in the previous stage and resolving their racial identity conflict, Asian Americans in Stage Five no longer have a driving need to be exclusively with other Asian Americans. They also recognize that while racial identity is important, it is not the only social identity of importance to them. The hallmark of this last stage is the blending of individuals' racial identity with the rest of their social identities, as evidenced in the following words:

What I also discovered was that my needs got less driving. That I had a lot more in common with people who were Caucasians in some cases. I accepted that. That just because we're Asian American doesn't mean we're going to be kindred spirits. I'd say that writing that book was a commitment to seeing it through to really try to get some blood flowing in that part of myself and find that missing limb, that missing corner of my heart and spirit.

Key features of the Incorporation Stage include:

Social environment: general.
Critical factor: clear and firm Asian American identity.
Self-concept: positive as a person.
Ego identity: whole person with race as only a part of their social identity.
Primary reference group: people in general.
Hallmark of the stage: blending of Asian American identity with the rest of an individual's identities.

Current Issues and Future Research

When this theory was developed in the 1980s, there were no other theories of Asian American racial identity development. Two decades later, this theory continues to be relevant to Asian Americans. Research has been done on specific ethnic groups and specific aspects of the ethnic and racial identity development of Asian Americans.[10] There is research that examines whether it is possible for different Asian ethnic groups to view themselves as a racial group and under what circumstances this unity might occur.[11] The general conclusion that one can draw from these works is that racial unity among Asian Americans is possible when it is politically and economically advantageous to do so, often in response to adversity. Examining how and when a racial group might come together is a different discourse than exploring the psychological processes that lead to a person's racial identity formation.

The Asian American Identity Development theory specifically focuses on racial identity development rather than ethnic identity development. This focus was fueled by the belief that much of what influences AAID is Asian Americans' status as a racial minority in the United States and the social and psychological consequences of this status. This is not to deny the existence of real cultural diversity among Asian ethnic groups. In fact, a study of college students by Yeh and Huang (1996) which focused on ethnicity, found that Asian Americans explicitly separate race and ethnicity and focus on ethnicity. Their research indicated that Asian Americans are largely affected by external forces and relationships in determining their affiliation with their cultural group and ultimately in forming ethnic identity. Yeh and Huang highlight the importance of acknowledging the collectivistic nature of ethnic identity development among Asian Americans.

However, the reality of everyday experience is that all Asian ethnic groups are perceived and treated from a common set of racial prejudices and stereotypes (Chan and Hune 1995). For the most part, we do not accord different status or treat an Asian person differently depending on the ethnic group (Chinese, Japanese, Korean, Vietnamese, and the like) he or she represents. The murder of Vincent Chin[12] in 1982 is a painful example of this reality. In fact one of the stereotypes of Asian Americans is that they all look alike. Just as a Black person is treated primarily on the basis of the color of his or her skin in this country regardless of ethnic membership (for example, African, Jamaican, Cape Verdean, mixed race, and so on), Asian Americans experience a similar social dynamic. It is their racial membership, not their ethnic membership, that impacts how Asian Americans feel about themselves in this country. This is the primary reason for formulating AAID as a racial identity theory.

While I have received much anecdotal information from Asian Americans of different ethnic backgrounds that the theory is applicable to their personal experience, it has not been tested by research among different Asian ethnic groups. This could be a fruitful area of future research. Relatedly, on college campuses today, there are more Asian ethnic associations, such as organizations for Korean students or Chinese American students, than Asian American associations. This shift implies a greater ethnic than racial orientation among modern college students. Future research could examine why this is so.

Although Ethnic Awareness is a stage of AAID, Asian American identity development is not primarily a process for finding one's heritage, although this does occur for some Asian Americans. As evident in the AAID theory, understanding and proclaiming one's Asian heritage is a necessary but not a sufficient condition for developing an Asian American racial identity. A critical factor is the acquisition of a coherent political point of view and a new paradigm, which are often gained through involvement in political movements. That new perspective recognizes the subordination of people of color in this country, including Asian Americans.

The political climate in the United States has changed significantly since the 1960s and the 1970s. There is more acceptance of the racial status quo, more political backlash about affirmative action, and more resistance to dealing with social oppression and injustice.[13] Given the importance of the sociopolitical environment in facilitating the development of an Asian American identity, how will the current, politically less progressive, environment affect Asian Americans? Will Asian American identity still evolve as outlined in the AAID theory if there are fewer opportunities to become involved in political movements that challenge current racial dynamics and institutions? Responses to the AAID theory from college students I've worked with indicate that the shifting of their paradigm during the third stage is much more subtle and at times hard to distinguish from the fourth stage. That is, the Awakening to Social Political Consciousness and Redirecting to Asian American Consciousness seem to blend into one stage. It will be important to study current college students and those in their mid- to late twenties to see how they resolve their racial identity conflict, and how similar or different their experience of racial identity conflict resolution is to the stages of AAID. Future research in this area could lead to a modification of the AAID theory.

Another potential impact of the post-1960s and 1970s political environment is that the importance of racial identity is beginning to be questioned. Two recent books by Asian American writers, *Native Speaker* by Chang-rae Lee (1995) and *The Accidental Asian* by Eric Liu (1998), provide some evidence of this. In his own way each author focuses more on the American part of his experience than on the Asian. Both authors are second-generation Asian American males in the White Identification stage, albeit passively, but they do not deny the existence of racial discrimination. One consequence of the changed political environment may be that Asian Americans spend more time in the White Identification stage, and perhaps never leave it. If this outcome is documented by future research, it would support one of AAID's theoretical assumptions of the importance of shifting one's paradigm by enhancing one's sociopolitical understanding, without which one remains in the White Identification stage.

Future research on Asian American racial identity must explore the length of time it takes for racism to affect the racial identity of Asian

Americans, and whether this effect is the same for all generations of Asian Americans. Differences between the experiences of foreign-born and native-born Asian Americans warrant additional attention.

Responses gained from sharing the AAID model with different generations of Asian Americans indicate that the theory primarily fits the experience of the 1.5 plus generation. The first generation of immigrants, who come to this country as adults, seem less affected psychologically by racism. Since the theory was developed using second-, third-, and fourth-generation Asian Americans, it may not accommodate the experiences of the immigrant generation. This is an important group to research, especially since fully 62 percent of Asian Americans in this country are immigrants.

Another significant social change that has occurred since the AAID theory was developed relates to the marriage patterns of Asian Americans. Specifically, more Asian Americans are marrying out of their Asian ethnic groups (for example, Chinese Americans marrying Korean Americans) and especially marrying out of their racial group (for example, Asians with White partners, Asians with Black partners, and so on). The AAID as currently written does not account for the experiences of interracial and interethnic people. Therefore, future research needs to examine the kinds of identity conflict that arise for Asian Americans who are in interracial marriages, or who are children of interracial or interethnic marriages. How these conflicts are resolved by these populations should also be studied. I believe the identity conflict issues are greatest for interracial people, especially if their background includes a blending of Asian and another race of color (that is, Black, Latino, or American Indian) because of their physical appearance. On the other hand, the mixed Asian ethnic families and children would probably have similar experiences as Asian Americans in general and would follow the AAID model because of the saliency of race over ethnicity that was discussed earlier. Additional research is needed to explore these topics more fully.

Summary: Synthesis

In summary, the Asian American Identity Development (AAID) theory is comprised of five stages which explore how Asian Americans gain a positive racial identity in a society where they must deal with various negative messages and stereotypes about who they are. The cultural tendency for Asian Americans to have a group and public orientation and to avoid shame contributes to the assimilation strategy evident in the White Identification Stage. Access to information and increased understanding about White racism can help an Asian American to move out of the White Identification Stage and start on the road to a positive racial identity.

While there are a number of research topics that could shed light on Asian Americans' racial identity conflict and its resolution, the AAID theory still seems very relevant today. This is due in part to the fact that as a society we have not made significant progress toward eliminating White racism, and therefore the societal setting in which Asian Americans experience life has not changed significantly. If anything, our society seems to be more reactionary toward issues of affirmative action and politically more conservative about race relations now than a few decades ago. In such an environment, there is a shortage of progressive social political movements and agendas. Consequently, it may be more difficult than before for Asian Americans to work through the AAID stages and positively resolve their racial identity conflicts.

NOTES

1. The AAID was created in the 1980s, based on doctoral dissertation research on the experiences of Japanese American women.

2. I have shared the AAID theory with many Asian Americans professionals in large corporations, both male and female. On one such occasion, a Chinese American woman rose up in a crowded room of over two hundred people to say how much of her own life experience was reflected in the AAID stages. Through her tears she talked about the pain of spending many years in the White Identification stage. In 1999, I taught an undergraduate course composed primarily of Asian American students from various ethnic backgrounds. The AAID theory was discussed as a part of the course. I wasn't sure how relevant the AAID stages would be for young people who grew up in the post–civil rights and the race pride movement era. However, I was pleasantly surprised by their recognition of AAID stages in their young lives.

3. Studies that have compared culturally diverse groups found that Asian American subjects provide more collective responses, 20 to 52 percent, than European American subjects who only gave 15 to 19 percent collective responses

(Higgins and King 1981). When compared to European Americans, Asian Americans tend to depend more heavily on the situation and values of the society to define who they are (Triandis 1989).

4. Specifically, Critical Race theorists believe that race is a conceptual mechanism by which power and privileges are distributed in this country. Furthermore, the concept of race was constructed as a political device to keep people of color subordinated to Whites. Therefore Critical Race theorists believe that progressive racial identity must reflect more than appreciation of common ancestry and include a common political agenda based on a shared worldview. This agenda should seek to terminate the subordination of people of color in this country (Iijima 1997).

5. There are a few books that chronicle the experience of Asian Americans in this country. Ronald Takaki (1989) is a great primer that describes the experiences of the major Asian ethnic groups in America. Another good source is a report of the U.S. Commission on Civil Rights (1992).

6. For further information on the history of racial discrimination suffered by Asian Americans and a critique of the model minority thesis, see Chin et al. (1996:13–23).

7. Much research done in the area of racial identity concludes that a child between the ages of three and six becomes aware of different ethnic groups and begins to identify with the appropriate one. However, both minority and majority children develop preferences for White racial stimuli (Clark 1955; Clark and Clark [1947] 1958; Clark 1980; Brand, Ruiz, and Padilla 1974).

8. Since completing the original study, I have processed the results with hundreds of Asian Americans in different adult stages of development, generations, ethnic backgrounds, and social environments. These encounters have illustrated that for the most part the theory of five stages is still viable. However, I have become more aware of the interplay between the way Asian Americans experience the various stages and Asian cultural values, especially of *group orientation* resulting in greater focus on the external social environment and the role of *shame* as a preferred control mechanism among Asian cultures.

9. Major political influences of this era were the Black liberation movement and Black nationalism. These movements believed that the way to reduce racial domination was to directly transform the power relationship between Blacks and Whites. The birth of the Asian American movement itself coincided with these movements for Black liberation. Asian American activists focused on raising questions of oppression and power and not so much on racial pride. To them, Asian American identity was primarily a means of uniting for political struggle rather than acquiring racial identity solely for its own sake (Iijima 1997).

10. Two unpublished theses, Ray (1996), Alvarez (1996), document the ex-

periences of Asian Americans as they adjust to living in this country. Others who have written on Asian American identity development are Phinney (1989), Lee (1989), Yeh and Huang (1996), DesJardins (1996), Oyserman and Sakamoto (1997), Ponpipom (1997), Ibrahim, Ohnishi, and Sandhu (1997), Sue, Mak, and Sue (1998), Lee (1999), Tse (1999), and Sodowsky, Kwan, and Pannu (1995).

11. Espiritu (1996) contains many chapters that examine various Asian ethnic group experiences and the circumstances under which Asian Americans unite and view themselves as a racial group. The book does not contain any theories of racial identity development of Asian Americans but does examine various circumstances under which Asian ethnic groups come together. The dominant examples are in the areas of national politics, responding to social service agency funding requests, responses to violence directed against Asian Americans, reactions to discrimination, and so on.

12. In 1982 Vincent Chin was murdered by a group of laid-off auto workers in Detroit. His Asian appearance made him a target. In an area where there was a lot of anti-Japanese feeling due to competition in the auto industry, Vincent was thought to be Japanese, though he was Chinese American. The fact that the White men who murdered Chin received minimum sentences of probation is an example of institutional racism directed against Asian Americans in our legal system.

13. It was during the 1990s that we saw the passage of proposition 206 in California that eliminated affirmative action in contracting, selection, and hiring in businesses, and admissions to universities. A number of other states, including Washington State, have followed suit. Other evidence of this changing social climate are the Texas Law school case and the Maryland scholarship case, both of which questioned the legality of affirmative action and the value of diversity in higher education in professional school admissions.

REFERENCES

Alvarez, Alvin N. 1996. "Asian American Racial Identity: An Examination of Worldviews and Racial Adjustment." Doctoral dissertation, Department of Psychology, University of Maryland, College Park.

Begley, Sharon. 1995. "Three Is Not Enough: Surprising New Lessons from the Controversial Science of Race." *Newsweek* (February 3):67–69.

Bernal, Martha E., and George P. Knight. 1993. *Ethnic Identity: Formation and Transmission among Hispanic and Other Minorities.* Albany: State University of New York Press.

Brand, Elaine S., Rene A. Ruiz, and Amado M. Padilla. 1974. "Ethnic Identification and Preference: A Review." *Psychological Bulletin* 81(11):860–890.

Carnevale, Anthony P., and Susan C. Stone. 1995. *The American Mosaic: An In-Depth Report on the Future of Diversity at Work*. New York: McGraw-Hill.

Chan, Kenyon S., and Shirley Hune. 1995. "Racialization and Panethnicity: From Asians in America to Asian Americans." Pp. 205–233 in *Toward a Common Destiny: Improving Race and Ethnic Relations in America*, ed. W. D. Hawley, A. W. Jackson, et al. San Francisco: Jossey-Bass.

Chin, Gabriel J., Sumi Cho, Jerry Kang, and Frank Wu. 1996. *Beyond Self Interest: Asian Pacific Americans, Towards a Community of Justice: A Policy Analysis of Affirmative Action*. Los Angeles: UCLA Asian-American Studies Center.

Chin, Pei-Ngo. 1970. "The Chinese Community in L.A." *Social Casework* (51)(10):591–598.

Clark, Kenneth B. 1955. *Prejudice and Your Child*. Boston: Beacon Press.

———. 1980. "What Do Blacks Think of Themselves?" *Ebony*: 176–182.

Clark, Kenneth B., and M. P. Clark. [1947] 1958. "Racial Identification and Preference in Negro Children." Pp. 169–178 in *Readings in Social Psychology*, ed. T. Newcomb and E. L. Hartley. New York: Holt.

Crenshaw, Kimberle. 1995. *Critical Race Theory: The Key Writings That Formed the Movement*. New York: New Press.

Delgado, Richard. 1995. *Critical Race Theory: The Cutting Edge*. Philadelphia: Temple University Press.

DesJardins, Kunya S. 1996. "Racial Identity Development and Self Concept in Adopted Korean Women." Doctoral dissertation, Boston University.

Espiritu, Yen Le. 1996. *Asian American Panethnicity*. Los Angeles: Asian American Studies Center, UCLA.

Gay, Geneva. 1985. "Implications of the Selected Models of Ethnic Identity Development for Educators." *Journal of Negro Education* 54(1):43–55.

Harklau, Linda, Kay M. Losey, and Meryl Siegal, eds. 1999. *Generation 1.5 Meets College Composition: Issues in the Teaching of Writing to U.S.-Educated Learners of ESL*. Mahwah, N.J.: Lawrence Erlbaum.

Helms, Janet E. 1990. *Black and White Racial Identity: Theory, Research and Practice*. Westport, Conn.: Greenwood.

Higgins, E. Tory, and Gillian King. 1981. "Accessibility of Social Constructs: Information-Processing Consequences of Individual and Contextual Variability. Pp. 69–121 in *Personality, Cognition and Social Interaction*, ed. N. Cantor and J. F. Kihlstrom. Hillsdale, N.J.: Lawrence Erlbaum.

Huang, Larke N. 1994. "An Integrative View of Identity Formation: A Model for Asian Americans." Pp. 43–59 in *Race, Ethnicity, and Self: Identity in Multicultural Perspective*, ed. E. P. Salett and D. R. Koslow. Washington, D.C.: National MultiCultural Institute.

Ibrahim, Farah, Hifumi Ohnishi, and Data Singh Sandhu. 1997. "Asian American Identity Development: A Culture Specific Model for South Asian Americans." *Journal of Multicultural Counseling and Development* 25(1):34–50.

Iijima, Chris K. 1997. "The Era of We-Construction: Reclaiming the Politics of Asian Pacific American Identity and Reflections on the Critique of the Black/White Paradigm." *Human Rights Law Review* 29:47.

Kasindorf, Martin. 1982. "Asian-Americans: A 'Model Minority.'" *Newsweek* (December 6):39.

Kim, Jean. 1981. "Process of Asian American Identity Development: A Study of Japanese American Women's Perceptions of Their Struggle to Achieve Positive Identities as Americans of Asian Ancestry." Doctoral dissertation, School of Education, University of Massachusetts, Amherst.

Knowles, Louis L., and Kenneth Prewitt, eds. 1969. *Institutional Racism in America*. Englewood Cliffs, N.J.: Prentice-Hall.

Kohatsu, Eric L. 1993. "The Effects of Racial Identity and Acculturation on Anxiety, Assertiveness, and Ascribed Identity among Asian American College Students." Doctoral dissertation, University of Maryland, College Park.

Lee, Chang-rae. 1995. *Native Speaker*. New York: Riverhead Books.

Lee, Sally R. 1989. "Self-Concept Correlates of Asian American Cultural Identity Attitudes." Doctoral dissertation, University of Maryland, College Park.

Lee, Stacey J. 1999. "'Are You Chinese or What?' Ethnic Identity among Asian Americans." Pp. 107–121 in *Racial and Ethnic Identity in School Practices: Aspects of Human Development*, ed. R. Hernández and E. R. Hollins. Mahwah, N.J.: Lawrence Erlbaum.

Liu, Eric. 1998. *The Accidental Asian*. New York: Random House.

Moritsugu, John, and Stanley Sue. 1983. "Minority Status as a Stressor." Pp. 162–173 in *Preventive Psychology: Theory, Research, and Practice*, ed. R. D. Felner, L. A. Jason, J. N. Moritsugu, and S. S. Farber. Elmsford, N.Y.: Pergamon.

Omi, Michael, and Howard Winant. 1994. *Racial Formation in the United States: From the 1960s to the 1990s.* New York: Routledge.

Oyserman, Daphna, and Izumi Sakamoto. 1997. "Being Asian American: Identity, Cultural Constructs, and Stereotype Perception." *Journal of Applied Behavioral Science* 33(4):435–453.

Phinney, Jean S. 1989. "Stages of Ethnic Identity Development in Minority Group Adolescents." *Journal of Early Adolescence* 9(1):34–49.

Ponpipom, Ada. 1997. "Asian-American Ethnic Identity Development: Contributing Factors, Assessment, and Implications for Psychotherapy." Doctoral dissertation, Institute for Graduate Clinical Psychology, Widener University, Chester, Pennsylvania.

Ray, Indrani E. 1996. *Racial and Ethnic Identity: South Asian American Youth's Experiences and Perceptions, a Thesis*. Doctoral dissertation, University of Massachusetts, Boston.

Smith, Elsie J. 1991. "Ethnic Identity Development: Toward the Development of a Theory within the Context of Majority/Minority Status." *Journal of Counseling and Development* 70:181–188.

Sodowsky, Gargi R., Kwong-Liem K. Kwan, and Raji Pannu. 1995. "Ethnic Identity of Asians in the United States." Pp. 123–154 in *Handbook of Multicultural Counseling*, ed. J. G. Ponterotto, J. M. Casas, L. A. Suzuki, and C. M. Alexander. Thousand Oaks, Calif.: Sage.

Sue, Stanley, and Harry H. Kitano. 1973. "Stereotypes as a Measure of Success." *Journal of Social Issues* 29(2):83–98.

Sue, David, Winnie S. Mak, and Derald W. Sue. 1998. "Ethnic Identity." Pp. 289–323 in *Handbook of Asian American Psychology*, ed. L. C. Lee, N. W. S. Zane et al. Thousand Oaks, Calif.: Sage.

Sue, Stanley, and Derald W. Sue. 1971. "Chinese-American Personality and Mental Health." *Amerasia Journal* 1:36–49.

———. 1990. *Counseling the Culturally Different: Theory and Practice*. New York: John Wiley.

Suzuki, Bob H. 1975. "The Broader Significance of the Search for Identity by Asian Americans." Lecture presented at the AA Conference held at Yale University, New Haven, Conn. (April 12).

Takaki, Ronald. 1989. *Strangers from a Different Shore: A History of Asian Americans*. Boston: Little Brown.

Triandis, Harry C. 1989. "The Self and Social Behavior in Differing Cultural Contexts." *Psychological Review* 96(3), 506–520.

Tse, Lucy. 1999. "Finding a Place to Be: Ethnic Identity Exploration of Asian Americans." *Adolescence* 34(133):121–138.

United States Commission on Civil Rights. 1992. *Civil Rights Issues Facing Asian Americans in the 1990s*. Washington, D.C.: The Commission.

Wijeyesinghe, Charmaine L., Pat Griffin, and Barbara Love. 1997. "Racism Curriculum Design." Pp. 82–109 in *Teaching for Diversity and Social Justice: A Sourcebook*, ed. M. Adams, L. A. Bell, and P. Griffin. New York: Routledge.

Yeh, Christine J, and Karen Huang. 1996. "The Collectivistic Nature of Ethnic Identity Development among Asian American College Students." *Adolescence* 96(31):645–661.

Chapter 4

Reflections on American Indian Identity

Perry G. Horse

In this chapter I address some issues that arise in general discourse about American Indian identity. I approach these issues with my own sense of identity as an Indian person. Working, living, and interacting with Indian people from dozens of tribes and Alaska Natives over a period of forty years also informs my thinking on this topic.

Generalization about Indians is risky. However, there are identity issues that affect most, if not all, American Indians. In this essay I strive to illuminate some of those. Those who are searching for a single racial identity model that fits all American Indians are cautioned that such a model would assume coherent and commonly held ideas of race and ethnicity among American Indians. Such may not be the case, given the wide diversity among Indian peoples.

In what follows, I discuss my tribal heritage and the influence of one's culture and native language on identity. Then I offer an Indian perspective on American history that views the settlement of North America by Europeans as colonialist expansion. This perspective reveals that Indians are now emerging with a postcolonial sensibility similar to that of other indigenous groups around the world who recently gained their political independence. This sensibility sets the stage for a renewed consciousness of us as Indians going into the twenty first century. The colonization of Indian Country was driven by economic imperatives. I will touch on issues that pertain to identity. In concluding, I posit a paradigm of Indian identity and raise some questions about the future.

Language, Culture, and Identity

The traditional Indian understanding of self begins with our respective tribes' creation stories. My Kiowa ancestors called themselves
T'eyp da. The word means coming out. In Kiowa legend the origin of
our people began underground. Out of darkness into light the people
emerged on Earth's surface. And so the story goes. The story is very
old.[1] In the oral telling it would seem fresh in the Kiowa psyche because the oral tradition keeps experience direct rather than in the abstract as occurs in writing. Discourse in one's native tongue touches a
wellspring of knowledge and emotion not accessible in any other
way. Language shapes a culture and is shaped in turn by that culture.
If one is not fluent in one's native tongue one can read translated versions in written form to become familiar with one's culture as an academic exercise. But the direct linguistic connection or meaning from
the original telling is lost.

Today we Kiowa refer to ourselves as *Koi-gu.* The exact translation is
obscure but the meaning may be linked to the identity of one of the six
bands that originally comprised the tribe, *Kco-koi-gu,* or Elk People.
Kiowa history locates our origin in the northwestern United States.
Many of our tribal surnames reflect that region in terms of references to
wildlife common in the mountain ranges of the west. Traditional
names, as we shall see, are important in the identity equation.

I came of age in the 1950s when my grandparents and great-grandparents were still vigorous and clear of mind. They in turn had come
of age in the nineteenth century with memories of what life was like
before our people were colonized. They instilled in me a strong sense
of connection to a way of life I would never know firsthand. That connection helped anchor my personal sense of worth and identity.

Part of me hearkens back to a past that grows dimmer with the
steady passage of time. Another part of me looks ahead to an imagined range of possibilities. Most of all, I tend to reflect on my experiences as an Indian person in the twentieth century. Thus, my consciousness as an Indian person is an amalgamation of perceptions influenced by a complex interplay of culture, political sensibility,
language ability, and a kind of synchronistic sense of events.

I use the term tribe as synonymous for an Indian nation and vice-
versa. Indeed, this is done across Indian Country and in official documents of the United States government. Thus, one's tribal affiliation

is usually the first criterion of Indian identity. For many, the second criterion of identity is often knowledge of one's tribal language. As a practical matter, however, the latter is highly arbitrary. Nevertheless, language is a powerful determinant of one's membership or recognition in just about any group. As Trask observes,

> Every person needs to maintain an individual identity. One of the most important aspects of that identity is membership of a group, and language provides a powerful way of maintaining and demonstrating group membership. . . . Language is a very powerful means of declaring and maintaining one's identity." (1995:85)

Trask notes that out of the five thousand languages spoken around the world, most are not written. For many Indians the task of language preservation is synonymous with identity preservation. As each generation loses its facility with the native language of a given tribe, the task becomes ever more challenging.

The extinction of some native Indian languages is a short-term threat. For many tribes the threat is only one generation away from becoming critical. Language and culture are learned. Therefore, the laws of learning should apply. However, if there is a genetic aspect to language learning, Indian educators may have to rethink teaching strategies. Trask and other linguists report that there seems to be a specific time frame within which humans acquire a language naturally. Usually the prime window for this is from birth to twelve years. Then a genetic switch seems to turn off, making language learning more difficult.[2]

Once learned, though, a language must be used consistently. If not used, it becomes easier to understand native words than to actually speak them. There is a "use it or lose it" quality to language facility in that regard. Our native languages represent a direct link to our past and our cultures. If we lose our languages some things are bound to be lost in translation. Thomas Kuhn has observed that:

> Language learning and translation are, I have in recent years been emphasizing, very different processes: the outcome of the former is bilingualism, and bilinguals repeatedly report that there are things they can express in one language that they cannot express in the other. . . . Language learning is a process that need not, and ordinarily does not, make full translation possible. (1993:324)

My personal experience with bilingualism supports these observations. The translation problem is particularly troublesome as it pertains to basic concepts of racial identity. For example, the concept of race as used in English is relatively new for Indians. To my knowledge there is no precise linguistic counterpart for that word in the Kiowa language. We have borrowed the English practice of color coding, using Kiowa words for the various colors that coincide with the hue of skin color.

In the Kiowa language—and I suspect in other Indian languages as well—the concept of race as a biological reality is vague. Indeed, some geneticists believe that the concept of race is so vague that practically any of the hundreds, even thousands, of subdivisions in the human species could be called a race.[3] Be that as it may, many people tend to think of race in terms of those major biological subdivisions of humankind distinguished by skull size, hue of skin, eye color, and other physical attributes. As a practical matter we act as though race exists. Or we believe it exists.

Among Indians, identity development begins with the family, extended family, kinship, or clan affiliations. Then it extends to the tribal group, and then to identification with the general Indian populace. At the individual level, self-identity as an Indian is important. Acknowledgment of that identity by the group is equally important. In our tribe acquisition of a name in the tribal language reinforces that identity. One can inherit the name of an ancestor or be given a name unique to oneself. Naming is usually done in a public ceremony whereby the meaning of the name is explained and payment is rendered by giving articles of value to others in honor of the naming. It is an important ritual. It is our way of being publicly acknowledged by our fellow Kiowas and solidifies our status as Kiowas.

Official recognition by a tribe's government is important too, as we shall see. Culture, language, and racial concepts, however, are powerful denominators of Indian identity in the eyes of many. Cultures and languages change. The Indian response to such changes will probably impact on the identity issue in ways yet to be seen. Theories about social and organizational change abound in the literature. Perhaps these theories can help us understand our racial identity as that identity changes.

Economic pressure is a major driving force behind many of the changes in Indian societies. Adaptation to the economic scheme of things in America is an ongoing phenomenon in Indian Country. Indeed, the traditional subsistence economies are gradually being replaced by what we have now. We will continue to adapt economically for the sake of survival. But we can still preserve what we think is worthy of preservation, be it our language, traditions, customs, or the land. Our identity will evolve accordingly. Key to the way this evolution plays out is the matter of how we adapt to new realities.

Consciousness and Identity

If one thinks of identity development as a process that occurs over time and goes through different stages, it is possible to consider such development in historical perspective through different eras. I find it useful to think of such eras in American history as described by futurist writers and others. For example, in *The Greening of America* (1971), Charles Reich identified the three eras that affected the consciousness of White Americans as: the colonial era, the industrial revolution, and the contemporary era. Reich argues that consciousness plays a key role in shaping a society and that, "Every form of consciousness is a reaction to a way of life that existed before, and an adaptation to new realities" (1971:22). He labels those eras as Consciousness I, II, and III, respectively.

Consciousness I (C.I) focused on the individual, the self. It saw self in harsh and narrow terms, accepting self-repression and allowing one to be cut off from the larger community of man and from nature. Nature was defined as the enemy. Success in C.I was determined by character, morality, hard work, and self-denial. Reich calls this the Puritan Ethic. Up until the industrial revolution, the economy of the colonial era was agrarian. Much was made of the rugged individualist.

Consciousness II (C.II), according to Reich, created the corporate state. Under C.II, the organization was predominant and the individual had to make his or her way through a world directed by others. It was a turn away from individualism. At the heart of C.II was the insistence that the power of man's reasoning alone could overcome the intangible aspects of life. Under C.II the economy moved from agrarian dominance to industrial and corporate life. It seemed to rest on organizational interests, status, prestige, and power.

Consciousness III (C.III) took root in the mid-1960s with liberation from the corporate state as its ideal. It began to look at the world as a community instead of as a jungle with every person for him or herself. It rests on two integrated concepts, respect for the uniqueness of each individual and the idea expressed by the word. C.III rests on those interests which, in the view of many, the economic and organizational parts of American society have failed to supply.

Reich's discussion is instructive as a non-Indian reflection of historical eras and stages of consciousness. Returning to his observation that consciousness is a reaction to a previous way of life and an adaptation to new realities as well as the key to shaping a society, it seems to follow that the consciousness of American Indians was affected similarly or in parallel. However, it must be kept in mind that the Indian adaptations took place external to the White consciousness per se. Indeed, if anything, Whites probably considered us as part of the C.I mind-set that pertains to nature, that is, the enemy.

The colonization of America occurred over a relatively brief span of time. To this day it has had a profound effect on Indians in ways that impact on the identity issue. By 1790, the colonists had taken lands from the Carolinas to New England. From the Declaration of Independence until the end of the Civil War, there was a tenuous balance of power between the Indian nations and the new settlers. Soon thereafter, power shifted dramatically to the new Republic. From about 1860 to 1890, the western half of the United States was flooded with immigrants seeking gold and land. In the short space of one hundred years, the native people of America were effectively displaced and relegated to small remnants of their original land base. This is a thumbnail sketch of the dizzying pace at which Indians were forced to deal with major changes in their economies and lifeways.

The need for historical consciousness among Indian people cannot be overstated. By clearly understanding our own history we can better transcend otherwise counterproductive attitudes such as bitterness, victimhood, and anti-White feelings. Many of today's Indians speak of the need to heal before we can go forward. Bringing our consciousness up to date would be a logical first step in the healing process.

Under C.II, in step with the industrial revolution, the westward expansion phase in American history decimated Indian economies with the loss of immense tracts of land. The cattle industry and the proliferation of railroads became a reality. Before the end of the nineteenth century Indian landholdings, which had comprised virtually all land west of the Mississippi were reduced to isolated reservations. Consciousness II extended into the twentieth century.

The pace of change accelerated. United States citizenship was bestowed unilaterally on Indians in 1924. By 1934 new systems of government were introduced to Indian tribes. Indian children were taken to federally operated boarding schools where acculturation into American life was enforced. This pattern of forced acculturation into non-Indian society continued well into the 1950s, when the government sought to abrogate its treaty obligations by implementing a policy of termination of the trust relationship between Indians and the United States. Indians were encouraged to leave their reservations under a program called relocation. Many responded and moved to urban areas of the country.

Reich's Consciousness III emerged in the land along with what is now known as the counterculture of the 1960s. Then, in 1970, the federal policy of self-determination for Indians was promulgated. This continues to this day. Indian tribes seized the opportunity and aggressively exercised their governmental powers under the rubric of tribal sovereignty. Tribal sovereignty is a touchstone of current Indian policy. It is a legal and political concept and is traced, as far as federal courts are concerned, to the Constitution. Its powerful impact on the issue of tribal membership will be discussed shortly. Even though Indian sovereignty is alluded to in the Constitution, there is no actual guidance in that document for "regulating commerce with foreign nations and the Indian tribes." Instead, there is a massive volume of Federal Indian Law and hundreds of regulations issued by the courts and executive agencies of the federal government with which Indian tribes must contend.

Tribal sovereignty is a doubled-edged sword. On the one hand, it has the virtue of acknowledging the presence of independent Indian governmental structures that predate the coming of the White man. On the other, it has the effect of replacing those preexisting structures with Euro-American concepts of government. In the eyes of many, this may or may not be a good thing.

The isolation of Indians from the mainstream of White America's economy parallels the three epochs mentioned earlier. Indians were effectively excluded from all three economic eras—the agrarian, the industrial, and the postindustrial. Our lands were usurped, leaving little for agrarian or other purposes. Starting with the so-called Doctrine of Discovery and continuing with unilateral legislative action, Indians were effectively dispossessed of their original land base except for approximately one hundred million acres in all (Kickingbird and Duchenaux 1973:227–228).

The economic isolation of Indians and the seizure of their land was a successful military strategy in the westward expansion phase of U.S. history. It evolved into a government policy of systematic acculturation with similar goals. The tactics changed but the strategy remained intact. That strategy said: if Indians lose their identity as Indians altogether and become more like full-fledged White Americans, the Indian problem will be solved.

When self-sufficient Indian economies disappeared, the very basis of life as Indians knew it began to fade. Whether those economies were based on agriculture, hunting, or harvesting the sea the loss of traditional ways of making a living had devastating consequences that persist to this day. The introduction of a new economy as practiced by the White man demanded a different philosophy from that of America's aboriginal societies. It demanded ways of making a living that were often antithetical to Indian sensibilities.

The introduction of capitalism began a process of exclusion of Indians from their land and from the economy of White America. The lack of fruitful occupations, the lack of access to education and capital, and the lack of political clout all contributed to the general malaise of Indian economic life for most of the twentieth century. The economic dependency of Indians was further exacerbated by the paternalistic policies and practices of the federal government that had oversight over services for Indians.

Dependency is enervating. It undermines the self-esteem and dignity of people. It goes directly to the issue of identity. How many times have we heard people say, "When we were kids, we were poor but we didn't know it." In fact, poor children learn quickly that they are indeed poor. This is because they can perceive prosperity all around them. The Indian tribes, too, could see prosperity all around their reservations in America. And they remained at the bottom of America's economic ladder for a long time. The term second-class citizens was routinely applied to Indian people.

For many Indians, the journey from economic dependency to real prosperity has barely begun. Others are well on their way. The latter have learned that economic prosperity can actually strengthen the cultural identity of Indian people. A case in point is the Mississippi Band of Choctaw Indians. In less than thirty years, the Mississippi Choctaws rose from economic dependency to self-sufficiency. They gained control of their own school system. Their number one goal is cultural preservation through education. Chief Phillip Martin is the Choctaw leader. Martin says,

> An economically prosperous tribe would have resources to devote to preserving its cultural heritage. It could undertake cultural education and preservation of the heritage of the past. Such prosperity would hold the tribe together and keep its members home. Without job opportunity on the reservation, the tribe would begin to scatter, particularly its most able and productive members. As the tribe dispersed, its culture would diminish and disappear. (Ferrara 1998:54)

The Choctaws' economic success is credited to their vigorous exercise of tribal sovereignty and self-government. Ironically, as they and other economically successful tribes became more astute about capitalism, they drew the attention of non-Indian business interests. This attention has not always been favorable. In fact, many non-Indian businessmen and politicians are challenging tribal sovereignty in ways that have become a serious threat to Indians. Many of today's Indian leaders consider tribal sovereignty to be the bedrock on which the revitalization, of Indian economies must be built. Cultural revitalization and identity go hand in hand with economic revitalization as the Choctaws have proven.

When the traditional Indian economies were diminished or obliterated, Indians were forced for the sake of survival to begin living like White people. This, of course, put them in a double bind, being Native but having to emulate the ways of Whites. To the extent that this caused them to be alienated from their internal and external worlds, they inevitably suffered some loss of identity. They experienced deep psychological trauma (Duran and Duran 1995:36–39). Indeed, the effect of such trauma on one's consciousness could be profound. For example, in the area of religion, coexisting in the White man's world while remaining spiritually independent was a dilemma for Indian people as they dealt with the missionary influence.[4]

Be that as it may, the roots of Indian pride run deep. Such pride is not necessarily vainglorious.[5] Rather, it is more like fanning a fire where the spirit resides. This is especially so when Indians gather for ceremonial or religious purposes. Just as philosophers in the ancient Western tradition speculated that an ethereal music of the universe was the force which held the cosmos together, the music and rhythms of Indian life holds us together. In my opinion one of the last bastions of Indian identity lies in this realm.[6]

The victimization of Indians is a matter of history and public record. Even though most of our land was taken by conquest, or by unfair congressional legislation, or by unscrupulous transactions, we still have a semblance of our land base.[7]

A Paradigm of Indian Identity

When discussing Indian identity I prefer to focus on factors that influence our individual and group consciousness as either tribal people or as American Indians. I prefer to couch Indian identity in terms of an overall ethic which informs our consciousness over time. Ethics refers to the principles or moral values which guide the actions of individuals or groups. Consciousness is not the same as politics. It is an individual issue. But in my view, large groups of people guided by a common ethic can create a tacit collective consciousness about themselves. We must look at ourselves against the entirety of all other cultures to see what is unique about ourselves and our own tribes or nations.

Part of this consciousness is fleeting. I have had experiences of this fleeting awareness by listening to the prayers of our elders in the native language, by singing our traditional songs, by dancing to the music of our ancestors, and by meditation. It bespeaks a harmony with an unseen order of things. It is like a tribal cosmology that seems to emerge in both the unconscious and conscious states. Contact with our native consciousness is often metaphorical, sometimes instinctive.

For Indians, I believe this consciousness is influenced in at least five ways:

1. How well one is grounded in the native language and culture;
2. Whether one's genealogical heritage as an Indian is valid;
3. Whether one embraces a general philosophy or worldview that derives from distinctly Indian ways, that is, old traditions;
4. The degree to which one thinks of him or herself in a certain way, that is, one's own idea of self as an Indian person; and
5. Whether one is officially recognized as a member of a tribe by the government of that tribe.

We identify first with the environment of the home and community. We come of age with a sense of who we are by learning the language, customs, traditions, and beliefs of our community. These are nonbiological, nongenetic factors, that is, our cultural identity. If we learn the native language and culture as part of our early life experience, we are likely to think of ourselves in that way for a long time. This observation is validated by historical fact. It comes from the story of Kiowa captives.

In prereservation days, the taking of captives was a common practice in the tribe. Many of those captives were young children and toddlers, usually White or Mexican. They were cared for and raised as Kiowas, and some intermarried within the tribe. Some captives were returned at their request, but many opted to stay, having become acculturated as Kiowas. They had come to think of themselves as Kiowas.

This raises an interesting question about the importance of the genealogical factor. It would seem that one's history as a member of a given tribe would be sufficient validation that one belonged to that tribe. But the current interpretation of tribal law regarding membership nowadays could effectively negate that as a legal matter. Nevertheless, one's consciousness as an Indian person tends to rest not on the laws of man but on one's upbringing and belief in oneself as being Indian as a consequence.

Growing up Indian in the old traditional ways, required sensitivity to and instruction in those ways. Through observation, instruction, and practice we develop that sensitivity consciously and unconsciously. We take note of a worldview that emphasizes the need for balance or harmony in one's life. This can be thought of in terms of one's relationship to all things, including one's religious predilections. It is a philosophical matter that I find difficult to articulate adequately in this space. It would touch on the spirituality of traditional Indian cultures, and most traditional Indians who are taught in those ways are reticent about such matters.

Suffice it to say that many Indians feel they are Indian because they have earned that entitlement in some way. Only they can tell you how that came to be. It requires knowledge and experience of the things discussed above. Personally, I feel I am Kiowa because I have direct experience of being one.

Eventually, we come to understand that tribes are political entities with our own governments and laws. Our tribal identity emphasizes culture as a practical matter. But we realize that our tribes are recognized as sovereign nations with the power to act accordingly. Such powers extend to determining who is or is not an officially recognized member or citizen of the tribe.[8] It is possible that one can demonstrate four of the above-mentioned five considerations but not be officially recognized as a member by the tribe's government. This is because tribes retain absolute authority over who is and who is not a tribal member. This is based on the principle of tribal sovereignty and has been upheld by the United States Supreme Court.

Postcolonial Sensibilities

The political resurgence of Indian tribes is a defining aspect of Indian life today. The political and legal status of tribes is perhaps their most distinguishing characteristic vis-à-vis other ethnic groups in the United States. Unlike other countries around the world that were colonized and then regained their independence, American Indian nations are subtended if not subsumed permanently under the United States of America. Yet Indian tribes enjoy legal recognition as sovereign political entities with simultaneous recognition as American citizens.

Just over two hundred years ago American colonists were subjects of another political power prior to the Declaration of Independence. American history is temporal compared with the longer lived histories of Indian tribes. This point is the touchstone for Indian policy and recognition of tribal sovereignty.

Self-governance and tribal sovereignty are the foundation for economic development and prosperity in Indian Country. This means that stability in tribal government should be the top priority for Indians. This requires not only political, business, and economic astuteness but also a more statesmanlike approach to dealing with constituencies, stakeholders, and other governments. Revitalizing or strengthening Indian cultures is closely tied to economic and political self-determination.

The changes we have experienced as Indians, especially in the last one hundred years, have undoubtedly taken a psychological toll. I am not a trained psychologist, but it makes sense to me that today's Indian would be in a state of recovery from old psychological wounds. Indians' consciousness is buffeted by the forces of rapid change and a basic unwillingness to completely sever ties to a psychological legacy which defined them as Indians in the first place. Boyd and others put it this way:

> Throughout the millennia these Native Americans also developed customs and beliefs which they wove into a total way of life. This separate cultural development, completely unrelated to the cultures evolving in Europe, Africa, and Asia, produced a people with unique psychological traits (Boyd and Pauahty 1981:2)

This refers to the sensibility about oneself touched on earlier, defined by one's individual consciousness as an Indian and by one's tribal affiliation. At the individual, tribal, and ethnic levels Indian people face tremendous challenges such as retaining their native languages, beliefs, customs, and traditions and once again weaving them into a way of life that reflects who they are as they understand themselves to be. This would be akin to a redefinition of self as individuals and as tribal cultural entities.

For many American Indians cultural transmission occurs in the family environment. For others it does not. Most of those who live in urban areas must deal with geographical dislocation from the tribal homeland. And, of course, all are affected by the mass media, popular American culture, the internet, American schooling, and peer pressure. Even those who live in their tribal homelands do not necessarily receive systematic cultural or language instruction in the home.

The future of cultural transmission among Indians may lie in the schooling arena. The Mississippi Choctaw experience, mentioned earlier, is a case in point. Once the Choctaws gained control of their own formal schooling system, they were able to use that system for the purpose of cultural transmission. At the postsecondary level, at least thirty one different tribal groups have established their own tribal colleges. A significant feature of the mission of these colleges is preservation of the tribal culture. It remains to be seen whether this approach to sustaining cultural integrity across the generations will be effective.

The early European colonizers brought three distinct languages with them to America: Spanish, French, and English. Of the three, English has outstripped the others by far in displacing native tribal languages at an alarming rate. However, we know that American English has accommodated or integrated native words and vice versa. As mentioned earlier, the word race does not seem to have an exact counterpart in many native Indian languages. Nor does racism or racist. Yet Indians certainly experience and feel the effects of the latter. And even though racial identity per se is a relatively new concept among Indians, it would seem to be of utmost importance as a future issue in terms of dealing with an American mind-set which uses race as synonymous with a nation or people. Race seems to be a misnomer in scientific terms. It is probably more accurate to consider race as a social construct.

Racist attitudes toward Indians are likely to continue into the twenty first century. Such attitudes give rise to misguided legislative attempts by congressional politicians, state politicians, and others to curtail or erode tribal sovereignty.[9] Such attitudes also manifest themselves in the use of Indian icons and imagery by commercial businesses, schools, colleges, professional team sports, and non-Indian artists.[10] The misuse of Indian icons and imagery works a not-so-subtle message on the minds of non-Indians and Indians alike. That message says it is all right to exploit Indians in this way because they are essentially powerless to stop it.

On the other hand, there are those in America and elsewhere who genuinely admire and respect American Indian people and their cultures. There are those seeking spiritual solace and harmony who look to Indian cultures for guidance in these areas. I once observed that people exploring alternative sources of spiritual wisdom are often inevitably drawn to the traditional beliefs of Native Americans.[11]

Our native elders spoke of coping with the dilemma of coexisting in the White man's world while remaining spiritually independent and cohesive as tribal people. They also spoke of the need for personal dignity and hope. To me, this goes to the crux of Indian identity today. We are engaged in a cultural struggle that is becoming more and more one-sided in favor of non-Indian influences. Yet we persist in the hope that our cultures will be preserved in ways that make sense to us. In those cultures, ultimately, lies our identity as native people. As individuals too, we draw much of our personal identity from those cultures.

NOTES

1. Boyd and Pauahty (1981:1–5). This volume and a companion, volume 2 Boyd and Pauahty (1983) grew out of a project approved by the Kiowa Tribal

Council in 1975 under the auspices of the Kiowa Historical and Research Society. All the stories and anecdotes therein were provided and approved by
Kiowa historians and elders. The origin stories of Indians, often characterized by Whites as myths, are not intended to inform White paradigms, biases,
or sensibilities. Rather, they are told from the perspective of ancient people
who had different perceptions of space and time. Cataclysmic events in
Earth's past were observed and recorded by ancient Indians, many of whom
may have survived such events and preserved old memories of reemergence
in these stories.

2. See Trask (1995:150). Some attempts are currently being made in Indian
communities to address this issue by introducing language instruction in
schools serving young Indian children. In other tribes usage of the native language is still strong enough in the home to give young children the opportunity to learn through family discourse. This was true in my experience, personally, but I cannot claim to have been fully fluent as a child although I certainly could understand what was being said in most cases. Because our
language was spoken at home I was able to discern the nuances of sound and
inflection that are so important to the language learning process.

3. See Cavalli-Sforza and Cavalli-Sforza (1995:227–244).

4. In the first two or three decades of the twentieth century many Kiowas'
sense of identity was severely shaken as the tribe was in transition from the
old religion (the Sun Dance) to newer beliefs as represented by the Native
American Church (Peyotism) and Christianity. Boyd and Pauahty note of this
period,

> In their search for identity, many Kiowas turned to Peyote. They felt the
> need for myth consciousness. The white man's emphasis on objective or
> rational consciousness denied the Kiowas' need for contact with the uni-
> versal rhythms. Their search for universal vitality required consciousness
> expansion, because their future is in a realm beyond reason. Peyote en-
> ables the celebrant consciously to submit to the impulses of the uncon-
> scious and thus be led to a path that would overcome his disorientation
> with the 'real' world limited by its rational objectivity. (1983:283)

Today's Kiowas embrace both Christianity and Peyotism for spiritual suste-
nance. Indeed, both are now complementary and celebrants of each have the
highest respect for the other.

5. In the context of ethnicity—as opposed to race—Indian people are in-
tensely proud of their respective cultures. This pride runs very deep and results in friendly rivalry between neighboring groups or overtones of resentment from ancient enmities. In this way Indians can be ethnocentric if not
ethnic chauvinists.

6. In an unpublished essay, I wrote about the importance of song, music,
and dance among Kiowas and other Indians, expressing it this way:

The ancient Greeks pondered the universe and speculated that the movement of heavenly bodies or spheres produced an ethereal music. If there is a music of the spheres, might the universe of a tribal body politic produce its own music, ethereal or otherwise? Beautiful music evokes an emotional response. It moves the spirit of individuals and tribes. The spirit lives and is expressed in the music. Such music will always strike a responsive chord in those who are so vested. The drum is the heart beat. The songs are the rhythm of life; the lyrics the poetry of existence. Part of one's identity, then, can be expressed in the songs of one's people no matter what one's race may be.

Kiowa culture places strong emphasis on traditional music and songs for practically any occasion. This was documented most recently in Lassiter (1998).

7. See Kickingbird and Ducheneaux (1973:225–232). Displacement from our lands was a crucial factor in our struggle to adapt to the capitalist equation of land, labor, and capital. In most cases we have plenty of labor but barely enough land and not much capital.

8. At Santa Clara Pueblo in Northern New Mexico a dispute arose when the Pueblo refused to grant official membership in the tribe to the children of a tribal member who had married a nontribal member. The tribal ruling was in accordance with tribal law which grants membership to children only when both parents are on the membership rolls of the tribe. The case eventually wound up in the Supreme Court which ruled in favor of the tribe. This is another instance where the courts have upheld the jurisdiction of tribal governments over domestic issues based on tribal sovereignty. In this case the court agreed with the Pueblo argument that its membership laws were rooted in its traditional culture. Therefore, control over the criteria for belonging to the tribe was basic to its exercise of tribal sovereignty.

9. A recent manifestation of such challenges to tribal sovereignty and Indian rights is illustrated by the efforts of Donald Trump to stop the competition represented by Indian gaming to established gambling interests. See also Ferrara (1998:135–141).

10. The exploitation of Indian icons and imagery, in my opinion, arises basically out of a racist mentality which is perhaps best illustrated by the team logos of the Cleveland Indians, the Atlanta Braves, and the Washington Redskins. Other examples are distillers and wine makers who have attempted to label their products as "Crazy Horse Whiskey," and "Kachina Wine," names deeply offensive to Indians in general and the tribes from which they come in particular. Other examples abound. In the mind of the public, apparently, the affront to Indians is too innocuous for serious consideration.

Another arena of commercial exploitation of Indians is the genre of fine art known as Western art, some of which purports to depict Indian life, history, and themes. There are artists of Indian descent who also profit monetarily from the genre of Indian art but one assumes that at least they do so with deep respect, humility, and accuracy. I know of no Indian artists who make a living depicting White people or cultures other than their own.

11. Horse (1996).

REFERENCES

Boyd, Maurice, and Linn Pauahty. 1981. *Kiowa Voices, Ceremonial Dance, Ritual and Song.* Volume I. Fort Worth: Texas Christian University Press.

———. 1983. *Kiowa Voices.* Volume II. Fort Worth: Texas Christian University Press.

Cavalli-Sforza, Luigi Luca, and Francesco Cavalli-Sforza. 1995. *The Great Human Diasporas: The History of Diversity and Evolution.* Reading, Mass.: Addison-Wesley.

Duran, Eduardo, and Bonnie Duran. 1995. *Native American Postcolonial Psychology.* Albany: State University of New York Press.

Ferrara, Peter J. 1998. *The Choctaw Revolution: Lessons for Federal Indian Policy.* Washington, D.C.: Americans for Tax Reform Foundation.

Horse, Perry G. 1996. "Spirituality and New Science in Organizations: A Tribal Perspective." *St. Thomas Law Review* 9 (fall):49–57.

Kickingbird, Kirke, and Karen Ducheneaux. 1973. *One Hundred Million Acres.* New York: Macmillan.

Kuhn, Thomas. 1993. *World Changes: Thomas Kuhn and the Nature of Science,* ed. Paul Horwich. Cambridge Mass.: MIT Press.

Lassiter, Luke. 1998. *The Power of Kiowa Song.* Tucson: University of Arizona Press.

Reich, Charles. 1971. *The Greening of America.* New York: Bantam.

Trask, Robert L. 1995. *Language: The Basics.* London: Routledge.

Chapter 5

Reflections on White Identity Development Theory

Rita Hardiman

In the years prior to the development of the first model of White identity development (Hardiman 1982), Du Bois (1973), among other Black scholars, urged Whites to turn their lens of analysis about race around and look at themselves in the mirror. In more recent times, scholars have increasingly turned their focus to Whites as part of the American racial equation, in fields as diverse as anthropology, counseling psychology, and film studies. Models of White racial identity and White racial consciousness have been formulated, researched, critiqued and reformulated, primarily in the area of counseling psychology.[1] In addition, a plethora of books, essays, and articles from other disciplines have also focused on Whiteness.

This chapter explores the current understanding of Whites and "Whiteness" in the United States: From whence have we come, where are we going, and where do we need to go with regard to race? First, I review the earliest models of White identity development which emerged from the fields of education and counseling psychology, notably the White Identity Development model or WID (Hardiman 1982) and the White Racial Identity Development or WRID (Helms 1984). My goals here are to understand the origins of these models within their disciplines, their political and historical context, and the assumptions upon which they were based. I examine the limitations of both models, and discuss the major criticisms made of each by others in the field.

The second section of the chapter shifts the focus away from models of White identity development per se, and reviews emergent thinking on the issues of Whiteness and White identity from scholars outside the fields of education and psychology. The recent dramatic upsurge in Whiteness studies has produced work that I believe can inform and reshape the current White identity development models. I conclude the chapter with my thoughts on the direction that research on White identity should take, as well as the essential questions that I think future White identity models should address.

Hardiman Model of White Identity Development (WID)

In the late 1970s, I began work on the development of a model of White racial identity to understand and explain how race and racism in the United States affected White people. I undertook this work because I was certain that in a society with racism at its core, racism affected Whites as the dominant and privileged racial group as certainly as it affected people of color, albeit in different and obvious ways. I knew that I had been trained since infancy to see race, think racially, and assume my position as a member of the dominant race in a racially stratified society.[2]

I was self-aware enough to know that not only was I prejudiced, having believed lies, stereotypes, and distortions about U.S. racial history, but also that those beliefs, attitudes, and feelings were not of my own making. I didn't construct them. They were presented to me, to my White peers, and indeed to people of all races in the United States through stories, folklore, the mass media, schooling, and by living in a racially polarized, segregated, and stratified society.

An important first step in my study was to shift the focus to the dominant group, the willing as well as the unknowing participants in a system of racial oppression: White people. As a female and a feminist, I knew that any form of oppression such as racism, sexism, or anti-semitism was a relationship between a dominant, powerful group and a subordinated or oppressed group. I knew that sexism would not be undone by studying its effects on women, or solely by women fighting their oppression. The system of male dominance had to change. The creation, operation, and maintenance of any system of oppression needed to be understood and analyzed in the service of figuring out how to undo it or overthrow it. I applied the same principle in looking at racism, noting in 1982 that "race relations research . . . is dominated by a focus on the victims of racial oppression, or the effects of racial oppression, not on the perpetrators of racism, the dominant white group" (Hardiman 1982:3).

In my original work, I also wanted to understand whether and how Whites could escape from the effects of their racist programming. Was becoming unprejudiced or antiracist possible for Whites? Could they undo their socialization? If so, how? Third, I wanted to contribute to the construction of a new way to be White that was not dependent on the subjugation or denigration of people of color. I knew that as the end of the twentieth century approached, Whites needed to figure out how to be one race or culture among many—rather than the center or core—in a nonoppressive and multiracial society. This work was both a personal quest and a professional mission. I was directly influenced by the work of Robert Terry, who in the 1970s began asking the question—what does it mean to be White and how can we redefine ourselves, so that as "new whites" (Terry 1975:22) we reject racism and work toward a pluralistic society?

The WID and the Helms model (1984, 1990a, 1995), which will be discussed in a later section, emerged in the aftermath of the contemporary civil rights/Black Power movements, which roughly spanned the decades of the mid-1950s to the early 1970s. The WID was written subsequent to the development of models of Black Identity or Nigrescence, and arose at a time when a new consciousness about race and gender—two key social identities—were a major focus of attention in several disciplines, including sociology, psychology, political science, and education. Prior to challenges by Blacks and women in academia which arose from these movements, most academic disciplines were marked by the White male dominance of the researchers and scholars who framed the discourse on race and racism. Reflecting this racial bias in particular, most of the studies and writing that focused on questions of race ignored the dominant racial group, Whites, as a subject of study. This White hegemony and focus on the "racial other" had been noted since the 1970s by such scholars as Blauner and Wellman (1973), Chesler (1976), Bowser and Hunt (1981), and more recently by critical race theorists such as Delgado and Stefancic (1997), Frankenberg (1993), and Giroux (1997). Exceptions to this bias were the handful of scholars who attempted to describe White responses to Black people or to the racial ethos of U.S. society by creating typologies of Whites or of liberals (Caditz 1976; Terry 1978).

The WID model also clearly arose out of a racism analysis, which required an understanding of the way oppression impacts individuals, rather than from a "cultural difference" analysis in which the focus is directed at White identification with White culture. At that time I wasn't clear that there was a "White" culture. Therefore this model, the first to look at the development of White identity, was very much a model of how Whites came to terms with their Whiteness with respect to racism and race privilege.

Stages of the WID Model

The WID model, originally developed in 1982 and updated in 1992 (Hardiman 1982, 1994; Hardiman and Jackson 1992), has five stages that describe the development of racial identity in White Americans. To briefly summarize here, the first stage is characterized by *No Social Consciousness of Race or Naivete* about race, marked by a lack of awareness of visible racial differences. Whites at this stage have no understanding of the social meaning of race or the value attached to one race over another. This naive period, which ends in early childhood, is followed by a stage of *Acceptance*, whereupon the White person accepts or internalizes racism and a sense of himself as racially superior to people of color, although this sense of dominance, privilege, or entitlement is often unconscious. The WID model assumes that it is impossible in this society to escape racist socialization in some form because of its pervasive, systemic, and interlocking nature. This is not a matter of choice for Whites, it is a by-product of living within and being impacted by the institutional and cultural racism which surrounds us.

The third stage, called *Resistance*, is marked by an individual questioning the dominant paradigm about race, and resisting or rejecting his racist programming. It is also a stage wherein Whites can become antiracist or active in efforts to reduce, eliminate, or challenge racism. In reference to the person's own race, this stage is often characterized by embarrassment about one's Whiteness, guilt, shame, and a need to distance oneself from the White group.

The fourth stage, *Redefinition*, occurs when the White person begins to clarify his own self-interest in working against racism, and begins to accept and take responsibility for his Whiteness. Rather than estrangement from Whiteness and their peers, Whites at this stage attempt to redefine themselves as "new whites" (Terry 1975:22). They take ownership of their Whiteness rather than trying to deny it or embracing another racial identity, such as taking on the most visible elements of Black or Native American culture.

The fifth and final stage, *Internalization*, involves integrating or internalizing this increased consciousness regarding race and racism, and one's new White identity into all aspects of one's life.

Analysis of the WID Model

In retrospect, it is clear that the WID model, like any model or theory, is imbedded in a particular historical context. When the WID was developed, the overriding issue impacting—or some would argue, creating—racial identity was racism. Therefore it is understandable, if unfortunate, that the model ignored or underemphasized the question of how Whites identified culturally with their Whiteness, thus making the model less about "identity" in the typically understood sense of the term and more about confronting one's personal racism. Also, it is clear that the WID was heavily influenced by the work of Black Identity or Nigrescence theorists, such as Jackson (1976) and Cross (1973) and by the work of social identity theorists who were looking at the socially defined/constructed roles of male and female (Block 1973; Pleck 1976; Rebecca, Hefner, and Oleshansky 1976).

The WID was articulated as a model that described the experience of a small number of Whites—those who were activists in the struggle against racism. It is grandiose and a gross oversimplification to say that the WID defined the racial identity experience for all Whites in the United States. Unlike the Helms (1984) model which followed it, the WID was not empirically researched, and as such has had a limited impact on the discourse of racial identity in the counseling psychology field. Most of the research on White identity in counseling has been the testing of, or expansion on, Helms's model. The WID model has been more widely used by practitioners, notably educators and those involved in conflict resolution (see Wing and Rifkin, this volume), to inform the design of training related to racism and racial identity. The WID model has had some influence on other theorists, notably Schapiro (1985), who focused on how men develop a gender identity that is not based on sexism or male dominance. Additionally, the WID model has had some influence on the Sabnani, Ponterotto, and Borodovsky model of White identity development (1991), which incorporated elements of the Helms model as well.

Finally, the WID stages were and still are more of a prescription for what I felt Whites needed to do than a description of experiences that Whites shared. As noted in the original report of the model (Hardiman 1982), there was little if any evidence of a Redefinition or Internalization stage, even in the anecdotal reports of White activists' autobiographies. Instead, these were stages that I saw as necessary and important next steps for Whites in the evolution of a liberated racial identity.

The Helms Model of White Racial Identity Development (WRID)

Coming from a different discipline than me, and as a Black woman investigating the interplay between Blacks and Whites in counseling relationships, Janet E. Helms (1984) proposed another model of White racial identity development. In her 1984 paper, Helms shared the frustration that all the attention in the counseling relationship was focused on people of color, the assumption being that Blacks were always the client and the therapist or counselor was always White. While the issues or pathology of the Black client were frequently discussed and dissected, the race of the White counselor was unremarked upon. Helms suggested looking at the White person as the subject of analysis and understanding as well. Her intention in developing the WRID model was to promote better psychotherapy relationships and to get "acknowledgment of race as a psychological characteristic of Whites as well as people of color . . . [to] . . . reduce the emphasis on changing clients who are people of color to adapt to White theorists' interpretations of such clients 'aberrant' behavior" (Helms 1995:195–196). The premise of her White Racial Identity model is that Whites, "indeed all people regardless of race, go through a stagewise process of developing racial consciousness wherein the final stage is an acceptance of race as a positive aspect of themselves and others" (Helms 1984:154).

Helms developed her initial WRID model by interviewing a few White friends and colleagues to determine how they viewed the development of their racial consciousness. In Helms's words, "Since their coping strategies seemed rather reminiscent of the manner in which members of a visiting culture might adjust to a host culture, theories of culture shock . . . were adapted to explain the attitudinal evolutionary process" (1984:155). Helms's original model had six stages. Her latest work proposes six "statuses," not stages of White identity development. Helms now says that the

> construct of stages has been inadequate for describing the developmen-
> tal processes surrounding issues of race for the following reasons: (a)
> An individual may exhibit attitudes, behaviors and emotions reflective
> of more than one stage (Helms 1989; Parham & Helms 1981); (b) to
> many researchers, stage seems to imply a static place or condition that
> the person "reaches" rather than the dynamic interplay between cogni-
> tive and emotional processes that identity models purport to address;
> and neither theory nor measurement supports the notion of the various
> stages as mutually exclusive or "pure" constructs (Helms 1989,
> 1990[b]). (1995:182–183)

Helms also notes that she "began substituting status (of the ego) for stage without intentionally changing the essential meaning of the concepts underlying either term" (Helms 1995:183). She writes that the

> general developmental issue for Whites is the abandonment of entitle-
> ment whereas the general developmental issue for people of color is
> surmounting internalized racism. In both circumstances development
> potentially occurs by way of the evolution or differentiation of succes-
> sive racial identity statuses, where statuses are defined as the dynamic
> cognitive, emotional and behavioral processes that govern a person's
> interpretation of racial information in her or his interpersonal environ-
> ments. Statuses give rise to schemata, which are behavioral manifesta-
> tions of the underlying statuses. (1995:184)

As with the earlier conception of stages, the statuses are sequential, and developmental in the sense that later stages permit more "complex management of racial material" (Helms 1995:184). Dominance describes the status that generally governs the person's racial reactions, whereas accessability pertains to whether a status is strong enough to permit the person ever to react in the status-relevant manner. Despite the new language—use of statuses versus stages—to describe her model, Helms's most recent description of her model for Whites is virtually the same as her original WRID model (1984).

The six racial identity ego statuses in Helms's model each build upon the previous one. The first status, *Contact*, is marked by the White person's "obliviousness to racism and one's participation in it" (Helms 1995:185). It also describes a point where Whites are comfortable with the racial status quo, not challenging themselves or White society and the dominant racial patterns. Contact is followed by the *Disintegration* status, marked by "disorientation and anxiety" (Helms 1995:185) which occurs when racial situations give rise to moral dilemmas that "force one to choose between own-group loyalty and humanism" (Helms 1995:185). The anxiety and disorientation of this status is followed by *Reintegration*, whereupon the White person resolves the negative feelings of the previous status by idealizing his or her own race—Whites—and expressing intolerance for other races. Helms's fourth status, *Pseudoindependence*, is marked by an "intellectualized commitment to one's own socioracial group and deceptive tolerance of other groups" (Helms 1995:185). The final two statuses, *Immersion/Emersion* and *Autonomy* involve the development of a positive racial identity for Whites that is free of racism. As the name implies, the Immersion/Emersion status involves an internal search for the redefinition of Whiteness, coupled with an "understanding of the personal meaning of racism and the ways by which one benefits" (Helms 1995:185). The *Autonomy* status, the final point of White identity development, is marked by the "capacity to relinquish the privileges of racism" (Helms 1995:185).

Analysis of the WRID model

The Helms model has been subjected to significantly more testing, critique, and debate than the WID model. There are four major criticisms directed at the WRID. The first faults the WRID for being based on the models of Black Identity, or the "oppression-adaptive models explaining ethnic minority identity development" (Rowe, Bennett, and Atkinson 1994:131), which Rowe et al. feel is the wrong approach to take in understanding the experience of the racially dominant group. A second criticism is that the WRID (and the WID as well) does not focus on White identity per se but on "how Whites develop different levels of sensitivity to and appreciation of other racial/ethnic groups" (Rowe, Bennett, and Atkinson 1994:131). Third, it is said that the WRID model is not a developmental model because Helms allows for the possibility of skipping stages and backward as well as forward movement through the stages. Finally, the WRID model is faulted for focusing exclusively on White-Black relationships to the exclusion of White interaction with other races.

Helms and Carter's White Racial Identity Attitude Scale (WRIAS), which is used to measure White racial identity development according to Helms's stages/statuses has also been criticized, notably by Behrens (1997) with regard to its reliability and validity. Beyond the questions he raises about the psychometric properties of the Helms scale, Behrens and Yu (1995) are concerned that the core problem of White identity theory stems from its conceptualization. The measurement problems, while significant, are secondary. The outcome of their critique is that Behrens and his coauthors (Rowe, Behrens, and Leach 1995) propose their own model, which focuses on White racial attitudes and which they refer to as types of White racial consciousness.

Synthesis

I believe the preceding critiques of the WID and WRID models have merit. Given the historical context from which they arose, the direction that these two models took is quite understandable. Both the WID and WRID models followed the civil rights/Black Power eras, and were part of the emerging study of social identity and the way identity was influenced by oppression. Both WID and WRID were affected by the antiracism orientation of their respective authors, perhaps my model even more so than Helms's. Helms was concerned with the dominant bias in counseling psychology, which focused on the pathology of Blacks. She also saw from the experience of her White colleagues that their relationships with people of color were so rarefied that they resembled those who experience culture shock when visiting or living in another country.

I was very focused on the WID as a model of antiracist development, and only included the life stories of antiracist White activists in the study which led to the development of the WID. However, both WID and WRID imply that they represent the identity development process of all White Americans. This is a major limitation of the models—they are too simplistic in explaining the diverse experiences of Whites and the ways in which they respond to or create their racial identity. For example, the WID and WRID do not acknowledge the possibility that

White identity development might entail different processes for individuals raised in all- or mostly White environments, and Whites who were raised in close proximity to people of color. In addition, neither model differentiates between northern and southern White communities, or Whites raised in White supremacist households in contrast to those raised in leftist, liberal, or progressive environments.

These limitations notwithstanding, both the WID and the WRID have had a major impact on the field of counseling psychology, and particularly on the development of theory and practice in multicultural counseling. By challenging the unmarked, dominant, and normative character of the White group against which all other races are measured, the WID and WRID have contributed to the reduction of racism and White cultural bias in the practice of counseling. This de-centering of Whiteness and the concomitant study of the impact of White racism on the identity and psychological health of Whites has been an important focus in cultural identity theory and the emergence of what Pedersen calls "the fourth force" (Pedersen 1990) in counseling psychology.

The Emergence of Whiteness Studies

Since my early work and the work of Janet Helms which mostly affected counseling psychology, a focus on Whiteness has emerged in a wide range of disciplines, including cultural studies, history, sociology, literary studies, and film studies. In fact, contributions in the field of Whiteness studies exploded in the 1990s. Dyer notes that the recent works by White people about Whiteness "arise predominantly out of feminism . . . labour history . . . and lesbian and gay studies, in other words what has come to be called identity politics" (Dyer 1997:8).

There is now a national multiracial organization called the Center for the Study of White American Culture, with a mission "to examine White American culture in the context of the greater American culture . . . and to educate White people about how White culture and values can find expression in non-dominant and non-oppressive ways" (Center for Study of White American Culture 1995, pamphlet). This organization, which has convened three national conferences on Whiteness, has featured presentations on the social construction of Whiteness and the role of Whites in the contemporary racial milieu.

None of the critical race theorists or others analyzing Whiteness such as Ignatiev are studying the development of White identity stages or statuses in the mode of the WID or WRID, nor has a new stage model to explain racial identity development for Whites emerged. However, an enormous outpouring of work, analysis, critique, and important dialogue has been created about Whiteness, how Whites grapple with their racial identity, and the role of Whites in creating coalitions and working for racial justice. Responses to the questions: "What is Whiteness?" and "What are Whites to do with it?" have produced a number of answers and much debate. In the next section, I discuss the various positions taken by major groups grappling with Whiteness.

The Race Traitors

Roediger (1991) and Ignatiev (1995) clearly articulate the social construction of Whiteness and describe the history of the evolution of Whiteness as a social tool. They focus on the use of race as a wedge to divide the working class and as a tool to compensate Whites psychologically with racial supremacy while they experienced class oppression. Beyond providing important historical analyses, both Ignatiev and Roediger are also activists with an agenda. They urge Whites to abandon "Whiteness" and seek solidarity with others (people of color) based on common self-interests. Ignatiev and Roediger feel that if Whites could see past the false construction of their race, they would identify ways in which they are oppressed, or otherwise share common cause with other oppressed people—most likely along lines of class, although coalitions across other lines are also possible. The race traitors, or new abolitionists as they are sometimes called, want Whites to reject race privilege and in effect become "race traitors" by refusing to collude with other Whites and a White-dominated society. This is done by a range of actions, from confronting racist humor to refusing tangible skin color privilege which comes through job opportunities and social contacts.

The new abolitionists are concerned with understanding the history of Whiteness, its construction, and use in order to further the end of Whiteness. Ignatiev, at least, does not see Whiteness as anything but "an expression of white privilege . . . there is no 'white' culture—

unless you mean Wonder Bread and television game shows" (1997:609). He is not interested in the discourse on Whiteness or White identity. He does not believe that there is a White culture and wants Whites to let go of race as a false construction. Ignatiev does acknowledge the difficulty of doing this, not the least of which is that White society won't allow it. In fact, he notes that

> The white race does not like to relinquish a single member, so that even those who step out of it in one situation find it virtually impossible not to join it later, if only because of the assumptions of others. (Ignatiev 1997:608)

The problem with Ignatiev's position is that if or when Whites succeed in rejecting or disowning Whiteness, this does not answer the question of what is left for them. Ignatiev and *Race Traitor's* emphasize "crossing over" or adopting cultures of color, especially Black culture, which raises the question of where the line is between crossing over and ripping off (1997:609). Crossing over can be seen as just another replication of what Whites have always done—dominate or conquer, borrow, steal, rename, and claim the accomplishments, culture, and technology of people of color. Ignatiev (1997) does not answer the question of what Whites should do, noting that while it may also be an option for Whites to find roots in pre-White cultures, such as Celtic or Germanic ones, this is not likely for most Whites who are too far removed from their ethnic culture for it to be meaningful. He proposes the alternative model of amalgamation for Whites, referencing the Seminoles of Florida who became a people comprised of runaway African slaves, various native tribes, and (presumably White) deserters from the army, united by their opposition to the U.S. government. Thus Whites cease to be White by finding common cause with other groups (Ignatiev 1997:610).

Redefining Whiteness

Unlike those individuals or activists who urge Whites to abandon their racial identity, others such as Giroux (1997), Kincheloe and Steinberg (1998), and Winant (1997) advocate working on redefining or reconstructing a White identity that is pro–racial justice. They take particular issue with the suggestion of the new abolitionists or race traitors that Whiteness can and should be discarded. Winant views the new abolitionist project as not taking seriously the complexities of the social construction of race, and asks: "[I]s the social construction of race so flimsy that it can be repudiated by a mere act of political will?" (1997:48). The limitation in the thinking of the race traitors is that by viewing Whiteness as solely a function of race privilege they miss seeing Whiteness as embedded in culture. As Rodriguez notes, "[T]he problem with attempting to erase Whiteness is that it would have to be erased both within social structures and within culture" (1998:60). Winant argues that,

> [W]hiteness may not be a legitimate cultural identity in the sense of having a discrete, "positive" content, but it is certainly an overdetermined political and cultural identity nevertheless, having to do with socioeconomic status, religious affiliation, ideologies of individualism, opportunity, and citizenship, nationalism, etc. Like any other complex of beliefs and practices, whiteness is embedded in a highly articulated social structure and system of signification; rather than trying to repudiate it, we shall have to rearticulate it. (1997:48)

Charles Gallagher, in his study of White college students and their sense of Whiteness, notes:

> Whiteness is in a state of change. . . . The meaning of whiteness is not to be found in any single description(s). . . . Whites can be defined as naive because they attach little meaning to their race, humane in their desire to reach out to nonwhites, defensive as self-defined victims, and reactionary in their calls for a return to white solidarity. (1997:6)

Rather than there being a single model that can identify or explain the complex nature of White identity, Gallagher says, his college-age respondents "generate similar disparate (and at times schizophrenic) renderings when asked what meaning they attach to their race" (Gallagher 1997:6). Gallagher feels that if Whites were ever unaware of their Whiteness, that time has passed, noting that Whites have gone through what Omi and Winant (1994) refer to as "racialization," or becoming marked by their race in the popular media, the conservative press, as well as scholarly discourse on Whiteness.

Winant agrees with Gallagher that while previously Whites tended to be unaware of their race, being unconscious of their position and race privilege, this is no longer the case. He notes that the Du Boisian notion of racial dualism, or a fracturing of the self by race, applies to Whites in the late twentieth century as surely as it has consistently applied to Blacks. Winant argues that Whiteness has been "deeply fissured by the racial conflicts of the post–civil rights period" (1997:40), thus making it impossible for Whites to maintain a "normalized" invisible sense of Whiteness. Winant says that White identities have been "displaced, and reconfigured: they are now contradictory, as well as confused and anxiety-ridden, to an unprecedented extent" (1997:41). This shift has occurred because Whiteness has been impacted by the moral and political challenges of the Black, and affiliated, movements. Winant goes on to describe the various "white racial projects" (1997:41) that have emerged from this challenge to Whiteness, including responses from the political right, liberal, center, and left, with different ways of being White embedded in each project.

Implications for New Thinking on White Identity

What have we learned about Whiteness and White identity from the recent discourse of the new abolitionists, critical race theorists, and others?

From historians such as Allen (1997), Ignatiev (1995), and Roediger (1991), we have a greater understanding of the construction of Whiteness as a social tool. We also have a deeper sense of the fluidity of Whiteness; as a political and social construct it is subject to change, even allowing some to become White who were previously not.[3] This work helps us understand at a more complex level how racial identity for Whites, as one aspect of social identity, is created and sustained by powerful forces beyond the individual. This understanding can aid in reducing guilt and anxiety as White educators and counselors work with fellow Whites to learn about and redefine our White identity.

From Winant and Gallagher, we are learning how the post–civil rights era, the rise of identity politics, and what has been referred to as the "browning" of American pop culture (Whitaker 1991) has prompted a racialization of Whiteness and a destabilization of the old definitions of Whiteness. These scholars also clearly point to the many different directions that Whites are taking in defining Whiteness, from a resurgence of active White supremacists on the far right, to "Wiggers"—White youth adopting or co-opting Black culture—to race traitors or new abolitionists. Winant's descriptions of these

White racial "projects" suggest that there are many different paths of White identity, and that a single model of White identity development is not likely to explain the wide variety of positions that Whites are taking regarding the meaning of their race. Gallagher's work has also informed us about the degree to which Whiteness is conscious rather than unconscious among college-age youth, and how White students in his samples are handling this new race consciousness.

Kincheloe and Steinberg suggest compelling reasons why educators in particular need to create a pedagogy of Whiteness that helps Whites construct a "progressive, antiracist white identity as an alternative to the white ethnic pride shaped by the right wing" (1998:12). They concur with Winant and Gallagher that a new consciousness of Whiteness has emerged and that it is more difficult at this period in history for Whites to be unconscious about their race. The heightened consciousness of the race and culture of people of color has created a void for Whites. In some ways the critical multiculturalists like Kincheloe and Steinberg bring us full circle to the question posed by Bob Terry in 1975, "What alternative models can replace the present American white-male-dominated society?" (1975:1).

The Future of Research on White Identity Development

What do we currently understand about the development of racial identity in Whites, and what direction should future work take? A major achievement, initiated in the helping professions by Hardiman and Helms, and later in other disciplines, is the decentering of Whiteness and the marking of Whites as a race that should be the subject of study. Despite this important contribution, the WID, WRID, and subsequent positions in White identity focus primarily on the way racism and racial isolation affect Whites. We understand more about how Whites are socialized to take on a privileged, racist sense of Whiteness. However, we lack understanding about how and why some Whites come to reject that privilege and racist-defined sense of self, while others see themselves as victims of affirmative action, and champions of the English-only movement, "standards," "family values," and other codes for race-based privilege. A much needed area for future study is related to the factors affecting how and why Whites choose to take their Whiteness in such different directions.

Another area that current thinking on White identity has not adequately investigated is the question of belonging: To what group or groups do Whites belong at a cultural level? Do some Whites have a racial culture or ethnic culture to which they belong and from which they derive a sense of belonging, history, or nurturing? Ignatiev and others suggest that Whites don't have a culture other than "Wonder Bread and television game shows." Thus when racism and race privilege are subtracted from Whiteness, there is no race or culture to belong to. While I support the notion that a sense of superiority and dominance pervades our definition of Whiteness, I lean toward the notion that there is more to Whiteness than racism, and yes, more than Wonder Bread. I think the question of the identity "vacuum" for Whites is an important one to explore further. Some who are cited in this chapter note the phenomenon of White youth adopting the cultural style of various people of color, a phenomenon that my colleague Judith Katz refers to as "cultural drag" (1988). This phenomenon leads to several interesting questions, such as: How do young Whites in particular identify culturally? Do they experience a cultural emptiness as Whites, and are they searching for an identity and style in the hip-hop culture of the 1990s or other cultural manifestations? Do they feel there is no other option than to be a Black *wannabe*? Is this "crossing over" a positive step or is it a sign that Whites are avoiding dealing with their own sense of history, culture, and identity that may have been discarded, lost, diluted, or embedded in unnamed traits? I believe that a significant piece of White resistance to Latinos or any other group retaining their language, and to multicultural celebrations of all kinds in schools and communities, comes from this feeling of a void, or from Whites' confusion about their own sense of identity at the racial or cultural level. This resistance is evidence of resentment toward others who express or hold on to something that many of our European ancestors lost, discarded, or had taken away as the price of admission to the White club in the United States.

Future Research on White Identity Development

A major new direction for work on White identity development is the exploration of how Whites deal with their racial identity as a source of privilege, and their racial, ethnic, or other cultural identity as a source of nurturance. In a society where racial dominance is contested and the expression of social identity (racial and cultural in particular) is part of our culture, Whites have to deal concomitantly with two key aspects of our identity: internalized dominance, racism, and privilege, and the search for cultural meaning and identification. The current work on White identity has yet to explore these intersecting dimensions of Whiteness. Instead it focuses almost exclusively on the dominance or racism aspect of White identity, and gives scant attention to the way Whites identify in a cultural sense with their race.

Some additional areas that future research on White identity should address include:

(1) A White Identity Development model should help us understand how Whites feel, think, and reflect upon their Whiteness and their own racial group, as well as how they relate to other races. Thus it should address how Whites view and feel about their physical and cultural characteristics—pride, revulsion, embarrassment? Why do Whites appear to be so focused on changing their own skin color and how do Whites feel about the way Whiteness is represented culturally?

(2) The intersection between race and ethnicity yields several questions such as: How do Whites experience their ethnicity within the racial construct of Whiteness? If, as Ignatiev suggests, "In becoming white, the Irish ceased to be Green" (1995:3), do some Whites claim an ethnic identity and ignore their racial identity as a cultural group? How do Whites react to the loss of ethnicity as part of the price of becoming White? With anger, sadness, or indifference? And how does this impact how they see themselves as part of a racial group in America? What are the various intersections of race and ethnicity for Whites in America? Are Whites who have a strong sense of ethnic heritage and pride more or less racist than those who don't? Does a strong sense of ethnicity better equip Whites to participate constructively in a nonracist, equitable, multicultural society?

(3) Are there Whites who have created a new sense of cultural identification that replaces their lost ethnicity and their rejection of aspects of White "wonder bread" culture? If so, what constitutes this culture? Do Whites see it as different from Black, Latino, Indian, or Asian culture? Or is it a multicultural blend of cultures from all continents as they are played out on American soil?

(4) It has been suggested that Whites react to the "identity movements" of others and the struggle and gains made for racial justice by people of color, by adopting a victim stance. Are there other ways that Whites have responded to these changes that are not defensive, reactionary, or oppressive?

These are some of the important questions that further work on Whiteness should address. In reflecting back on almost twenty years of focus on the question of White identity, it is exciting to see how far we have come, yet challenging to see how much we still do not know. Much work is needed to further our development toward the elimination of a White identity that is based on the racial oppression of others, and that damages each of us who are White in the process.

NOTES

1. In addition to Hardiman and Helms, discussed in this essay, see also Carney and Kahn (1984), Sue and Sue (1990), and Sabnani, Ponterotto, and Borodovsky (1991).

2. This process of being socialized as a member of a particular social group has been described by Miller (1976), Bell (1997), and Wijeyesinghe, Griffin, and Love (1997), among others.

3. For example, the Irish as described in Ignatiev (1995), and Jewish Americans, Italian Americans, and Latinos, as described in Frankenberg (1993:11).

REFERENCES

Allen, Theodore W. 1997. *The Invention of the White Race*. Vol. 2. London: Verso.

Behrens, John T. 1997. "Does the White Racial Identity Attitude Scale Measure Racial Identity?" *Journal of Counseling Psychology* 44(1): 3–12.

Behrens, John T., and Chong-Ho Yu. August 1995. "A Meta-Analytic Review of the White Racial Identity Attitude Scale." Paper presented at the 103rd Annual Convention of the American Psychological Association, New York, N.Y.

Bell, Lee Anne. 1997. "Theoretical Foundations for Social Justice Education." Pp. 3–15 in *Teaching for Diversity and Social Justice: A Sourcebook*, ed. M. Adams, L. Bell, and P. Griffin. New York: Routledge.

Blauner, Robert, and David Wellman. 1973. "Toward the Decolonization of

Social Research." Pp. 310–330 in *The Death of White Sociology*, ed. J. A. Ladner. New York: Vintage.

Block, Jeanne H. 1973. "Conceptions of Sex Role: Some Cross-Cultural and Longitudinal Perspectives." *American Psychologist* 28(6):512–526.

Bowser, Benjamin P., and Raymond G. Hunt, eds. 1981. *Impacts of Racism on White Americans*. Newbury Park, Calif.: Sage.

Bowser, Benjamin P., Raymond G. Hunt, and David C. Pohl. 1981. "Introduction." Pp. 13–26 in *Impacts of Racism on White Americans, 1st ed.*, ed. B. P. Bowser and R. G. Hunt. Newbury Park, Calif.: Sage.

Caditz, Judith. 1976. *White Liberals in Transition*. New York: Spectrum.

Carney, Clarke G., and Karen B. Kahn. 1984. "Building Competencies for Effective Cross-Cultural Counseling: A Developmental View." *Counseling Psychologist* 12(1):111–119.

Chesler, Mark A. 1976. "Contemporary Sociological Theories of Racism." Pp. 21–71 in *Towards the Elimination of Racism*, ed. P. Katz. New York: Pergamon Press.

Cross, William E., Jr. 1973. "The Negro-to-Black Conversion Experience." Pp. 267–286 in *The Death of White Sociology*, ed. J. A. Ladner. New York: Vintage.

———. 1978. "The Thomas and Cross Models of Psychological Nigrescence." *Journal of Black Psychology* 4(1):13–31.

Delgado, Richard, and Jean Stefancic, eds. 1997. *Critical White Studies: Looking Behind the Mirror*. Philadelphia: Temple University Press.

Du Bois, William E. B. 1973. *The Philadelphia Negro*. Millwood, N.Y.: Kraus-Thomson.

Dyer, Richard. 1997. *White*. New York: Routledge.

Frankenberg, Ruth. 1993. *White Women, Race Matters: The Social Construction of Whiteness*. Minneapolis: University of Minnesota Press.

Gallagher, Charles A. 1997. "White Racial Formation: Into the Twenty-First Century." Pp. 6–11 in *Critical White Studies*, ed. R. Delgado and J. Stefanic. Philadelphia: Temple University Press.

Giroux, Henry. 1997. "Rewriting the Discourse of Racial Identity: Towards a Pedagogy and Politics of Whiteness." *Harvard Educational Review* 67(2): 285–320.

Hardiman, Rita. 1982. "White Identity Development: A Process Oriented Model for Describing the Racial Consciousness of White Americans." Doctoral dissertation. University of Massachusetts, Amherst.

———. 1994. "White Racial Identity Development in the United States." Pp. 117–140 in *Race, Ethnicity, and Self: Identity in Multicultural Perspective*, ed. E. P. Salett and D. R. Koslow. Washington, D.C.: National MultiCultural Institute.

Hardiman, Rita, and Bailey W. Jackson. 1992. "Racial Identity Development: Understanding Racial Dynamics in College Classrooms and on Campus."

Pp. 21–37 in *Promoting Diversity in College Classrooms: Innovative Responses for the Curriculum, Faculty, and Institutions*, ed. M. Adams. San Francisco: Jossey-Bass.

Helms, Janet E. 1984. "Toward a Theoretical Explanation of the Effects of Race on Counseling: a Black/White Model." *Counseling Psychologist* 12(4): 153–165.

———. 1989. "Considering Some Methodological Issues in Racial Identity Counseling Research." *Counseling Psychologist* 17(2):227–252.

———. 1990a. *Black and White Racial Identity: Theory, Research, and Practice*. Westport, Conn.: Greenwood.

———. 1990b. "An Overview of Black Racial Identity Theory." Pp. 9–32 in *Black and White Racial Identity: Theory, Research, and Practice*, ed. J. E. Helms. Westport, Conn.: Greenwood.

———. 1995. "An Update of Helms's White and People of Color Racial Identity Models." Pp. 181–198 in *Handbook of Multicultural Counseling*, ed. J. G. Ponterotto, J. M. Casas, L. A. Suzuki, and C. M. Alexander. Thousand Oaks, Calif.: Sage.

Ignatiev, Noel. 1995. *How the Irish Became White*. New York: Routledge.

———. 1997. "Treason to Whiteness Is Loyalty to Humanity: An Interview with Noel Ignatiev of *Race Traitor* Magazine." Pp. 608–612 in *Critical White Studies: Looking Behind the Mirror*, ed. R. Delgado and J. Stefancic. Philadelphia: Temple University Press.

Jackson, Bailey. 1976. "The Function of a Theory of Black Identity Development in Achieving Relevance in Education for Black Students." Doctoral dissertation, University of Massachusetts, Amherst.

Katz, Judith. July 18, 1988. Personal Communication, Amherst, Mass.

Kincheloe, Joe L., and Shirley R. Steinberg. 1998. "Addressing the Crisis of Whiteness: Reconfiguring White Identity in a Pedagogy of Whiteness." Pp. 3–30 in *White Reign: Deploying Whiteness in America*, ed. J. L. Kincheloe, S. R. Steinberg, N. M. Rodriguez, and R. E. Chennault. New York: St. Martin's Press.

Miller, Jean Baker. 1976. *Toward a New Psychology of Women*. Boston: Beacon Press.

Omi, Michael, and Howard Winant. 1994. *Racial Formation in the United States from the 1960s to the 1990s*. 2d edition. New York: Routledge.

Parham, Thomas A., and Janet E. Helms. 1981. "The Influence of Black Students' Racial Identity Attitudes on Preferences for Counselor's Race." *Journal of Counseling Psychology* 28(3): 250–257.

Pedersen, Paul B. 1990. "The Multicultural Perspective as a Fourth Force in Counseling." *Journal of Mental Health Counseling* 12:93–95.

Pleck, Joseph H. 1976. "The Male Sex Role: Definitions, Problems and Sources of Change." *Journal of Social Issues*, 32(3): 155–164.

Rebecca, Meda, Robert Hefner, and Barbara Oleshansky. 1976. "A Model of Sex Role Transcendence." *Journal of Social Issues* 32(3):197–206.

Rodriguez, Nelson M. 1998. "Emptying the Content of Whiteness: Toward an Understanding of the Relation between Whiteness and Pegagogy." Pp. 31–62 in *White Reign: Deploying Whiteness in America*, ed. J. L. Kincheloe, S. R. Steinberg, N. M. Rodriguez, and R. E. Chennault. New York: St. Martin's Press.

Roediger, David. 1991. *The Wages of Whiteness*. London: Verso.

Rowe, Wayne, John T. Behrens, and Mark M. Leach. 1995. "Racial/Ethnic Identity and Racial Consciousness: Looking Back and Looking Forward." Pp. 218–236 in *Handbook of Multicultural Counseling*, ed. J. G. Ponterotto, J. M. Casas, L. A. Suzuki, and C. M. Alexander. Thousand Oaks, Calif.: Sage.

Rowe, Wayne, Sandra K. Bennett, and Donald R. Atkinson. 1994. "White Racial Identity Models: A Critique and Alternative Proposal." *Counseling Psychologist* 22(1):129–146.

Sabnani, Haresh B., Joseph G. Ponterotto, and Lisa G. Borodovsky. 1991. "White Racial Identity Development and Cross-Cultural Counselor Training: A Stage Model." *Counseling Psychologist* 19(1):76–102.

Schapiro, Steven A. 1985. *Changing Men: The Rationale, Theory, and Design of a Men's Consciousness Raising Program*. Doctoral dissertation, Department of Education, University of Massachusetts, Amherst.

Sue, Derald Wing, and Sue, David. 1990. *Counseling the Culturally Different: Theory and Practice*, 2nd edition. New York: John Wiley and Sons.

Terry, Robert W. 1975. *For Whites Only*. Grand Rapids: Eerdsman.

———. 1978. "White Belief, Moral Reasoning, Self-Interest, and Racism." Pp. 349–374 in *Belief and Ethics: Essays in Ethics, the Human Sciences, and Ministry in Honor of W. Alvin Pitcher*, ed. W. W. Schroeder and G. Winter. Chicago: Center for the Scientific Study of Religion.

Wellman, David. 1977. *Portraits of White Racism*. Cambridge: Cambridge University Press.

Whitaker, Charles. 1991. "The Browning of White America: Impact of Black Creativity and Leadership on American Culture." *Ebony* 46(10):25–26.

Wijeyesinghe, Charmaine L., Pat Griffin, and Barbara Love. 1997. "Racism Curriculum Design." Pp. 82–109 in *Teaching for Diversity and Social Justice: A Sourcebook*, ed. M. Adams, L. Bell, and P. Griffin. New York: Routledge.

Winant, Howard. 1997. "Behind Blue Eyes: Whiteness and Contemporary U.S. Racial Politics." In *Off White*, ed. M. Fine, L. Weis, L. C. Powell, and L. M. Wong. New York: Routledge.

Chapter 6

Racial Identity in Multiracial People
An Alternative Paradigm

Charmaine L. Wijeyesinghe

Multiracial identity is the newest chapter in the evolving field of racial identity development.[1] The heightened interest in the experience of Multiracial people is fueled by changing social demographics, an increasing number of Multiracial people who identify with all their racial ancestries, and the emergence of groups advocating the rights of Multiracial people. These forces, as well as the recent spate of media coverage of Multiracial people,[2] foster the perception that much is known about Multiracial identity. In reality, a critical mass of research on Multiracial people is still in development. Like the earliest theories of Black and White identity, existing models of Multiracial identity represent initial attempts at understanding an emerging topic.

This chapter explores Multiracial identity as it has been framed by select developmental models. The chapter begins with a discussion of key terms that appear in the text, and assumptions underlying some of the literature on Multiracial identity and the approach taken in this chapter. This section is followed by a brief discussion of the impact of Black and White identity development theories on Multiracial identity models. Two models of Multiracial identity development are then reviewed and critiqued. Next, the chapter presents and discusses the Factor Model of Multiracial Identity (FMMI), a model based on my own research on Black and White Multiracial adults. The chapter concludes with a summary of areas that present both opportunity and challenge to the field of Multiracial identity in the future.

Definitions

The following definitions of key terms used in this chapter reflect my understanding and interpretation of the literature on racial identity development and Multiracial identity.

Race and racial groups refer to socially constructed concepts that divide the human population into subgroups based on real or perceived differences in such things as physical appearance or place of ancestral origin.[3] *Ethnicity and ethnic groups* are socially constructed subcategories of racial groups that emphasize the shared geographical, historical, and cultural experiences of different groups of people.

The terms *racial ancestry* and *ethnic ancestry* represent the race and ethnicity claimed by, or attributed, to a person's ancestors. The term *racial identity* is the racial category or categories that an individual uses to name him or herself based on factors including racial ancestry, ethnicity, physical appearance, early socialization, recent or past personal experiences, and a sense of shared experience with members of a particular racial group.

Ascribed racial group membership is the racial group or groups that are applied to an individual by other people and social institutions based on factors such as physical appearance, racial ancestry, and the social construction of race at a given point in time. This ascribed racial group may or may not be consistent with the racial group that the individual actually identifies with, defined in this chapter as *chosen racial group membership*.

The last two definitions incorporate several of the previously defined terms. *Monoracial* and *Multiracial* can refer to (1) a person's racial ancestry, (2) a person's chosen racial identity, (3) a racial group membership ascribed to a person, or (4) a person's chosen racial group membership. Monoracial represents any of these concepts when they reflect a single racial group. Multiracial refers to any of the concepts based on two or more racial groups. In the text of this chapter, Monoracial and Multiracial refer to an individual's racial ancestry, unless otherwise noted.

Assumptions

This chapter assumes that Multiracial people and issues related to their identity are not neutral topics. The subject of Multiracial people can heighten the emotions (Wardle 1989; Root 1992), cause suspicion, create division within communities of color, and give rise to fears of losing ground in the struggle for racial equality.[4] This climate is supported by centuries of racism and racial oppression in the United States, and can lead to Multiracial identity being viewed as irrelevant, or as secondary to research on Monoracial populations. This chapter takes the perspective that Multiracial identity researchers and theorists need to be informed by the history of race in the United States, while moving ahead in their efforts to address emerging social and historical trends.

Although the public perception of Multiracial people is becoming more positive, the assumption that Multiracial people are confused, distraught, and unable to fit in anywhere in the American racial landscape remains common. A number of factors perpetuate this negative image. Stereotypes based on decades of misinformation are difficult to discard.[5] Research revealing identity conflict and ambiguity in Multiracial people—such as the work of Gibb (1987), Logan, Freeman, and McRoy (1987), Brandell (1988), Lyles et al. (1985), and Brown (1990)—has sometimes been lifted from its specific clinical contexts and generalized to Multiracial people as a whole. In addition, these works are often not discussed in conjunction with studies—such as those by Poussaint (1984), Shackford (1984), and Wijeyesinghe (1992)—that present a more positive picture of Multiracial people and their experience of racial identity. Another mental health-related assumption is evident when particular choices of racial identity by Multiracial people are deemed more positive than others. For example, the Multiracial identity models by Poston (1990) and Kich (1992), reviewed in this chapter, link positive mental health to the development of a Multiracial identity.

The FMMI, presented later in this chapter, assumes that there is no one right or more appropriate choice of racial identity for Multiracial people. Racial identity in this model is determined by each Multiracial individual, as opposed to being assigned by other people or by society. This is not to say that outside influences have no effect on Multiracial people's racial identity. The section of the chapter that discusses FMMI addresses the impact of external factors, such as early socialization, on the internal process of racial self-definition.

Contributions of Monoracial Identity Development Models to Models of Multiracial Identity

Although the Black identity development models offered by Thomas (1971), Cross (1971), and Jackson (1976) differed in the number and names of their individual stages, each framework described a Black person's shift from an identity based on the internalization of the norms and values of White society to one based on a new awareness and definition of self, racial group membership, and racism. As part of this process of change, the models reported a withdrawal from the White world coupled with an immersion in the Black community in order to gain knowledge, support, experience, and a new definition of Blackness. The models noted that racial identity development included emotional components and changes in beliefs, behaviors, and attitudes.

The White identity development models by Hardiman (1982) and Helms (1984) described a sequence of stages through which Whites could achieve a redefined sense of racial identity that acknowledged and addressed White privilege and racism. The Hardiman and Helms models also included descriptions of the emotions and behaviors associated with the progress of White identity development.

Models of Black and White identity development provided the structure, *stages of identity development*, adopted by certain subsequent models of Multiracial identity (Poston 1990; Kich 1992). In addition, some of the content and themes from the Black and White theories appeared in these Multiracial identity development models, including (1) a stage characterized by an immersion-like experience into the culture, practices, and politics of particular racial groups; (2) the presence of strong emotions at various stages of identity development; and (3) an identity in the later stages of development that reflected a heightened understanding of race and racism, and a greater appreciation of self.

The FMMI is structured around factors affecting choice of racial identity rather than stages of development. However, a number of these factors were evident in the earlier Monoracial identity development models. For example, the models by Cross, Jackson, and Hardiman all include reference to physical appearance, cultural attachment, and political involvement in the description of various identity stages of racial identity development. The FMMI focuses more specifically on the impact of these and other factors on racial identity, rather than on a particular developmental process.

Lastly, unlike the models proposed by Cross, Jackson, and Hardiman, the FMMI assumes that racial identity is a choice made by each individual. In the formative Monoracial models, racial identity reflected the individual process of understanding one's experience and the experience of Blacks (Cross, Jackson) or Whites (Hardiman) within a system of racism. Less attention was paid to Black or White identity as a choice or label that a person took on during the process of identity development. In effect, a person was Black or White, most likely based on racial ancestry, whether or not he or she chose to identify as such. In this context, the Monoracial theories addressed the meaning and understanding people made of an identity presumed to be a given. The FMMI, in a sense, moves back a step and begins with the question of how Multiracial people come to choose certain identities (that is, identity is not already assigned). The model then moves to questions of how individuals understand and make meaning of these chosen identities in light of their experiences.

Stage Models of Multiracial Identity Development[6]

The Poston Model of Biracial Identity Development

Based on the findings of Hall (1980) Poston proposed a developmental model of Biracial identity.[7] This five-part process described a Biracial person's transition from an initial stage characterized by lack of awareness of racial identity to a final stage marked by the achievement of a Multiracial identity. Throughout the process, Biracial people experienced various choices related to racial identity as well as feelings associated with these choices.

Stage one of Poston's model, *Personal Identity*, described young peoples' sense of self that could include an awareness of race and ethnicity. However, self-definition was generally not defined by ethnic background. People entered the second stage of the model, *Choice of Group Categorization*, when pushed to choose a racial identity. According to Poston, most Biracial people chose Monoracial identities, since an identity based on multiple ethnicities required "some level of knowledge of multiple cultures and a level of cognitive development beyond which is characteristic of this age group" (1990:154). Factors influencing a person's choice of racial identity in Stage two included variables that provided support or status, as well as physical appearance, cultural knowledge, political involvement, and personality difference.

In the third stage of Poston's model, *Enmeshment/Denial*, Biracial individuals experienced guilt and confusion for choosing identities that did not fully match their racial and ethnic ancestry. In addition, Poston noted that people in this stage could feel "self-hatred, and lack of acceptance from one or more group" (1990:154). Resolution of these feelings and the development of an appreciation of both parental cultures moved individuals to later stages in the model.

Although Biracial people tended to claim a monoethnic identity in the fourth stage, *Appreciation*, there was a greater valuation of all their identities. In the fifth and final stage of Poston's model, *Integration*, Biracial people were disposed to recognizing and appreciating all their racial ancestries. Poston noted that "individuals at this stage experience wholeness and integration." (1990:154).

The Kich Model of Biracial and Bicultural Identity

Based on his research on Biracial adults of Japanese and White ancestry, Kich developed a three-stage model that ended with the achievement of what the author termed a Biracial or Bicultural identity.

Stage one of Kich's model, *Awareness of Differentness and Dissonance*, occurred between the ages of three and ten, when an individual sought peer and referent groups beyond the immediate family. The subsequent acknowledgment of difference between self and other people engendered feelings such as not belonging totally to any one group. Dissonance occurred when this sense of self-as-different was judged negatively, and where comparisons with other people resulted in the devaluing of self. According to Kich, early experiences of differentness and dissonance were universal to Biracial people.

The second stage of the Kich model, *Struggle for Acceptance*, reflected Biracial people's pursuit of acceptance by others in the face of increasing experiences of differentness and dissonance. Kich noted that "passing" (1992:312), defined as attempting to take on behaviors of a racial group usually of higher status in order to gain acceptance, afforded some relief from feelings of difference and alienation. However, this strategy stemmed from a temporary devaluing of people's

Biracial selves. While the second stage of the model could be emotional and difficult, it offered opportunities for self-exploration, understanding, and identity resolution.

The final stage of the Kich model, *Self-Acceptance and Assertion of an Interracial Identity*, represented increasing acceptance of a self-determined Biracial and Bicultural identity. In this stage, the skills related to passing during Stage two were seen more positively, in that they allowed Biracial people to move among different racial groups.

Analysis of Poston and Kich Models

The models formulated by Poston and Kich contributed to the understanding of Multiracial identity by: (1) providing two foundational models of Multiracial identity development; (2) noting the potential impact of factors such as physical appearance, level of parental support, racial makeup of surrounding community, and extent of cultural knowledge about Multiracial identity; (3) acknowledging the effect of outside prejudices and values on identity development in Multiracial people; and (4) providing direction for future research on Multiracial identity. The following analysis of the Poston and Kich models highlights issues that might limit their use as comprehensive models of Multiracial identity development and raises questions for future research.

The Poston and Kich models are based on stages of development, with the final stage of each model representing the achievement of a Multiracial identity. As the middle three stages of Poston's work reflect the choice of a largely Monoracial identity, this model may not represent the experience of people who choose Multiracial identities throughout their lives, or who choose Monoracial identities without experiencing identity confusion, guilt, self-hatred, and anger potentially associated with Poston's Enmeshment/Denial stage. Similarly, Kich's model does not account for Multiracial people who choose Monoracial identities without experiencing identity conflict, confusion, or self-hatred.

In both the Poston and Kich models, the achievement of personal wholeness and integration is associated with the development of a Multiracial identity.[8] However, the history of slavery, immigration, and racial oppression in the United States has resulted in millions of people who are Multiracial by ancestry, but who by majority do not claim Multiracial identities due to personal choice or socially imposed restrictions. It would be difficult to characterize these people as experiencing ongoing dissonance because their racial identities do not reflect all their racial ancestries. In fact, claiming a Multiracial identity was not even an option until recent decades. In light of this context, linking psychological wholeness to the development of a Multiracial identity is a very recent phenomenon, and hence may limit the application of the Poston and Kich models to older Multiracial people.

Lastly, the Poston and Kich models seem to characterize Multiracial people as a single group, the determining characteristic being that people have more than one racial ancestry. However, like all racial populations, Multiracial people represent different ethnic backgrounds, geographical locations, historical periods in which they were raised, number of generations in the United States, cultural practices, and other social identities such as gender, sexual orientation, class, and disability. Each Multiracial population is also affected by its unique experiences and history in the United States. For example, Multiracial people of African American/European American ancestry probably have some experiences that differ from those with Vietnamese/European American backgrounds. Given this kind of diversity and what is currently known about Multiracial identity, it seems premature to attribute a singular experience like dissonance, or a singular process made up of several stages, to Multiracial people as a group.

Synthesis

The preceding analysis makes an important distinction between models that describe *the development of a Multiracial identity*, such as the work of Poston and Kich, and models that address *racial identity in Multiracial people*. Models that fall within the latter category need to represent the diversity of experience within and between groups of Multiracial people. Given that the literature on Multiracial identity is still fairly limited, it is questionable whether a model that accounts for the range of choices of identity and experiences found among Multiracial people can be developed at this time. Perhaps it is more realistic to create additional models that speak to aspects of diverse Multiracial experiences. When taken together, these models would form a mosaic for understanding various aspects of Multiracial identity. The FMMI, presented in the next section of the chapter, represents another contribution to this mosaic.

The Factor Model of Multiracial Identity (FMMI)

The FMMI was developed from a qualitative study of African American/European American Multiracial adults. Participants in the study chose a range of racial identities, including Black, White, and Multiracial. In addition, participants varied in age, life experience, economic class, and gender. Quotations that appear in this section of the chapter are taken from the data of the study.

FIGURE 6.1
The Factor Model of Multiracial Identity (FMMI)

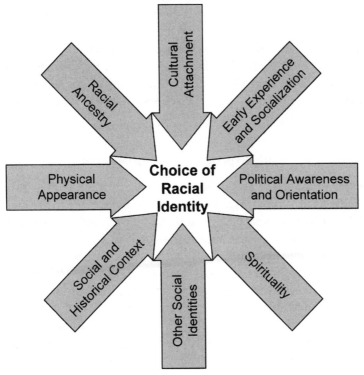

Modified from Wijeyesinghe 1992.

The FMMI consists of eight factors that affect choice of racial identity by Multiracial people.[9] A Multiracial person's choice of racial identity can be based on some, but usually not all, of these factors. Although the factors are represented by distinct circles, many of them are interrelated. The chapter now turns to an elaboration of each of the factors and its effect on racial identity.

Racial Ancestry

Racial ancestry, defined as the racial groups reflected in an individual's ancestors, is discussed first because for many people, being Multiracial and having a Multiracial identity are matters of family tree. Some people who identify as Multiracial base their identity in large part on the racial makeup of their families. However, Multiracial people who choose Monoracial identities may rely on racial ancestry to a lesser degree, if at all, when establishing their racial identity. For example, participants in the study who identified as Black acknowledged and appreciated their White ancestry and the experiences they had in relation to it. However, they felt it had little relevance to their day-to-day lives since they looked Black, lived as Black people, and felt a strong connection to Black culture. The FMMI does not necessarily link mental health concerns with the choice of a Monoracial identity. This allows it to accommodate Multiracial people who choose Monoracial identities without guilt, anxiety, or conflict.

Early Experiences and Socialization

Early socialization and experiences often provide Multiracial people with overt as well as subtle messages about their racial identity, racial ancestry, or racial group membership. A major source of this socialization is exposure to cultural aspects of one or more of the racial groups represented in the family, such as food, music, celebration of various holidays, and the use of various languages or dialects. In addition, interaction with extended family members can provide information about Multiracial children's racial ancestry and family expectations related to their racial identity. For some Multiracial individuals, family and extended family members provide safety, support, and affirmation should Multiracial children encounter negative reactions from others.

Parental assignment of children's racial identity can also affect Multiracial people's choice of racial identity. Assigned racial identities can be retained throughout the lifetime. Such was the case with a woman who identified as Black, who noted,

> I've always said the same thing, which is that I'm Black. And if they say, "Well, what are your parents?" Then I say, "My father's this and my mother's that." I remember having a conversation with my father when he told me that because of the history of race in this country, that people who had any Black ancestry were considered Black. (Quoted in Wijeyesinghe 1992:23)

Other Multiracial people may change their racial identities from the one they received in childhood, in response to experiences beyond the realm of their family. Multiracial people who receive little or no information about their racial ancestries or identities in childhood may choose a racial identity later in life, when racial identity becomes more of an issue due to outside influences, or when they become more aware of issues of race and racism.

Lastly, interactions with peers, teachers, and even strangers can influence Multiracial people's choices of racial identity. Questions about racial ancestry or identity are often part of these encounters, and can stem from perceived uniqueness or ambiguity of some Multiracial people's physical appearance. In childhood, these inquiries may result in family conversations about race and identity. Later on in life, recurring questions about ancestry and identity can raise feelings of embarrassment, shame, or dissonance for Multiracial people who feel negatively about part of their racial background. These kinds of feelings may underlie the sentiments expressed by a Multiracial man who identified as White, when he indicated that "To me [my identity] means that [I] never have to deal with any racism from people, which I'm lucky that I don't have people not want to talk to me because I'm Black or not trust me because I'm of mixed heritage. I always feel that I'm one step ahead as far as, yes I am of mixed heritage, but I do not have to deal with any of the hardships" (quoted in Wijeyesinghe 1992:176).

In summary, Multiracial people's family, community, and social institutions create a system of socialization which can have a strong effect on choice of racial identity. While some Multiracial people retain their original racial identity throughout their lives, others may change their choice of racial identity in response to later experiences in life.

Cultural Attachment

Aspects of culture that Multiracial people are exposed to in their past and present environments can also affect their choice of racial identity. Cultural experiences in childhood, and throughout life, can include all sides of a Multiracial person's ancestry, or only some of them. A Multiracial person's choice of a Multiracial identity may reflect, in part, exposure and attachment to cultural traditions that encompass all of a person's racial background. However, such experiences do not guarantee the choice of a Multiracial identity in childhood or adulthood. For example, Multiracial people who identify as Monoracial may appreciate their diverse cultural experiences, but feel that their current racial identity is based on cultural preferences that became more prominent in adulthood.

The relationship between cultural attachment and choice of racial identity is affected by at least some of the other factors represented in the FMMI. For example, claiming a Black identity, based on a strong preference for Black culture, may be less of an option for a Multiracial person who looks White than for a person who appears to be Black.

Physical Appearance

Physical appearance creates a strong context in which Multiracial people choose their racial identities. Characteristics such as skin color and tone, hair color and texture, eye color and shape, size and shape of facial features, and body structure are used by the general public and society to make assumptions about people's racial ancestry, racial group membership, and racial identity. Some Multiracial people are assumed to be Monoracial if they have physical characteristics attributed by society to single racial groups. Other Multiracial people have physical characteristics that appear inconsistent with, or span societal definitions of, who belongs to what racial group based on appearance. This perceived physical ambiguity often underlies the question, "What are you?" familiar to many Multiracial people.

Physical appearance can often facilitate Multiracial people's acceptance within particular racial communities, especially when their chosen racial identities are consistent with the racial groups ascribed to them by others based on physical appearance. While appearance can result in acceptance, it can also cause rejection or frustration when physical characteristics restrict choice of racial identity. For example, a Multiracial woman who looked White, noted:

> What I have to offer [the Black community] is a lot, but because of my physical appearance, I'm not gonna be taken serious. It's hard in a way that I almost want to be able to wear a sign or something letting people know of my background and whatever, so that they can accept me first and then hear what I got to say. (Quoted in Wijeyesinghe 1992:199)

This statement highlights the fact that while Multiracial people are often assumed to look like "people of color" or "racial minorities," as a group they reflect great diversity in appearance, and include individuals who both appear to be or who identify as White.

In summary, physical appearance can support some Multiracial people's choice of racial identity and facilitate their acceptance into a particular racial community. For others, appearance can lead to speculation or questions from people they encounter. Appearance can also create barriers for some Multiracial people choosing certain racial identities, or being seen as members of certain racial groups.

Social and Historical Context

How Multiracial people identify racially is affected by social responses to issues of race, racism, interracial relationships, and Multiracial people at a given time in history. Living with the legacy of the *one drop rule,*[10] the majority of Multiracial people born prior to the last two decades of the twentieth century could only identify with their "minority" ancestry, since social norms and practices treated them as if they were Monoracial, regardless of their actual racial ancestry. As a result of the growing number of Multiracial people, increased public awareness of their issues, and an emerging Multiracial rights movement, Multiracial people born during the 1980s and 1990s have greater options for claiming various racial identities, including a Multiracial identity. The most visible outcome of the changing times and circumstances can be seen in the U.S. Census forms, which began in the year 2000 to allow individuals to check more than one box to indicate their race.[11] In addition, numerous colleges and universities, such as Brown University, Stanford University, Amherst College, and Hampshire College have organizations for Multiracial students, indicating that some institutions are beginning to accommodate people with Multiracial identities and ancestries. However, societal accommodations related to Multiracial people are both few and new. The long-term impact of these changes on social perspectives on Multiracial people, and race in general, will become clearer with the passage of time and future studies.

Political Awareness and Orientation

For some Multiracial people, the choice of racial identity development is affected by their increased awareness and experiences that place race, racism, and racial identity in a larger historical, political, economic, and social context. Within this context, claiming a particular identity, whether Multiracial or Monoracial, can take on meaning as a political act or statement. The influence of political orientation on choice of racial identity was evident when a Multiracial woman who identified as Black, said: "If I were married to a White man and had a light-skinned son, that would also be for me a political implication because it would be in a sense watering down the African American, which I don't think needs to happen" (quoted in Wijeyesinghe 1992:151).

The 1990s produced organizations that provided support and networking for interracial families, and political advocacy for the rights of Multiracial people.[12] Given the emergence of these groups, and more vocal and active interracial families and Multiracial people, choosing a Multiracial identity may be seen by some people as a politically oriented response to social systems that, for the most part, still expect Multiracial people to choose a Monoracial identity.

Other Social Identities

Discussions of Multiracial identity often focus on how Multiracial people experience race. In fact, race may be the primary or sole basis for some Multiracial people's overall identity. However, for others racial identity may reflect an integration of racial and nonracial social identities, such as gender, ethnicity, sexual orientation, and socioeconomic class. For example, a Multiracial person may not distinguish between race and gender when she identifies as a "woman of color."

In other instances, nonracial social identities may take a more prominent role than race in Multiracial people's current sense of self. For instance, a young man who identified as Multiracial, said, "The majority of my life isn't spent thinking about racial anything. It's spent thinking about paychecks, and money, and moving, and day-to-day sort of things" (quoted in Wijeyesinghe 1992:240).

Therefore, other social identities beyond race can mediate the choice of racial identity for some Multiracial people. In some instances, immediate issues related to identity may not include race at all, but be based on nonracial aspects of Multiracial people's experience.[13]

Spirituality

Spirituality, while often associated with religious practice, is defined more broadly in the FMMI as the degree to which individuals believe in, seek meaning from, or are guided by a sense of spirit or higher power. In relation to racial identity in Multiracial people, spiritual beliefs can provide them with a source of strength and refuge from racism, sustain them through the process of racial identity development, or assist them in deriving greater meaning from their racial ancestry or identity.

In addition, spirituality can create a sense of connection between people that transcends racial labels and differences. A Multiracial woman who identified as Black and was also a Bah'ai, noted, "I think that man is the one that gives all these names, plus the need to identify certain things. When we break down man and say 'well, he's this and he's that,' but we're all one people" (quoted in Wijeyesinghe 1992:123).

Racial identity within the FMMI represents the result of an individual's internal meaning-making process at a given point in life. For some Multiracial people, part of this process is influenced by personal spiritual beliefs, traditions, or experiences.

Application of the FMMI

The FMMI presents racial identity for Multiracial people, much like identity for any other racial group, as complex and evolving. This section of the chapter summarizes how the content and context of the FMMI can be used to better understand racial identity in Multiracial people.

The factors in the FMMI provide helping agents, educators, parents, and others with an additional tool for organizing and understanding the experiences of Multiracial people and their choices of racial identity. For example, a person who identifies as Multiracial may base his identity mainly on his racial ancestry, early socialization, and physical appearance. In contrast, a Multiracial person who identifies as Monoracial may base her identity on her physical appearance and current political and cultural orientations. Used in this manner, the factors in the FMMI represent a filter for Multiracial people's experiences in order to create greater understanding of why and how they choose a range of racial identities.

Although I have identified them individually, many of the factors in the FMMI have an overlapping relationship. For example, racial ancestry has some effect on a Multiracial person's appearance, which in turn may affect his early socialization. In another instance, active involvement in the cause for racial justice may result in a Multiracial person seeking a cultural and political community that supports her work and choice of identity. Interaction between different factors can raise questions about how well various factors "fit" together in a particular Multiracial person's life. When there is a congruence between these factors, few if any intrapersonal or interpersonal conflicts may emerge. For example, a Multiracial person who looks Black, is seen by others as being Black, and identifies and lives as a Black person may not experience internal conflict about choice of identity, or face challenges concerning his ancestry or identity.

Greater possibilities for internal conflict may exist when there are wide discrepancies between the factors underlying choice of racial identity, and possibly external perceptions or forces. For example, a person who identifies as Multiracial because of her racial ancestry, upbringing, and cultural affiliation may face challenges or frequent questioning if her physical features lead others to believe she is Monoracial. Should this woman seek help under these conditions, a counselor might explore how she developed her current sense of racial identity; how she experiences situations that confirm her chosen identity, how she makes sense of situations that contradict her sense of racial identity, and how she reconciles any discrepancy between her racial ancestry, chosen identity, physical appearance, and experiences in the larger society.

Interpersonal conflict is often assumed to go hand in hand with having a Multiracial ancestry. Educators, counselors, and other helping agents should be aware that although some Multiracial people have concerns related to their racial identity, others may not feel the need to explore racial identity issues at all, or may feel that other social identities such as their gender, sexual orientation, religion, or class background are more pressing in their lives. When Multiracial people do seek assistance for issues related to their racial identity, helping agents might consider the extent to which the conflicts are internally grounded (as in the individual's struggle with identity issues) or a response to largely external forces (such as external expectations that the person choose a particular racial identity, or other people expressing negative personal opinions and feelings about Multiracial people).

Several existing models of Monoracial identity (Cross 1971; Jackson 1976; Hardiman 1982) and Multiracial identity (Poston 1990; Kich 1992) view changes in racial identity as movement to another stage of racial identity development. While authors of the Monoracial models, in particular, did not attach value to the different stages of racial identity development, people using them sometimes do. For example, a Black person in Jackson's stage of Acceptance may be seen by colleagues, friends, or counselors as less self-aware and self-affirming than someone in the stages of Redefinition or Internalization.

Although not framed as a stage-based developmental model, the FMMI can also be misread or misused, primarily when certain factors are deemed more legitimate indicators of racial identity than others. If, for example, a counselor feels that race and racial identity are based solely on racial ancestry, she may not accept a Multiracial person's choice of a Monoracial identity. In another case, a person who identifies as Multiracial may be challenged by someone who believes that such an identity denies the history of race and racism in the United States, or creates divisiveness in other racial communities. Therefore, helping agents and individuals working with Multiracial people may find FMMI a helpful tool to identify their own personal biases and beliefs about race, racial identity, and Multiracial people; acknowledge how these beliefs might influence their work with Multiracial people; and create greater personal openness to the range of experiences Multiracial people may have.

Looking Ahead

This section summarizes some of the key issues and questions presented in this chapter, and comments on the way exploration of these areas might advance both our understanding of Multiracial people and identity, and the field of racial identity development in general.

The FMMI and its perspective that Multiracial people choose a range of racial identities based on various factors creates a foundation for several future research questions. These questions include the following: (1) Do some factors represented in the FMMI play a more significant role in Multiracial people's choice of racial identity? (2) Which factors tend to underlie the choice of a Monoracial identity, and which ones tend to support the choice of a Multiracial identity? (3) How do individual Multiracial people address major discrepancies between the factors underlying their racial identity, such as when a person identifies as Multiracial but is perceived by others to be White, based on appearance? and (4) What factors, in addition to those represented in the FMMI, affect choice of racial identity in Multiracial people?

Individual factors from the FMMI warrant further investigation to clarify their relationship to racial identity development. For example, while the FMMI describes the impact of sociohistorical context on Multiracial people, the nature of this factor is constantly changing with time. Therefore the impact of evolving social and political processes related to race, Multiracial people, and the larger climate around Multiracial issues will remain a relevant area of study in the coming years.

Physical appearance and its relationship to Multiracial identity, as well as racial identity in general, remains a relevant and important area for examination. As the number of Multiracial people increases over time and the nation achieves even greater racial diversity, society's ability to assign racial group membership to individuals based on appearance may become increasingly difficult. The relationship between appearance and racial identity raises several areas for future study, including (1) the impact of evolving social understanding and practices linking race to appearance on racial categories, racial identity development, and Multiracial people; (2) the identity development of Multiracial people who are either presumed to be White, or who identify as White, based on their physical appearance; and (3) the experiences of Multiracial people whose chosen racial identity is inconsistent with their physical appearance, and the effect these experiences have on their racial identity development.

The relationship between other nonracial social identities and racial identity has received limited attention in both the literature on Monoracial and Multiracial populations. Future studies could focus on a number of areas, including the relation between racial identity and other identity processes occurring simultaneously in a person's life; the impact of other social identities on a Multiracial person's choice of either a Monoracial or Multiracial identity; and aspects of identity development that are similar, as well as unique, to groups based on race, gender, sexual orientation, and the like. The answers to these and related questions will serve to advance our understanding of racial identity development in Monoracial and Multiracial people.

In addition to the many questions about Multiracial people that remain, only a few of which have been noted in this section, the design of future studies needs to reflect research populations and diverse methodologies. Much of the existing literature examines the experiences of Multiracial people of Black and White ancestry, and employs qualitative research methods. While additional research on Black and White Multiracial populations is needed, future studies on other Multiracial populations—including people whose ancestry includes Whites and a racial group other than Black, and Multiracial people with no White ancestry at all—would make significant contributions to the literature.[14] In addition, increased understanding of Multiracial people hinges on the employment of both qualitative and quantitative measures.

Finally, it is important to note that a basic knowledge of Multiracial identity and Multiracial people is still being constructed. While questions focusing on future and evolving dynamics are a crucial component to this foundation, the fundamental questions of how a wide range of Multiracial people develop, make meaning of, and experience their racial identities remain relevant and pressing.

Closing Thoughts

Multiracial people and identity are often treated as flash points in the discussion of race and racism in the United States. An alternative to this reactionary and emotional approach is to position Multiracial people within the racial mosaic of the United States rather than outside it. In this inclusive context, the experiences of Multiracial people might throw light on the experiences of other racial populations. Exploring the question, What does it mean to be Multiracial in the twenty-first century? necessitates examining the question, What does it mean to be Latino, White, Black, or a member of any racial group in the United States?

The exploration of Multiracial people and their experiences related to racial identity contributes to the larger field of racial identity development by raising for examination, and in many cases reexamination, underlying questions and assumptions about racial identity development, questions such as the following: What do we mean when we talk of racial identity? Is racial identity given or chosen? and What are the strengths and limitations of models based on their underlying paradigm and assumptions about racial identity? While answers to these questions remain open for discussion it is clear that Multiracial people and identity will continue to influence the larger field of racial identity development and the understanding of race in American society.

NOTES

1. Within the context of modern racial identity development theories, research on and models of Multiracial identity are fairly new additions. However, research and commentary on Multiracial people have been a part of the social sciences for over a century (Kahn and Denmon 1997). In their review of the literature, Kahn and Denmon note that studies from the late 1800s to the mid-1900s focused mainly on the classification of mixed-race individuals and the alleged inferiority or superiority of some of their traits. Research conducted since 1980 represents a shift from attention to inborn factors to environmental influences on Multiracial identity, and from a perspective of Multiracial identity as a pathological experience to that of a normal developmental process.

2. The media have provided a number of perspectives on Multiracial identity over the last decade, including articles in major publications such as *Ebony* (Norment 1990), *Essence* (Njeri 1991), *Newsweek* (Leland and Beals 1997; Morganthau 1995), and *Time* (White 1997), as well as more specialized publications such as *Mothering* (Wardle 1999).

3. There are numerous essays addressing the social construction of race. Some examples include the work of Montagu (1951, 1963), Jordan (1974),

Lieberman, Stevenson, and Reynolds (1989), and Lopez (1995). Authors who write about the impact of the social construction of race on Multiracial people include Zack (1993), Ferber (1995), Spickard (1992), and Fish (1995).

4. Jones represents one example of this perspective. In his closing comments, Jones notes:

Most Blacks have no intention of claiming a special bi-racial status for themselves while leaving behind those Blacks who can make no such claim. Bi-racials who mislike this reality may, of course, and should continue their appeals to Whites for special recognition. Those who understand it should rejoin the African-American community and continue the struggle for racial justice. (1994:209)

5. The work of Kahn and Denmon (1997) provides an overview of historical research focusing on alleged physical, psychological, and emotional deficits in Multiracial people.

6. Several research studies conducted during the 1980s provided the context for emerging Multiracial theories. Several of these studies, drawn from the field of counseling, are noted on page 131, in this chapter. Additional references related to identity in Biracial children include the work of Ladner (1984), Shackford (1984), Sebring (1985), and Wardle (1987, 1989). Although not presented as a model of Multiracial identity, the Cultural Continuum that resulted from the work of Logan, Freeman, and McRoy (1987) may be viewed as an early attempt to describe various approaches to Multiracial identity.

7. *Biracial* and *Bicultural* are used instead of *Multiracial* in this section of the chapter, since they are the terms that appear in the Poston and Kich models.

8. This assumption is less evident in the Poston model, since a person in Stage four could identify Monoracially without the negative emotions evident in the previous stage. While Poston noted that people in the fifth and final stage of his model "tend to recognize and value all of their ethnic identities" (1990:154), people who claimed a multiethnic heritage were described as developing a "secure, integrated identity" (1990:154).

9. It should be noted that the factors of early experiences and socialization, past and/or present cultural attachment, and physical appearance appeared more often in the data, and more consistently across participants than the other factors.

10. See Zack (1993) and Fernandez (1996) for the impact of the one drop rule on Multiracial people and identity.

11. See Pearlman (1997) for a discussion of the impact of changes in Census categories, and related issues and questions.

12. The efforts of groups such as the Association of MultiEthnic Americans (AMEA) have gone beyond grassroots local organizing. In fact, the representatives of AMEA addressed a subcommittee of the U.S. House of Representatives. See Fernandez (1995) for a transcript of this testimony.

13. Cross and Fhagen-Smith (this volume) use the concept of "race salience" in their discussion of the relationship between other social identities and racial identity development among African Americans.

14. See Root (1997) and Spickard (1997) for discussion of some of the issues related to Asian Americans with multiple racial heritages.

REFERENCES

Brandell, Jerrold, R. 1988. "Treatment of the Biracial Child: Theoretical and Clinical Issues." *Journal of Multicultural Counseling and Development* 16 (October):176–187.

Brown, Philip, M. 1990. "Biracial Identity and Social Marginality." *Child and Adolescent Social Work Journal* 7(4) (August):319–337.

Cross, William E. 1971. "Discovering the Black Referent: The Psychology of Black Liberation." Pp. 96–110 in *Beyond Black and White: An Alternative America*, ed. V. J. Dixon and B. G. Foster. Boston: Little, Brown.

Ferber, Abby, L. 1995. "Exploring the Social Construction of Race: Sociology and the Study of Interracial Relationships." Pp. 155–167 in *American Mixed Race: The Culture of Microdiversity*, ed. N. Zack. Lanham, Md.: Rowman & Littlefield.

Fernandez, Carlos, A. 1995. "Government Classification of Multiracial/Multiethnic People." Pp. 15–36 in *The Multiracial Experience: Racial Borders as the New Frontier*, ed. M. P. P. Root. Thousand Oaks, Calif.: Sage.

———. 1996. "Testimony of the Association of MultiEthnic Americans before the Subcommittee on Census, Statistics, and Postal Personnel of the U.S. House of Representatives." Pp. 191–210 in *American Mixed Race: The Culture of Microdiversity*, ed. N. Zack. Lanham, Md.: Rowman and Littlefield.

Fish, Jefferson, M. 1995. "Mixed Blood." *Psychology Today* 28 (November/December):55–63.

Gibb, Jewelle, T. 1987. "Identity and Marginality: Issues in the Treatment of Biracial Adolescents." *American Orthopsychiatric Association* 57(2):265–278.

Hall, Christine. 1980. "The Ethnic Identity of Racially Mixed People: A Study of Black-Japanese." Cited in C. W. S. Poston 1990. "The Biracial Identity Development Model: A Needed Addition." *Journal of Counseling and Development* 69 (November/December):152–155.

Hardiman, Rita. 1982. "White Identity Development: A Process Oriented Model for Describing the Racial Consciousness of White Americans." Doctoral dissertation, School of Education, University of Massachusetts, Amherst.

Helms, Janet, E. 1984. "Toward a Theoretical Explanation of the Effects of Race on Counseling: A Black and White Model." *Counseling Psychologist* 17(2):227–252.

Jackson, Bailey, W. 1976. "The Function of a Theory of Black Identity Development in Achieving Relevance in Education for Black Students." Doctoral dissertation, School of Education, University of Massachusetts, Amherst.

Jones, Rhett, S. 1994. "The End of Africanity? The Bi-Racial Assault on Blackness." *Western Journal of Black Studies* 18 (4):201–210.

Jordan, W. D. 1974. *The White Man's Burden: Historical Origins of Racism in the United States.* New York: Oxford University Press.

Kahn, Jack, S., and Jacqueline Denmon. 1997. "An Examination of Social Science Literature Pertaining to Multiracial Identity: A Historical Perspective." *Journal of Multicultural Social Work* 6 (1/2):117–138.

Kich, George, K. 1992. "The Developmental Process of Asserting a Biracial, Bicultural Identity." Pp. 304–317 in *Racially Mixed People in America*, ed. M. P. P. Root. Newbury Park, Calif.: Sage.

Ladner, Joyce. 1984. "Providing a Healthy Environment for Interracial Children." *Interracial Books for Children Bulletin* 15 (6):7–8.

Leland, John, and Gregory Beals. 1997. "In Living Colors." *Newsweek* 29(18): 58–60.

Lieberman, Leonard, Blaine W. Stevenson, and Larry T. Reynolds. 1989. "Race and Anthropology: A Core Concept without Consensus." *Anthropology and Education Quarterly* 20(2): 67–73.

Logan, Sadye L., Edith M. Freeman, and Ruth G. McRoy. 1987. "Racial Identity Problems for Bi-Racial Clients: Implications for Social Work Practice." *Journal of Intergroup Relations* 15(2):11–24.

Lopez, Ian F. H. 1995. "The Social Construction of Race." Pp. 191–203 in *Critical Race Theory: The Cutting Edge*, ed. R. Delgado. Philadelphia: Temple University Press.

Lyles, Michael, R., Antronette Yancey, Candis Grace, and James H. Carter. 1985. "Racial Identity and Self-Esteem: Problems Peculiar to Biracial Children." *Journal of the American Academy of Child Psychiatry* 24(2):150–153.

Montagu, Ashley. 1951. *Statement on Race: The Story of UNESCO's Statement on Race Problems.* New York: Henry Shuman.

———. 1963. *Race, Science, and Humanity.* Princeton: D. Van Nostrand.

Morganthau, Tom. 1995. "What Color Is Black?" *Newsweek* 125 (7):63–65.

Njeri, Itaberi. 1991. "Who Is Black?" *Essence* 22(5):65–66, 115–117.

Norment, Lynn. 1990. "Who's Black and Who's Not?" *Ebony* 45 (5):134–136, 138–139.

Pearlman, Joel. 1997. "Multiracials, Intermarriage, Ethnicity." *Society* 34 (September/October):21–24.

Poston, Carlos, W. 1990. "The Biracial Identity Development Model: A Needed Addition." *Journal of Counseling and Development* 69 (November/December):152–155.

Poussaint, Alvin, F. 1984. "Study of Interracial Children Presents Positive Picture." *Interracial Books for Children Bulletin* 15(6):9–10.

Root, Maria, P. P. 1992. "Within, Between, and Beyond Race." Pp. 3–11 in *Racially Mixed People in America*, ed. M. P. P. Root. Newbury Park, Calif.: Sage.

———. 1997. "Multiracial Asians: Models of Ethnic Identity." *Amerasian Journal* 23(1):29–41.

Sebring, Deborah, L. 1985. "Considerations in Counseling Interracial Children." *Journal of Non-White Concerns in Personnel and Guidance* 13(1):3–8.

Shackford, Kate. 1984. "Interracial Children: Growing Up Healthy in an Unhealthy Society." *Interracial Books for Children Bulletin* 15(6):4–6.

Spickard, Paul, R. 1992. "The Illogic of American Racial Categories." Pp. 12–23 in *Racially Mixed People in America*, ed. M. P. P. Root. Newbury Park, Calif.: Sage.

———. 1997. "What Must I Be? Asian Americans and the Question of Multiethnic Identity." *Amerasian Journal* 23(1):43–60.

Thomas, Charles, W. 1971. "Boys No More: Some Social-Psychological Aspects of the New Black Ethic." Pp. 16–26. In *Boys No More*, ed. C. W. Thomas. Beverly Hills: Glencoe.

Wardle, Francis. 1987. "Are You Sensitive to Interracial Children's Special Identity Needs?" *Young Children* 42(2):53–59.

———. 1989. "Children of Mixed Parentage: How Can Professionals Respond?" *Children Today* 18(4):10–13.

———. 1999. "The Colors of Love: Raising Multiracial Kids Who Are Proud of Their Identities." *Mothering* 96 (September/October):68–73.

White, Jack, E. 1997. "I Am Just Who I Am." *Time* 149(18):33–36.

Wijeyesinghe, Charmaine. 1992. "Towards an Understanding of the Racial Identity of Bi-Racial People: The Experience of Racial Self-Identification of African-American/Euro-American Adults and the Factors Affecting Their Choices of Racial Identity." Doctoral dissertation, School of Education, University of Massachusetts, Amherst.

Zack, Naomi. 1993. "The Ordinary Concept of Race." Pp. 9–18 in *Race and Mixed Race*, Naomi Zack ed. Philadelphia: Temple University Press.

Chapter 7

Racial Identity Theories in Counseling
A Literature Review and Evaluation

Amy L. Reynolds and Suraiya Baluch

Racial issues in counseling and therapy were first written about during the 1950s. As society began to directly address the issues of racism and discrimination during the 1960s, the counseling profession was criticized for focusing therapy on the needs of White Americans (Jackson 1995). Attention to racial issues and multicultural concerns flourished during the 1970s and generated a surge of innovative articles and research in counseling and psychology (Reynolds and Pope 1991). Some mental health professionals believe the increased attention to racial and multicultural issues in the counseling literature over the past two decades is unprecedented (Jackson 1995). Others, while supporting the notion that the focus on multicultural issues has expanded, believe that such reports on the heightened coverage have been inflated (Sue and Sue 1999).

Racial identity theory was first developed in the 1970s when counselors and psychologists, who were part of the genesis of multicultural counseling, attempted to educate the larger profession about the unique issues of people of color. These initial racial identity theories explored how African Americans and Asian Americans made sense of themselves as racial beings. They included the work of Cross (1971), Sue and Sue (1971), Thomas (1971), Vontress (1971), and Jackson (1975). Most of the multicultural counseling literature at that time focused on racial group differences. In order to prevent therapists from viewing people of color in monolithic ways and responding to them in a stereotypical manner, these fledgling racial identity theories put forth the powerful and unique notion that individual differences within racial groups were as compelling as those between racial groups. Racial identity theories focused the attention away from race per se by challenging the notion that "racial group membership alone dictates how people will react in counseling, respond to specific interventions, or show preference for the type of counselor" (Ridley, Espelage, and Rubenstein 1997:143).

While in the 1990s such a thought may seem rather obvious, two decades ago it was an innovative idea. According to Sue and Sue, "[O]ne of the most promising approaches to the field of multicultural counseling/therapy has been the work on racial/cultural identity development among minority groups" (1999:123). During the past twenty years, a variety of racial identity models have been proposed, several of which have been widely researched (for example, Cross 1971; Helms 1984). The majority of racial identity theories and research have focused on Black and White identity, although additional models and studies have explored the racial identity concerns of Asian Americans (Kim 1981; Lee 1991; Sodowsky, Kwan, and Pannu 1995), Latino/a Americans (Bernal and Knight 1993; Casas and Pytluk 1995; Ruiz 1990), and American Indians (Choney, Berryhill-Paapke, and Robbins 1995; Sue and Sue 1999). In addition to the racial identity models for specific racial groups other models have focused on the racial identity similarities of people of color as a group (Atkinson, Morten, and Sue 1979; Carter 1995), on Whites and people of color (Sue and Sue 1999), on the commonalities among oppressed groups (Myers et al. 1991), and on multiple identities and oppressions (Reynolds and Pope 1991). Research on racial identity has addressed a wide range of therapeutic and multicultural issues such as counselor preference, working alliance, social attitudes, emotional well-being, and multicultural competence. While racial identity theory was initially applied primarily to the individual counseling/therapy setting, it has more recently been utilized in a wide range of settings and situations (for example, group and family therapy, consultation and diversity training, organization development, law, schools and teaching, supervision, and conflict mediation).

This chapter briefly reviews the trends and patterns of racial identity counseling and supervision research and offers an analysis of this literature. Recommendations about how to explore racial identity in various therapy and supervision settings are also examined. Some illustrations of how to apply racial identity theory in both the counseling and supervision context are offered. Finally, emerging trends and future research in the racial identity counseling literature are explored.

Before focusing on the topic of racial identity, it is important to acknowledge that such discussions often lead to differing viewpoints. Some individuals are more familiar or comfortable with certain terminology and may even be offended by the use of some words (for example, minority, people of color). Some professionals have concerns about some of the language and values surrounding racial identity models, especially stage models. Assumptions about what constitutes a healthy racial identity and language such as "visible racial groups" may be unsettling to some professionals. Common concerns about stage models themselves include the risk of focusing more on the various stages and how growth "should" occur rather than on an individual's unique growth in the context of her or his life and the inherent assumption that later stages of identity development are better. Some authors, such as Cross (1985) and Cross and Fhagen-Smith (this volume), believe that while racial self-hatred has significant negative effects, individuals can function effectively and sometimes positively at all levels of racial identity. Other authors, such as Carter (1995), Thompson and Carter (1997), and Parham and Helms (1985a, 1985b) believe there is a strong connection between psychological functioning and racial identity.

Many of these language and philosophical differences are not easily resolved and continue to be addressed in the literature. As authors of this chapter, we have chosen to present these varying views without offering our own opinions. We believe such differences and debate are healthy as long as they honor the process of growth as a dynamic and unique experience for each individual.

Definitions and Conceptualizations of Racial Identity

In this section we briefly review definitions of racial identity and their potential impact on the counseling context. Definitions and conceptualizations of racial identity have evolved as various theories and models have put forth diverse and unique constructs and perspectives. There is no uniform or unified definition of racial identity, although most theories or models conceptualize racial identity as one's identification with a particular racial group. While some racial identity models are based on typologies (for example, Root 1990; Rowe, Bennett, and Atkinson 1994; Sue and Sue 1971) and others utilize a linear developmental or stage/status perspective (for example, Cross 1971; Parham 1989; Helms 1990), most models examine individual attitudes toward one's own racial group and the racial groups of others. According to Carter, "each level of racial identity is presumed to be associated with a distinct worldview that corresponds to emotional, psychological, social, and interpersonal preferences consistent with that worldview" (1995:139). Another way to view racial identity is that "the development of racial identity is said to reflect a process of racial self-actualization" (Thompson and Carter 1997:xvi).

Diverse views and perspectives in the racial identity literature have encouraged increasingly complex theoretical discussions. Cross (1985, 1987) described racial identity as being a combination of two different aspects of identity (reference group orientation and personal identity) and focused his research in that direction. Parham (1989) proposed a more complex developmental process which incorporated recycling or revisiting prior stages throughout the life span. Rowe, Bennett, and Atkinson (1994) suggested that developmental or stage models are inadequate in their conceptualization of White racial identity and proposed a typological model of White racial consciousness. Helms (1995) proposed that racial identity did not reside in a single stage but was a profile of stages in which individuals maintained attitudes reflective of multiple stages simultaneously. Helms (1996) further expanded her conceptualization by discarding the term stages, which she believed encouraged a static and limited view of development, in favor of the term status, which she viewed as being more dynamic, fluid, and interactive. Such revisions and enhancement of racial identity theory only further strengthen its meaningful application to the process of counseling and supervision.

Regardless of the theoretical conceptualization of racial identity, most authors agree that racial identity has a significant effect on the therapeutic process. Without racial identity models, therapists often rely on group knowledge about diverse races which may lead to stereotyping and failure to explore within-group differences (Sue and Sue 1999). Without exposure to racial identity theory therapists (of all races) may pay more attention to racial group membership, which research shows is not the most relevant factor (Carter 1995). Unless therapists learn about racial identity, they may mistakenly focus on clients' race without exploring what meaning their race and culture has for them as therapists. This focus leads to assumptions which may cause clients to be misunderstood, misdiagnosed, and their behavior misinterpreted. Helms (1984, 1990) first emphasized the importance of assessing a client's racial identity as a means of understanding and improving the therapeutic relationship. The diagnostic value of racial identity theories helps therapists know how to work most effectively with clients (Sue and Sue 1999). According to Helms and Cook, therapists must ask whether racial identity is "germane to the problem for which the client is seeking assistance"(1999:96). If racial identity is viewed as relevant to the client's concerns, then analysis of the racial identity of the client and its impact on her or his life can assist in the creation of hypotheses that can be examined through the therapeutic process. However, knowledge about racial identity can just as easily lead to stereotyping and over interpretation of a client's attitudes and behaviors as relying on racial group knowledge alone. In addition, it is vital that racial identity theory be applied to the counselors' racial identity to further enhance self- understanding and the ability to work with others. According to Sue and Sue, "an understanding of cultural identity development should sensitize therapists and counselors to the role that oppression plays in a minority individual's development"(1999:137).

In addition to the significant role that racial identity plays in the counseling process, its impact on supervision and counselor training has been increasingly examined in the literature. Thompson observed that "supervision is an integral aspect in the progression of counseling and psychotherapy training"(1997:51). Counselor supervision is the primary way in which supervisors pass along knowledge to trainees and is one of the most intense learning experiences in clinical training (Carter 1995; Ladany, Brittan-Powell, and Pannu 1997; Peterson 1991). Peterson (1991) noted that supervisors have the task of helping supervisees explore their own and their clients' racial identity attitudes. Jordan (1998) defined culturally specific supervision as involving both the supervisor and supervisee exploring how their ethnic background impacts the supervisory relationship. Examining how racial issues are handled in therapy and supervision seems crucial to the professional identity development of counselors.

The focus of most multicultural counseling research and application literature reviewed in this chapter are Cross's (1971) and Helms's (1990) theoretical and empirical work on racial identity development. Helms (1990) theorized that there are predictable relationship outcomes based on an individual's role (counselor, client) and the different levels of racial identity development. According to Helms, regressive relationships occur when the client possesses more advanced racial identity attitudes than the counselor. Progressive relationships occur when the client is at less advanced levels of racial identity than the counselor. Finally, parallel interaction occurs when both client and counselor possess similar racial identity statuses. These levels of racial identity are not specific to racial group membership and the interactions specified above can occur within and between all racial groups.

Racial Identity Counseling Research

Carter states that "as is the case with many theories, empirical research and instruments have not kept pace with theory building" (1995:139). Helms (1989) has highlighted the unique methodological issues that challenge racial identity research. Despite these challenges, the volume of counseling research that incorporates racial identity concerns appears to be growing. Ponterotto (1989) suggests that racial identity research is significantly influencing counseling research. The ability of this important line of research to develop and expand is affected by the measurement tools available. Currently there are primarily four measures of racial identity—Black Racial Identity Attitude Scale (RIAS-B), White Racial Identity Attitude Scale (WRIAS), Oklahoma Racial Identity Attitudes Scale (ORIAS), and Visible Racial/Ethnic Identity Scale (VREIS)—used in research to varying degrees.

The bulk of the counseling research that has examined racial identity has focused on White and Black racial identity. While there have been theoretical discussions about the meaningfulness of the racial identity construct for other people of color groups (for example, American Indians, Latino/a Americans, and Asian Americans), concerns about the applicability of racial identity have led to limited racial identity research on these groups (Choney, Berryhill-Paapke, and Robbins 1995; Sue and Sue 1999). For example, Choney, Berryhill-Paapke, and Robbins state, "[R]acial identity as a construct may perpetuate the homogeneity myth about American Indians and fail to reflect cultural variation found among tribes" (1995:76). In discussing Hispanics and Asians, some authors have chosen to use the term ethnic identity because they believe it more accurately represents these groups (Casas and Pytluk 1995; Sodowsky, Kwan, and Pannu 1995; Sue, Mak, and Sue 1998). Acculturation paradigms, an important and parallel construct in multicultural research, have been extensively used to study all three of these people of color groups. However, some racial identity models, similar to the Black racial identity models, have been proposed for two of the three groups: Asian Americans (Kim 1981; Lee 1991; Sodowsky, Kwan, and Pannu 1995), and Latino/a Americans (Bernal and Knight 1993; Casas and Pytluk 1995; Ruiz 1990). Unfortunately the instrumentation, and therefore the empirical research, necessary to assess the validity and meaningfulness of such racial identity models has yet to be adequately established. There are other racial identity models that address identity issues across groups (Sue and Sue 1999; Atkinson, Morten, and Sue 1979; Myers et al. 1991). However, the research and instrumentation for these models is also limited. Carter (1995) has attempted to address this problem through the creation of the Visible Racial/Ethnic Identity Scale which can be used for all people of color groups. Although this instrument is relatively new and the literature describing it is small, it offers measurement options for those seeking racially diverse samples without wanting to use multiple racial identity or acculturation instruments.

Carter (1995) offers an extensive review of racial identity research. He highlights studies that examine primarily Black and White racial identity, psychosocial constructs, and the therapeutic process. He has found that racial identity status attitudes affect the thoughts and behaviors of both counselor and client as well as the interaction between them. This interaction is, in fact, quite complex, being a product of the way the racial identity of both counselor and client interact in the therapy dyad. Carter also asks what influences the therapy process more–race or racial identity. He concludes that "racial identity issues were more useful for understanding the counseling process than race alone" (1995:175). Most of the studies he reports examine the racial identity of Blacks and Whites. However, Carter offers an important model for incorporating racial identity into counseling process and outcome research. While more counseling research, especially applied studies, needs to be completed across all levels of racial identity among all racial groups, we have enough evidence to consider how to more fully apply the racial identity theories to the counseling process in meaningful and effective ways.

Racial Identity Supervision Research

There is a limited but growing body of clinical and research literature addressing race and racial identity in counseling supervision. Although the majority of this literature also focuses on Black-White relationships, there is growing discussion of other racial groups (Bernard 1994; Jordan 1998; Porter 1994). Leong and Wagner (1994) have conducted an exhaustive review of the multicultural supervision literature. They classify their findings into three categories: articles which briefly mention cross-cultural supervision; articles which discuss specific clinical problems in multicultural supervision and possible solutions there to; and theoretical articles that offer supervision models to observe, predict, and explore multicultural issues. Their review found that the limited information which does exist is predominantly theoretical and not empirically based. According to Leong and Wagner, more research is needed to validate or dispute the proposed theories and to further our understanding of multicultural supervision.

In a review of the literature by the authors of this chapter, we identified seven significant quantitative and qualitative studies which examine racial issues in supervision (Constantine 1997; Cook and Helms 1988; Fukuyama 1994; Hilton, Russell, and Salmi 1995; Ladany, Brittan-Powell, and Pannu 1997; Reynolds et al. 1999). In addition, articles in journals and books that address the application of racial identity theories to clinical training and practice have been increasing in recent years (Cook 1994; Cook and Hargrove 1997; Jordan 1998; Peterson 1991; Porter 1994).

One of the first empirical studies to specifically address race in supervision was Cook and Helms's (1988) study which identified the characteristics of supervisory relationships and the perceptions that may predict the satisfaction of supervisees of a visible racial or ethnic group (Asian, Black, Hispanic, and Native American) with cross-cultural supervision. Cook and Helms found that several dimensions influenced supervisees' satisfaction, including a supervisor's liking, emotional discomfort, conditional interest, conditional liking, and unconditional liking. The dimensions that led to supervisees' greatest satisfaction were supervisor's liking and conditional interest (Cook and Helms 1988). Also, perceptions of supervisory experience varied by race or ethnicity of the supervisee. The study found that Native Americans and Blacks had the most difficulty in supervision while Asian Americans had the least difficulty, and that Black, Hispanic, and Native American supervisees believed that their supervisors were uncomfortable with them. Such discomfort might be caused by limited experience with cross-cultural supervision.

Other researchers have also examined characteristics and incidents that may impact cross-cultural therapy and supervision. Ochs (1994) surveyed four hundred White nationally certified counselors to find out whether they had received any training to help White clients with racial issues, the incidence of White racial issues, the appropriate resources available to them, and seven areas in which White clients may have encountered racial questions (that is, school, neighborhood, work, dating, socializing, affirmative action, and White identity). Ochs found that 45 percent of counselors reported their White clients raising racial issues and for another 26 percent, racial concerns were their primary counseling issue. Ochs noted that this exploratory study raised several questions, including whether White counselors receive effective training to work with White clients around racial issues, how White racial issues are handled in supervision, and what needs to be addressed in order to improve supervision in this context.

Fukuyama (1994) notes that there is limited knowledge regarding relevant variables in multicultural supervision. In order to help identify important issues in supervision, Fukuyama (1994) conducted a small survey of racial and ethnic minority students (n = 18). Her pilot study helped "to take a good deal of mystery out of the process of culturally sensitive supervision" (Bernard 1994:165). She elicited critical incidents that occurred in supervision that either facilitated or impeded students' professional development. Critical incidents were defined as "meaningful emotional or behavioral interpersonal experiences that make an impact on the supervisee's effectiveness" (Fukuyama 1994:143) and may cause the supervisee to change her or his perceived counseling effectiveness. In terms of positive critical incidents, three categories of responses were delineated: openness and support, culturally relevant supervision, and opportunities to participate in multicultural activities. Two categories of negative critical incidents were delineated: lack of supervisor cultural awareness and questioning supervisee abilities (Fukuyama 1994).

Reynolds et al. (1999), using a focus group qualitative methodology, identify six themes related to the facilitation and hindrance of multiculturally sensitive supervision: (1) limitations of the supervisory relationship to address multicultural issues; (2) supervisor insensitivity to multicultural issues and perspectives of students of color; (3) coping mechanisms and support systems; (4) importance of cultural worldview; (5) possible role of racial similarity in supervision; and (6) characteristics of multiculturally sensitive supervision. Certain facets of the supervisory relationship seemed to hinder the discussion and incorporation of multicultural issues, such as the power dynamic in the relationship and the supervisor's lack of familiarity with the multicultural literature. Supervisees often sought outside support systems and peer supervision as a means of compensating for what they did not receive in supervision. While this was a positive coping strategy, it did not encourage the supervisory relationship to change and grow.

Hilton, Russell, and Salmi (1995) have examined the effects of supervision support (high versus. low) and supervisor race (African American versus Caucasian) and supervisees' perceptions of supervision. These researchers found no significant influence of supervisor race on supervisees' rating of the supervision interaction. Level of supervisor support did play a major role in supervisees' evaluations of the supervisory process. Supervisees could distinguish between high- and low-support supervisory relationships. Individuals with high-support supervision evaluated supervision more positively. Constantine (1997) has conducted an exploratory study to identify the degree to which multicultural differences were present in supervision relationships, the level of supervisors' training in multicultural counseling, and their competence in providing adequate multicultural supervision. Perceptions of both supervisors and supervisees regarding the scope and range of multicultural issues in supervision, and how supervision would have been improved with regard to multicultural topics were also assessed. Constantine found that all supervision relationships involved participants who were culturally different on at least two demographic dimensions (for example, race, religion, and sexual orientation).

Although there are few studies that explore multicultural issues in supervision, there are even fewer that examine racial identity and supervision. As with the multicultural counseling literature, when exploring issues of racial identity the multicultural supervision literature tends to focus on Helms's (1990) conceptualization of the impact of racial identity on the relationship dynamics between supervisors and supervisees. Based on the varying roles and levels of racial identity, it is possible for the supervisory relationship to be progressive (when the supervisor has a more advanced level of racial identity), regressive (when the supervisor has a less advanced level of racial identity), or parallel (when they are at similar levels). In one significant study, Ladany, Brittan-Powell, and Pannu (1997) surveyed one hundred and five counselor trainees (White, African American, Asian, Latino, and Native American) and found that supervisee-supervisor racial identity interactions were related to the supervisory alliance, and racial identity interactions (for example the Helms 1984 model) and racial matching influenced supervisees' development of multicultural competence. These researchers reported that supervisees who were engaged in parallel-high interactions (when both individuals have similarly advanced levels of racial identity) had the highest agreements on the goals and tasks of supervision. Also, these relationships were found to have the strongest emotional bonds. Progressive relationships were found to have the second strongest working alliances for agreement on the tasks and goals and the emotional bond. Regressive interactions predicted the weakest supervisory alliance (Ladany, Brittan-Powell, and Pannu 1997).

These researchers found that in both parallel-high and progressive interactions, the supervisor appeared able to facilitate the supervisee's development of multicultural competence. Racial matching did not significantly predict aspects of the supervisory working alliances. However, racial matching did significantly relate to the supervisees' perception of the supervisors' influence on their multicultural competence. Supervisors of color seemed to have the most perceived impact on the supervisees' multicultural competence both among supervisees of color and White.

Racial Identity Interventions and Applications

The topic of racial identity in counseling and supervision has become increasingly visible and at times dominant in the multicultural counseling literature. While some of this writing is research based, even more of it is focused on the practitioner with suggestions and recommendations for how both counselors and supervisors may effectively incorporate information on racial identity into their therapeutic and supervisory relationships. Many of the salient recommendations from the literature are briefly reviewed below, along with two illustrations that highlight the centrality of racial identity to the therapeutic and supervision process.

Counseling Relationships and Processes

Research has built a case for the importance of exploring the impact of racial identity of both therapist and client on the counseling process. Sue and Sue (1999) believes that racial identity is a useful assessment and diagnostic tool that allows for implementation of counseling strategies best suited to a specific client. Once it has become apparent that race or racial identity is a significant issue for the client, therapists can complete an assessment of their clients as well as themselves. Such assessment should extend beyond racial identity and include other social influences, personality variables, environmental influences, and life experiences (Thompson and Carter 1997).

According to Thompson and Carter, "racial identity development entails a continual and deliberate practice of self examination and experiencing" (1997:17). Therapists may need to facilitate clients' racial identity development, especially when they "experience meaninglessness and emotional distress in their lives because of issues related to race" (Thompson and Carter 1997:17). Research has demonstrated that more advanced levels of racial identity may lead to better psychological functioning (Carter 1995). "How to decide to foster this development requires a considerable degree of skill—skill that is built largely on the practitioner's own racial identity advancement as well as his or her ability to integrate this understanding with other conceptualizations of client change" (Thompson and Carter 1997:17–18).

Further knowledge and integration is required when the complexity of racial identity interaction is considered. According to Thompson and Carter, "when matters of race enter into the discourse, either directly or indirectly, the quality of the interaction (that is, relationship types) will be influenced by the prevailing racial identity status of each person within the dyad" (1997:26–27). Once a client's racial identity level is known, the therapist may have some understanding of her or his readiness for various interventions. "The practitioner who uses racial identity theory as a framework in his or her own practice has to anticipate the problems that can occur in the relationship and to arm him or herself with strategies to develop or strengthen the working alliance so that meaningful work can occur" (Thompson and Carter 1997:40–41). According to Helms (1990), an assessment of clients' racial identity is necessary to determine if their presenting issues are aggravated by racial identity that is not integrated into their overall identity and attitudes. It is important to realize that challenging a client's racial identity can lead to feelings of anger, isolation, shame, or guilt as one examines her or his attitudes, behavior, and relationships with others who are racially similar or different.

Thompson and Carter (1997) identify three general intervention strategies to facilitate the development of racial identity in clients: (1) confronting dissonance and encouraging complex and flexible thinking; (2) didactic approaches; and (3) corrective socialization. The first step, confronting dissonance, aims to help clients uncover their racial dilemmas and to create opportunities for them to fully experience their dissonance. This may require challenging their resistance to addressing racial identity either directly or indirectly. By examining their attitudes and behavior and looking for contradictions in their logic and thought processes, clients' thinking will hopefully become less dichotomous and more complex. Obviously such an approach requires a therapist who is self-aware and sensitive to racial identity issues.

Once clients have begun to acknowledge the existence of racial issues and face the dissonance, they may need some information to assist them in their self-discovery (Thompson and Carter 1997). Such didactic approaches and resources can include readings, presentations, or films. It may even help a client to have theoretical frameworks, such as racial identity development models, to help them appreciate and understand their struggles.

For some clients, acknowledging their dissonance and resistance and gathering content knowledge may not be enough to bring about real change in their racial identity and acceptance of themselves (and others) as racial beings. Racial identity attitudes may be tied to many intra- and interpersonal aspects of a person's life that are not easily left behind. The racial identity attitudes of some people connect them to particular groups of people who are important to them and to the way they view themselves. At some point these relationships, whether past or present, as well as the beliefs and attitudes that go with them, may become problematic to the client's well-being and self-esteem. For example, many Whites have difficulty moving beyond racist beliefs because such beliefs are fostered and embraced in their family of origin. Changing one's racial identity attitudes often requires either indirectly or directly challenging one's family. The same dynamic can occur with other groups that take on that role in an individual's life, a peer group in one's childhood or college days. According to Thompson and Carter, "[A]dvancement of racial identity can threaten a person's sense of connectedness to the social environment" (1997:45).

Thompson and Carter's final intervention strategy is corrective socialization, which involves clients unlearning negative beliefs and relearning positive aspects of their racial identity so as to reconstruct themselves and the way they were socialized as racial beings. Individual or group therapy, workshops on racism, as well as journaling or other types of homework can assist clients in their efforts to redefine who they are and what they believe. Although Thompson and Carter (1997) focus on the client when discussing these strategies, such interventions could work just as effectively for a supervisee.

It is important to realize that the focus in therapy should not just be on the client but that "the benefits for the client can be maximized when interventions facilitate the racial identity development of both the client and counselor" (Ridley, Espelage, and Rubenstein 1997:145). Parham takes this position further when he writes that "identity attitudes of a client may influence the therapist's ability to establish a strong working alliance with the client" (1989:220). Helms (1990) and others (for example, Carter 1995; Ponterotto 1989) emphasize the importance of therapists doing a meaningful self-assessment of their own racial identity. While research is still tentative in this area, it appears that therapist racial identity may have major implications for the client and the therapeutic process.

Regardless of the level of racial identity a therapist maintains, self-understanding increases the possibility of a facilitative relationship. Some of the interventions discussed previously can benefit counselors in terms of enhancing their own racial identity. Supervision is an ideal forum for such growth and challenge to occur; unfortunately not all counselors are in supervision and even when they are, they may not have supervisors with enough awareness of their own racial identity or adequate levels of multicultural competence to effectively facilitate the counselor's process.

In addition to increasing understanding of the client and counselor, racial identity development theory can increase one's understanding of the therapeutic relationship itself. Helms (1984, 1990) and Carter (1995) describe the various types of therapy relationships that occur within and across racial groups in great detail, using the racial identity interaction model. They also offer specific interventions to facilitate a healthier racial identity. These interventions vary according to the level of racial identity and type of interaction between therapist and client. Counselors and supervisors can consult an increasing number of resources to aid them in the process of facilitating the racial identity development of themselves and their clients or supervisees.

It is often difficult to understand what it means to facilitate the racial identity development of others without examples or illustrations of such interactions and relationships. We now offer a brief vignette and analysis that reviews the way racial identity issues can enter into and affect the therapeutic relationship. While we do not have the space to fully explore all the possible types of racial identity interactions in therapy, this example will at least offer one situation and analyze how it might be viewed.

Vignette

The client is a forty-year-old White American lesbian who is also an evangelical and devout Christian. She is a social worker who works part-time in several different agencies (including a Jewish mental health agency), seeing a variety of clients in a large urban area. Her clientele is often racially and economically diverse.

This client has addressed several significant issues in therapy, including her relationship with her family of origin, her social isolation and increasing distrust of people, her intense emotionality and its impact on her work and social relationships, as well as career and body image concerns. Whenever under duress, this client focuses her anger and intolerance on individuals or groups that are racially or religiously different from her. On several occasions in therapy, the client expressed frustration or anger with Jews and Blacks because of specific work-related concerns. At times she presented a hypersensitivity and slight paranoia about their perceptions of her and their behavior (which often seemed to fit racial and religious stereotypes).

The counselor, who is a White American female, has a small private practice in a large urban city with a diverse client population. She has had extensive training in the area of multicultural counseling. She is often bothered and offended by some of the client's remarks. The counselor, who often confronts such prejudice and intolerance in other life settings, was unsure how to address the client's behavior within the session in a therapeutic fashion. When the client was challenged, she often became defensive and described herself as having no bias. Over time she was willing to admit that she had become increasingly intolerant and focused her energy on other people who had nothing to do with her unhappiness. The counselor had rarely worked with racial or racial identity issues within a White-on-White dyad and while she could assess and understand her client's level of racial identity, she sometimes had to monitor her emotional reaction within the session so it would not get in the way.

This is an example of a progressive relationship in which the counselor possesses a more advanced level of understanding regarding racial and cultural issues than the client (Helms 1990). The counselor in this vignette had explored racial and cultural issues a great deal yet had little experience working with cultural issues in a White-on-White dyad. The client was unaware of her racial identity issues and how it was affecting her emotional health and well-being. According to Ochs (1997), "[A] White client has a racial issue when his or her position of privilege, concretely or psychologically, is perceived as threatened by the presence and/or actions of non-Whites" (1997:70). The counselor's limited experience in addressing issues of race within a White-on-White dyad is reflective of the multicultural or racial identity literature which does not address this issue adequately (Carter 1995). Despite the limited literature, it is important that White counselors take the risk of addressing racial concerns with their White clients. According to Helms and Cook, "White therapists must be able to be very empathic without endorsing the client's racism" (1999:321). The client's self-awareness and openness will be enhanced by the openness and honesty of the therapist and might involve some self-disclosure about the counselor's own struggle with racism and racial identity issues. This requires a therapist willing to take personal risks to explore her or his own racism and countertransference. When a client's issues create powerful reactions within the counselor, it is important to fully examine the source of those reactions and understand what the counselor must own as her or his issues.

Taking this type of directive approach where multicultural issues are not the focus of therapy (but may be affecting the client's well-being and relationships) may be seen by some as controversial. While this approach is certainly value-laden, many professionals agree that all aspects of the counseling process are value-driven. As demonstrated in the previous vignette, racist and bigoted views very likely have mental health implications for clients and should not be overlooked as a possible target of intervention within therapy.

Supervision

While the literature on multicultural issues in supervision has been expanding in the past few years, limited attention has been paid to racial identity issues in supervision. D'Andrea and Daniels (1997) have made several recommendations regarding the application of theoretical models of racial identity to facilitate multicultural supervision. Their suggestions include assessing the supervisor's and supervisee's racial and ethnic identity status and applying the identity development models to conceptualize challenges and dynamics occurring in supervision, particularly the impact of the racial identity levels of each participant on the process. D'Andrea and Daniels encourage supervisors to begin by assessing their own level of multicultural competence, to collaborate with supervisees who share levels of multicultural competence, and to learn by inquiring from supervisees who have more multicultural awareness and knowledge than themselves. The authors provide a specific list of questions supervisors can use to assess their level of multicultural competence (D'Andrea and Daniels 1997).

Helms and Cook (1999) review the literature around socioracial (for example, racial composition) and psychoracial (for example, racial identity) issues in supervision. They note that racial identity as a variable has been found to significantly impact the supervisory process. Helms and Cook observe that the current focus in theoretical and empirical work is on examining racial and cultural issues among and between the supervisor, supervisee, and client. The authors emphasize the importance of a here-and-now focus on racial issues in supervision (for example, what is going on at the present moment), as well as being able to generalize the current experience to future situations involving similar dynamics and variables.

Fong and Lease (1997) discuss issues that may arise for White supervisors in the process of conducting multicultural supervision. The authors observe that although most supervisees have a White supervisor, little attention has been paid to this area in the literature. Fong and Lease suggest some intervention strategies for White supervisors, including addressing their own professional development in the area of multicultural competencies, creating a development plan to ensure ongoing growth, and supporting supervisees in their own multicultural professional development.

Williams and Halgin (1995) discuss issues in supervision that may arise between White supervisors and Black supervisees. They contend that there are very significant differences in the training and supervision of White students and Black students. The authors divide their discussion into five major topic areas: (1) minority training issues; (2) understanding cultural and racial differences; (3) verbal and nonverbal communication differences; (4) interpersonal issues, including prejudice and racism, affirmative action and assuming similarity; and (5) Black therapists working with Black and White clients with basically no independent model of multicultural supervision. Williams and Halgin emphasize the importance of supervisors understanding racial issues and the way they affect supervision, as well as utilizing a multiculturally sensitive framework with which to conceptualize supervision.

Ryan and Hendricks (1989) explore salient issues in the supervision of Asian and Hispanic supervisees. The authors stress that awareness of potential differences is key to a successful supervisory relationship with Asian and Hispanic supervisees. In addition, Ryan and Hendricks emphasize the importance of honest communication in supervision in facilitating the development of the supervisory relationship.

While noting that the literature jointly discussing multiculturalism and supervision is rare, Stone (1997) proposes recommendations for multicultural supervision. During the first phase of supervision or training, there is a learning set, including the basic assumption that all programs value and respect cultural differences and are committed to training multiculturally competent counselors. The second phase of the process, concrete experience, entails actually working with issues of diversity regardless of the specific background of the supervisor and supervisee. The third phase, reflection, involves reflecting on concrete experience in a systematic manner. The last phase, action, focuses on implementing what the supervisor or training program has learned. Stone notes that this can take several forms, including discussions with peers regarding learning, involvement in social justice movements, community involvement, and conducting research to gather empirical support for learning.

Using examples to further our understanding of the racial identity issues in supervision often clarifies the dynamics that must be addressed regardless of whether one is a supervisor or supervisee. What follows is a brief vignette and analysis that reviews how racial identity issues can enter into and affect the supervisory relationship.

Vignette

The supervisee is a Black Caribbean American twenty-four-year-old female. She is enrolled in a predominately White counseling psychology program. Her training has included extensive multicultural work, including emphasis on self-awareness and knowledge. Her race and racial identity are an important part of who she is. The supervisee is doing her fieldwork once a week at a community agency in a large city with a diverse client population. After initial sessions with a number of clients who were racially and ethnically different from the supervisee, she broached the subject of diversity with her supervisor. The supervisor is a White Italian American male in his fifties with a cognitive theoretical orientation.

The supervisee discussed her concerns, including her insecurities regarding working with clients who were racially and culturally different and older than she was. Her concerns included questions about establishing rapport and connecting to her clients and them with her. The supervisor replied that any counselor could work with any client. The supervisee interpreted this as the supervisor meaning that he thought culture was irrelevant to the counseling process. This shut down communication in this area. Neither one broached the topic again. The supervisee sought outside consultation with professors and peers in her program. During the year of supervision, issues of race and culture were not incorporated into supervision. The supervisee left the fieldwork site feeling unsatisfied with her supervision and angry with the supervisor for his perceived ignorance. She felt fragmented, having

been unable to be authentic in the process. The supervisor was unaware of her feelings.

This is an example of a regressive relationship, in which the supervisee
possesses a more advanced level of understanding regarding racial and
cultural issues than the supervisor (Helms 1990). The supervisor in this
vignette had not explored his own work and life in terms of racial and
cultural issues. Porter (1994) notes that this is a crucial aspect of providing multicultural supervision. This supervisory relationship was
characterized by a lack of direct, open, and honest communication
around issues of race and culture. Neither supervisor nor supervisee
was willing to share their different views, beliefs, and meanings. Morgan (1984) notes that the supervisor is responsible for being sensitive to
race and culture in both supervision and therapy. The supervisee, according to Morgan, also must be willing to explore issues of countertransference. What makes these types of relationships so challenging is
that they require the individual with the least amount of power (the supervisee) to take the most risk. Such interactions are not uncommon as
most supervisors have not been trained in multicultural counseling and
may have a different worldview than their supervisees.

Emerging Trends and Future Research

Racial identity research in counseling and psychology has been a significant component of the multicultural counseling literature for almost
three decades. Although new models are continually being introduced,
the bulk of theory development took place in the 1970s and 1980s.
Helms (1984, 1990), Carter (1995), Thompson and Carter (1997), and
others have begun to build a literature and research base that demands
that racial identity be incorporated into our assessment and analysis of
the therapeutic process. The racial identity interaction theory of Helms
(1984) advanced the racial identity literature to a completely different
level by focusing on how the racial identity of both the counselor and
client profoundly affect the type of relationship that a counselor or
client may develop. This relationship ultimately influences their level of
racial identity and whether that relationship has growth potential in the
area of racial identity for either person.

Carter (1995) took the conceptualization of the interactive process between counselor and client one step further with the development of his Racially Inclusive Model of Psychotherapy. His model suggested that race and racial identity are critical components of a person's personality and psychological development at both the intrapsychic and interpersonal level. Without a complex interactive conceptualization of the influence of racial identity on the counselor and client as well as the relationship itself, true and meaningful understanding of racial identity and the counseling process will not be achieved (Carter 1995).

An additional trend over the past decade has been the increased attention to racial identity issues for people of color who are not Black. More racial identity models have been created during the past ten years and some research is being completed that examines these models and populations. Ponterotto (1989) calls for the ongoing exploration of other people of color groups.

During the past decade there has been increased attention on racial identity and multicultural issues in supervision and counselor training. More research studies, theoretical models, and frameworks for practice have been made available. This expanded literature will hopefully enhance the multicultural knowledge and skill base of supervisors and faculty, thus having an important impact on future generations of therapists and supervisors.

Future research will benefit from as complex and interactive a view of racial identity as possible. Stone strongly states that "action in the form of research is desperately needed. So much theory, so little data. Speculation, experience, and advocacy are no replacement for careful experimentation" (1997:283). Helms (1989) suggests that racial identity constructs, methodology, and environment are dynamic and complex and researchers need a certain level of understanding to appreciate the ways in which racial identity may influence research design, implementation, and outcome. Akbar (1989) and Nobles (1989) both identify the source of methodological difficulties sometimes encountered in racial identity research as the conceptual basis of racial identity theories. The lack of attention to spiritual issues and transformations as well as the view that the conceptualization of Black identity as being influenced more by external environmental events rather than the result of a core identity are just a few of the conceptual issues that some argue plague racial identity theory.

Ponterotto (1989), on the other hand, believes that the strongest challenges to the racial identity literature are methodological and measurement-based. He argues for the creation of new racial identity measures that move beyond cognitive or attitudinal aspects of racial identity to a focus on behavioral and affective dimensions of racial identity. Both Helms and Ponterotto argue for a broader range of methodologies in racial identity research, specifically the increased use of qualitative research designs. Helms (1984, 1989) and Ponterotto have also emphasized the importance of studying and exploring White racial identity as fully as the racial identity of other groups. Too often in the multicultural counseling literature, individuals have focused their attention on studying people of color rather than incorporating the concerns, dynamics, and identities of all racial groups.

Bernard (1994) points out that we still have limited knowledge about multicultural supervision and that the profession should not accept supervisors who are not trained in supervision and multicultural issues. Similarly, Priest observes that it is essential "that supervisors have course work and practical experiences in supervision and multicultural work" (1994:156). Researchers have made several suggestions for improving models and future research. Leong and Wagner (1994) note that it will be important to determine whether multicultural supervision follows a developmental model. Ladany, Brittan-Powell, and Pannu (1997) contend that racial identity interaction and racial matching should perhaps be integrated into models of counseling or supervision.

Bernard contends that empirical research in the area of multicultural supervision is "grossly inadequate" (1994:170). She points out that the validity of the theoretical postulations must be proven with empirical data. Leong and Wagner (1994) also note that there is a paucity of knowledge based on empirical data. There has been a call for more in-depth case studies and quantitative research to obtain descriptive information regarding the actual process of cross-cultural supervision, including the needs of ethnic minority supervisees, outcome expectations, developmental stages of multicultural supervision, and communication styles (Jordan 1998; Priest 1994). In particular, Priest (1994) observes that culturally based cognitive learning styles and racial identity stages that impact the processing of information and feedback in supervision must be identified.

In addition, particular techniques to promote multicultural awareness and competence in supervisees need to be empirically examined (Leong and Wagner 1994). Cook (1994) suggests that the multiple dynamics and variables involved in supervision are exciting and untapped areas for study in counseling and racial identity research. Exploring how each participant's (that is, supervisor, supervisee, client) racial attitudes may affect the process and perceived variables such as expertise and trust is a relatively unexamined area. In particular, Ladany, Brittan-Powell, and Pannu (1997) suggest that a more thorough investigation of racial identity interactions is needed to expand racial identity theory.

In terms of methodology, some authors favor the use of measures that offer alternative perspectives of multicultural competence, rather than the global assessment employed in their study (Ladany, Brittan-Powell, and Pannu 1997; Ponterotto et al. 1994). Similarly, Leong and Wagner (1994) encourage the use of more complex terms and assessments and have further recommended that race and ethnicity be conceptualized as a multidimensional psychological variable that would account for the full diversity of what race and ethnicity mean. Ladany, Brittan-Powell, and Pannu (1997) also suggest that an instrument be created to measure racial identity interaction, specifically to assess the dynamics surrounding racial issues in supervision. Similarly, Cook and Helms (1988) note that one of the limitations of their empirical study was that they used measures designed specifically to assess the characteristics of counseling rather than supervision. An additional area of possible investigation is the examination of the influence of racial identity interaction on other aspects of supervision, such as the ability of supervisees to conceptualize clients who are culturally different from them (Ladany, Brittan-Powell, and Pannu 1997; Ladany et al. 1997). Furthermore, Ladany, Brittan-Powell, and Pannu (1997) recommend that researchers explore the dynamics of parallel process as applied to racial identity interactions between the supervisee-supervisor and client-supervisee. Lastly, Fukuyama (1994) recommends that researchers focus on multicultural critical incidents with White supervisees, and also expand the exploration of critical incidents to include other cultural differences, such as religious orientation, racial identity, and sexual orientation.

Summary

Based on the review of the theoretical and empirical research in the multicultural counseling and supervision literature, it is clear that racial identity plays a pivotal role in those relationships and may have a significant impact on the process and outcome of therapy and supervision. While it is vital that all therapists know and understand the racial identity development literature in order to be ethical practitioners, content knowledge alone is not enough. A significant aspect of what makes a construct like racial identity so powerful is that it encourages therapists to explore their own identity and relate it to the experience and identity of their clients. This self-reflection is vital to the development of a meaningful working alliance.

The dynamic nature of racial identity theory development and research may be one of the reasons it has, and will continue to have, an impact on the counseling profession. As therapists enhance their own self-awareness and level of multicultural competency through the incorporation of racial identity theory into the therapeutic process, they honor both the individual and cultural strengths and life experiences of their clients. Such understanding also leads to a more meaningful appreciation of racism and other forms of oppression and its impact on the psychological makeup of all clients. This process means that "practitioners develop and refine their craft by constantly learning from their personal and professional experiences and by allowing room for theoretical expansion and revision" (Thompson and Carter 1997:46–47).

REFERENCES

Akbar, Na'im. 1989. "Nigrescence and Identity: Some Limitations." *Counseling Psychologist* 17(2):258–263.

Atkinson, Donald, George Morten, and Derald W. Sue. 1979. *Counseling American Minorities: A Cross-Cultural Perspective.* Dubuque, Iowa: W. C. Brown.

Bernal, Martha E., and George P. Knight. 1993. *Ethnic Identity: Formation and Transmission among Hispanics and Other Minorities.* Albany: State University of New York Press.

Bernard, Janine M. 1994. "Multicultural Supervision: A Reaction to Leong and Wagner, Cook, Priest, and Fukuyama." *Counselor Education and Supervision* 34(2):159–171.

Carter, Robert T. 1995. *The Influence of Race and Racial Identity in Psychotherapy: Toward a Racially Inclusive Model.* New York: John Wiley.

Casas, J. Manuel, and Scott D. Pytluk. 1995. "Hispanic Identity Development." Pp. 155–180 in *Handbook of Multicultural Counseling*, ed. J. G. Ponterotto, J. M. Casas, L. A. Suzuki, and C. M. Alexander. Thousand Oaks, Calif.: Sage.

Choney, Sandra K., Elise Berryhill-Paapke, and Rockey R. Robbins. 1995. "The Acculturation of American Indians: Developing Frameworks for Research and Practice." Pp. 73–92 in *Handbook of Multicultural Counseling*, ed. J. G. Ponterotto, J. M. Casas, L. A. Suzuki, and C. M. Alexander. Thousand Oaks, Calif.: Sage.

Constantine, Madonna G. 1997. "Facilitating Competency in Counseling Supervision: Operationalizing a Practical Framework." Pp. 310–324 in *Multicultural Counseling Competencies: Assessment, Education and Training, and Supervision*, ed. D. B. Pope-Davis and H. L. K. Coleman. Thousand Oaks, Calif.: Sage.

Cook, Donelda. 1994. "Racial Identity in Supervision." *Counselor Education and Supervision* 34(2):132–141.

Cook, Donelda, and L.P. Hargrove. 1997. "The Supervisory Experience." Pp. 83–96 in *Racial Identity Theory: Applications to Individual, Group, and Organizational Interventions*, ed. C. E. Thompson and R. T. Carter. Mahwah, N.J.: Lawrence Erlbaum.

Cook, Donelda A., and Janet E. Helms. 1988. "Visible Racial/Ethnic Group Supervisees' Satisfaction with Cross-Cultural Supervision as Predicted by Relationship Characteristics." *Journal of Counseling Psychology* 35(3):268–274.

Cross, William E., Jr. 1971. "The Negro-to-Black Conversion Experience: Towards a Psychology of Black Liberation." *Black World* 20(9):13–27.

———. 1985. "Black Identity: Rediscovering the Distinction between Personal Identity and Reference Group Orientation." Pp. 155–171 in *Beginnings: The Social and Affective Development of Black Children*, ed. M. B. Spencer, G. K. Brookins, and W. R. Allen. Hillsdale, N.J.: Lawrence Erlbaum.

———. 1987. "A Two Factor Theory of Black Identity: Implications for the Study of Racial Identity Development in Minority Children." Pp. 117–133 in *Children's Ethnic socialization*, ed. J. S. Phinney and M. J. Rotheram. Beverly Hills, Calif.: Sage.

Cross, William E., Jr., and Peony Fhagen-Smith. "Patterns of African American Identity Development: A LifeSpan Perspective." Chapter 10 in this volume.

D'Andrea, Michael, and Judy Daniels. 1997. "Multicultural Counseling Supervision: Central Issues, Theoretical Considerations, and Practical Strategies." Pp. 290–309 in *Multicultural Counseling Competencies: Assessment, Education, and Training and Supervision*, ed. D. B. Pope-Davis and H. K. Coleman. Thousand Oaks, Calif.: Sage.

Fong, Margaret, and Suzanne Lease. 1997. "Cross-Cultural Supervision: Issues for the White Supervisor." Pp. 387–40 in *Multicultural Counseling*

Competencies: Assessment, Education, and Training and Supervision, ed. D. B. Pope-Davis and H. K. Coleman. Thousand Oaks, Calif.: Sage.

Fukuyama, Mary A. 1994. "Critical Incidents in Multicultural Counseling Supervision: A Phenomenological Approach to Supervision Research." *Counselor Education and Supervision* 34(2):142–151.

Helms, Janet E. 1984. "Toward a Theoretical Explanation of the Effects of Race on Counseling: A Black and White Model." *Counseling Psychologist* 12(3–4): 153–165.

———. 1989. "Considering Some Methodological Issues in Racial Identity Counseling Research." *Counseling Psychologist* 17(2):227–52.

———. 1990. *Black and White Racial Identity: Theory, Research, and Practice.* Westport, Conn.: Greenwood Press.

———. 1995. "An Update of Helms's White and People of Color Racial Identity Models." Pp. 181–191 in *Handbook of Multicultural Counseling,* ed. J. G. Ponterotto, J. M. Casas, L. A. Suzuki, and C. M. Alexander. Thousand Oaks, Calif.: Sage.

———. 1996. "Toward a Methodology for Assessing Racial Identity as Distinguished from Ethnic Identity." Pp. 143–192 in *Multicultural Assessment in Counseling and Clinical Psychology,* ed. G. R. Sodowsky and J. Impara. Lincoln, Nebr.: Buros Institute of Mental Measurement.

Helms, Janet E., and Donelda A. Cook. 1999. *Using Race and Culture in Counseling and Psychotherapy: Theory and Process.* Boston: Allyn and Bacon.

Hilton, Doreen B., Richard K. Russell, and Steven W. Salmi. 1995. "The Effects of Supervisor's Race and Level of Support on Perceptions of Supervision." *Journal of Counseling and Development* 73(5):559–563.

Jackson, Bailey W. 1975. "Black Identity Development." *Journal of Educational Diversity* 2:19–25.

Jackson, Morris L. 1995. "Multicultural Counseling: Historical Perspectives." Pp. 3–16 in *Handbook of Multicultural Counseling,* ed. J. G. Ponterotto, J. M. Casas, L. A. Suzuki, and C. M. Alexander. Thousand Oaks, Calif.: Sage.

Jordan, Karin. 1998. "The Cultural Experiences and Identified Needs of the Ethnic Minority Supervisee in the Context of Caucasian Supervision." *Family Therapy* 25(3):181–187.

Kim, Jean. 1981. "The Process of Asian American Identity Development: A Study of Japanese-American Women's Perceptions of Their Struggle to Achieve Personal Identities as Americans of Asian Ancestry." Doctoral dissertation, University of Massachusetts, Amherst.

Ladany, Nicholas, Christopher S. Brittan-Powell, and Raji K. Pannu. 1997. "The Influence of Supervisory Racial Identity Interaction and Racial Matching on the Supervisory Working Alliance and Supervisee Multicultural Competence." *Counselor Education and Supervision* 36(4):284–304.

Ladany, Nicholas, Arpana G. Inman, Madonna G. Constantine, and Elizabeth

W. Hofheinz. 1997. "Supervisee Multicultural Case Conceptualization Ability and Self-Reported Multicultural Competence as Functions of Supervisee Racial Identity and Supervisor Focus." *Journal of Counseling Psychology* 44(3):284–293.

Lee, Fu-lin Yang. 1991. "The Relationship of Ethnic Identity to Social Support, Self-Esteem, Psychological Distress, and Help Seeking Behaviors among Asian American College Students." Doctoral dissertation, University of Illinois, Urbana-Champaign.

Leong, Frederick T., and Nicole S. Wagner. 1994. "Cross-Cultural Counseling Supervision: What Do We Know? What Do We Need to Know?" *Counselor Education and Supervision* 34(2):117–131.

Morgan, Donald W. 1984. "Cross-Cultural Factors in the Supervision of Psychotherapy." *Psychiatric Forum* 12(2):61–64.

Myers, Linda J., Suzette L. Speight, Pam S. Highlen, Chikaco I. Cox, Amy L. Reynolds, Eve M. Adams, and C. Patricia Hanley. 1991. "Identity Development and World View: An Optimal Conceptualization." *Journal of Counseling and Development* 70 (1):54–63.

Nobles, Wade. 1989. "Psychological Nigrescence: An Afrocentric Review." *Counseling Psychologist* 17(2):253–257.

Ochs, Nancy G. 1994. "The Incidence of Racial Issues in White Counseling Dyads: An Exploratory Survey." *Counselor Education and Supervision* 33(4): 305–313.

———. 1997. "White Counselor and White Client: The Case of Mrs. Ames." Pp. 69–82 in *Racial Identity Theory: Applications to Individual, Group, and Organizational Interventions,* ed. C. E. Thompson and R. T. Carter. Mahwah, N.J.: Lawrence Erlbaum.

Parham, Thomas A. 1989. "Cycles of Psychological Nigrescence." *Counseling Psychologist* 17(2):187–226.

Parham, Thomas A., and Janet E. Helms. 1985a. "Relation of Racial Identity Attitudes to Self-Actualization and Affective States of Black Students." *Journal of Counseling Psychology* 32(2):431–440.

———. 1985b. "Attitudes of Racial Identity and Self-Esteem of Black Students: An Exploratory Investigation." *Journal of College Student Personnel* 26(2):143–146.

Peterson, Francine K. 1991. "Issues of Race and Ethnicity in Supervision: Emphasizing Who You Are, Not What You Know. Settings, Stages and Mind Sets." *Clinical Supervisor* 9(1):15–31.

Ponterotto, Joseph G. 1989. "Expanding Directions for Racial Identity Research." *Counseling Psychologist* 17(2):264–272.

Ponterotto, Joseph G., Brian P. Rieger, Ann Barrett, and Ricky Sparks. 1994. "Assessing Multicultural Counseling Competence: A Review of Instrumentation." *Journal of Counseling and Development* 72(3):316–322.

Porter, Natalie. 1994. "Empowering Supervisees to Empower Others: A Cultur-ally Responsive Model." *Hispanic Journal of Behavioral Sciences* 16(1):43–56.

Priest, Ronnie. 1994. "Minority Supervisor and Majority Supervisee: Another Perspective of Clinical Reality." *Counselor Education and Supervision* 34(2): 152–158.

Reynolds, Amy L., and Raechele L. Pope. 1991. "The Complexities of Diver-sity: Exploring Multiple Oppression." *Journal of Counseling and Develop-ment* 70(1):174–180.

Reynolds, Amy, Ketrin Saud, Kristin Schaefer, and Kellye Liew. 1999. "Multi-cultural Issues in Supervision: Incorporating Student Voices." Manuscript under review for publication.

Ridley, Charles R., Dorothy L. Espelage, and Karen J. Rubenstein. 1997. "Course Development in Multicultural Counseling." Pp. 131–158 in *Multi-cultural Counseling Competencies: Assessment, Education and Training and Su-pervision*, ed. D. B. Pope-Davis and H. L. K. Coleman. Thousand Oaks, Calif.: Sage.

Root, Maria P. 1990. "Resolving "Other" Status: Identity Development of Bira-cial Individuals." Pp. 185–206 in *Diversity and Complexity in Feminist Therapy*, ed. L. S. Brown, and M. P. P. Root. New York: Harrington Park Press.

Rowe, Wayne, Sandra Bennett, and Donald R. Atkinson. 1994. "White Racial Identity Models: A Critique and Alternative Proposal." *Counseling Psychol-ogist* 22(1):120–146.

Ruiz, Aureliano S. 1990. "Ethnic Identity: Crisis and Resolution." *Journal of Multicultural Counseling and Development* 18(1):29–40.

Ryan, Angela S., and Carmen O. Hendricks. 1989. "Culture and Communica-tion: Supervising the Asian and Hispanic Social Worker." *Clinical Supervi-sor* 7(1):27–40.

Sodowsky, Gargi R., Kwong-Liem K. Kwan, and Raji K. Pannu. 1995. "Ethnic Identity of Asians in the United States." Pp. 123–154 in *Handbook of Multi-cultural Counseling*, ed. J. G. Ponterotto, J. M. Casas, L. A. Suzuki, and C. M. Alexander. Thousand Oaks, Calif.: Sage.

Stone, Gerald L. 1997. "Multiculturalism as a Context for Supervision: Perspec-tives, Limitations, and Implications." Pp. 263–289 in *Multicultural Counseling Competencies: Assessment, Education and Training, and Supervision*, ed. D. B. Pope-Davis and H. L. K. Coleman. Thousand Oaks, Calif.: Sage.

Sue, David, Winnie S. Mak, and Derald W. Sue. 1998. "Ethnic Identity." Pp. 289–324 in *Handbook of Asian American Psychology*, ed. L. C. Lee and N. W. S. Zane. Thousand Oaks, Calif.: Sage.

Sue, Derald W., and David Sue. 1999. *Counseling the Culturally Different: The-ory and Practice*. New York: John Wiley.

Sue, Stanley, and Derald W. Sue. 1971. "Chinese-American Personality and Mental Health." *Amerasia Journal* 1:36–49.

Thomas, Charles W. 1971. *Boys No More*. Beverly Hills, Calif.: Glencoe.

Thompson, Chalmer E. 1997. "Applying Racial Identity Theory to Individual Psychotherapy and Dyadic Supervision." Pp. 49–54 in *Racial Identity Theory: Applications to Individual, Group, and Organizational Interventions*, ed. C. E. Thompson and R. T. Carter. Mahwah, N.J.: Lawrence Erlbaum.

Thompson, Chalmer E., and Robert T. Carter, eds. 1997. *Racial Identity Theory: Applications to Individual, Group, and Organizational Interventions*. Mahwah, N.J.: Lawrence Erlbaum.

Vontress, Clemont E. 1971. *Counseling Negroes*. Boston: Houghton Mifflin.

Williams, Steven, and Richard P. Halgin. 1995. "Issues in Psychotherapy Supervision between the White Supervisor and the Black Supervisee." *Clinical Supervisor* 13(1):39–61.

Chapter 8

Racial Identity Development and the Mediation of Conflicts

Leah Wing and Janet Rifkin

This chapter describes a new approach to conflict resolution that is informed by racial identity development and oppression theory. At the heart of this approach is the belief that oppression dynamics have an impact on every dispute. Through our analysis and concrete examples, we explore how an understanding of these dynamics can be incorporated into mediation training and practice. This chapter draws on the experience of the Multicultural Student Conflict Resolution Team, a program we first developed at the University of Massachusetts, Amherst.[1] In particular, it focuses on how mediators who are trained in racial identity development theory can make use of it in their intervention techniques.

From the outset we want to note that the use of oppression theory and racial identity development theory (Hardiman and Jackson 1997) in the course of mediation training or intervention is a significant departure from the way mediation has typically been practiced in the United States. The use of these theories reflects our assumptions about the relationships between the people involved in any mediation. We believe that the social group memberships of the disputing parties and of the mediators make an impact, regardless of the conflict that instigated the use of mediation (Wing 1996, 1997a; Wijeyesinghe and Kandel 1997). These assumptions are not wholly congruent with the widely held view of mediation in the United States and therefore provide a challenge to the development of a new mediation approach.

The predominant view of mediation reflects a devotion to the concept of neutrality which our approach challenges as impossible and undesirable in an oppressive society. In addition, the common approach to mediation focuses on each mediation participant as an *individual* with individual needs that can be negotiated according to their specific context. In this approach to mediation, the participants have the opportunity to describe their concerns and to work toward developing a mutually acceptable agreement or plan for the future for their specific relationship. Another hallmark of typical mediation practice in the United States is leaving the decision making in the hands of the participants. These characteristics are seen as benefitting each participant by promoting empowerment (Bush and Folger 1994) and democratic participation (Susskind and Cruikshank 1987). Yet despite these potential benefits, the focus on individual needs and participation does not sufficiently account for the fact that society is stratified by *group* membership. As a result, we argue, all disputes are influenced by group membership identities such as race, class, and gender. A focus on the impact of one's identity as related to larger social groups is crucial in mediation since people receive or lose out on privileges based on their social group's standing in society. It is this view, indicting oppression as the problem and defining all action even in mediation as tied to either perpetuating or dismantling it, which inevitably undermines the promotion of neutrality in conflict intervention (Wing 1996).

Therefore, as we were conceptualizing the development of the mediation program at the University of Massachusetts, Amherst, we faced the dilemma that our views on social justice and the typical approach to mediation appeared incompatible. Despite the fact that both mediation and social justice emphasize empowerment and democratic participation, as described above, the two fields also contain beliefs that clash. For example, mediators commonly promote neutrality and gear their interventions toward individual conflict resolution, while social justice advocates typically organize for value-driven systemic social change. How were we to reconcile these two approaches? Were they reconcilable? It became our goal to explore an approach to mediation that operationalized our interest in a social justice practice. In the process, we explored how a mediation practice driven by a commitment to neutrality could perpetuate social injustice and the ways in which a new approach to mediation practice might incorporate social justice. We discovered that at the center of these analyses for future practices were an understanding of social identity development and racial identity development.

This chapter begins with a brief description of the theories that have informed our mediation approach. We then describe a typical dispute that appears on many college campuses and illustrate how mediators' understanding of oppression and racial identity development theory could positively influence their intervention in such a dispute. We end with some of the questions and challenges that still remain for us as we continue to explore how to make mediation a social justice practice.

Our Assumptions

First, we would like to begin by acknowledging that it is as White women from the United States whose first language is English that we write this chapter. We assume that these and other aspects of our identities have informed our perspectives on social justice and mediation and our work in combining the two. It is from these positions that we write about our work.

Our mediation approach is rooted in a perspective on social justice and oppression dynamics: how power operates and how access to resources is distributed in society.[2] This is at the core of our approach since these factors often feed the development of conflicts and influence the dynamics that occur within a mediation session. In particular, they fundamentally influence access to the currency of power that exists within a mediation session and thereby influence the material results of a mediation (Wing 1997a).

To elucidate our approach to mediation, we briefly explain our analysis of oppression (the reality that exists in society at present) and social justice (a goal for society). In our view, social justice requires that structures in society be designed to meet the needs of all. Yet, at present, society's institutions favor certain starting places, identities, and positions over others (Rawls 1971) and this affects relationships across all strata of society. Therefore, actions such as mediation which affect the distribution of resources must take this stratification into account. In this way, mediation will invariably either undermine or perpetuate oppression.

This approach to social justice names the problem to be dismantled as oppression: the systematic subjugation of groups of people based on their real or perceived social group memberships (Hardiman and Jackson 1997). In a society in which oppression plays an integral part, many conflicts are likely to emerge as a direct result of the differing circumstances that people experience due to oppression. As a result, mediators must make efforts not to perpetuate this condition of oppression in their interventions.

According to this view of society, all relationships occur in a context influenced by social stratification. All of us are members of social groups (based on race, class, gender, sexual orientation, and the like) and experience the effects of oppression, which are tied to such social group memberships. "Social oppression then involves a relationship between an agent [dominant] group and a target [subordinate] group that keeps the system of domination in place" (Hardiman and Jackson 1997:17).

Another important concept is the developmental process individuals go through whether they are members of a dominant social group (receiving privilege) or of a targeted social group (being denied privilege). This process is well described in the Social Identity Development Theory (SIDT) (Hardiman and Jackson 1997). The SIDT is particularly useful for mediators since it highlights the role of conflict in the developmental process in relation to social group memberships and oppression.

Before briefly describing the stages of identity development and their implication for use by mediators, we want to offer a few caveats. While a developmental model implies unidirectionality and compartmentalization, the SIDT can be understood as more fluid and circular. In fact, it is most helpful to view it as a series of different lenses through which people may view the world. A person may tend to use a lens reflecting a particular stage and after a time may use the next lens in the developmental sequence most frequently. And while people may move from one stage to another in what appears to be a linear fashion, as they experience further oppression or develop a deeper understanding of oppression and/or their identity, they may instead move more deeply into what would appear to be an "earlier" stage. In effect, we can see this model as a spiral of movement, like the peeling of an onion, rather than as solely a linear process. An example of this might occur when a person moves more deeply into an "earlier" stage after experiencing identity-related violence. The movement through the stages of identity development will be further analyzed in the section below describing each stage.

The SIDT does account for the fact that while someone may be in one stage regarding their gender identity they may be in another stage regarding their racial identity (Hardiman and Jackson 1997; Wijeyesinghe and Kandel 1997). However, a limitation of the SIDT is that it does not account for the complex realities of how one aspect of one's social identity is affected by and interwoven with other aspects of one's social identity. For example, an African American woman and a White woman can experience gender identity quite differently due to their racial identities. In addition, SIDT does not provide a framework for the complexities of Biracial and Multiracial identities. Instead, it concentrates on the general commonalities of experience as people use each of the stages' lenses.

We have found it useful to introduce mediators to the SIDT in general. However, given that the focus of this chapter is on Racial Identity Development Theory (RIDT) and mediation interventions, we limit our discussion to racial identity development while noting that this is only one of the aspects of social identity development which we teach mediators.

Racial Identity Development Theory

According to the Racial Identity Development Theory (Hardiman and Jackson 1992) we use when training mediators, the first stage in the developmental process is Naive/No Social Consciousness. With this as the lens, a person is unaware of the rewards and sanctions associated with membership in a racial group and with breaking the rules of one's racial group. In particular, people utilizing this lens learn to accept the framework that Whites are superior to people of color. Once this unconscious acceptance happens, people enter the Passive stage of Acceptance (Stage two). In Passive Acceptance, a person is unaware of this outlook. However, in Active Acceptance conscious acceptance of these beliefs and perpetuation of racial stratification occurs.

Stage three is referred to as Resistance since it is during this stage that a person focuses on understanding and resisting the existence of racism and its manifestations. By doing this the person is questioning the dominant group's definition of acceptable reality—the status quo. When one uses the lens of this stage it often results in conflict. People in Passive Resistance may engage in confrontations only in relatively safe situations, or may seek to avoid them entirely. However, despite this, they may still experience internal conflict between their past views and values and the new understanding that emerges with the discovery that oppression exists as a problem. When people are focused on actively engaging with others in the struggle against racism even beyond safe confrontations they move into what Hardiman and Jackson (1997) refer to as Active Resistance. In this way an individual can move beyond being a subject acted upon by others within an oppressive system to being an actor in his or her own life.

Stage four of the RIDT is Redefinition. Here people focus on redefining their own racial group's history and culture. Conflict often emerges as people experience this stage. For example, people in other stages of identity development can become angered by the focus or actions of those in Redefinition, as when White Anglos (non-Hispanic or non-Latino Whites) in Resistance attempt to join a group of people of color (in Redefinition) who choose to come together without White Anglos present. Conflicts can also emerge because some people believe that conscious and unconscious self-segregation by groups of people of color is the source of racial discrimination and tension. Yet these same people often do not see the conscious and unconscious self-segregation of White Anglos as responsible for racial tensions. Yet people in Passive Resistance, who may sense the existence of racism, may still see the coming together of a group of people of color without White Anglos as discomforting to White Anglos. Unsure of what to do about racism, some individuals in Passive Resistance may prefer not to be confronted by reminders of racial identity.

We see this kind of conflict in our trainings when we discuss dividing the participants into two groups—people of color and White Anglos—for part of the activities on racism. Often several White Anglo trainees, while acknowledging that racism exists, comment that dividing into separate groups will exacerbate racial tension. We have observed that the comments made from the concerned participants at this point fall into two categories. Some people are uncomfortable with the idea of explicitly discussing each other's personal views on racism at all while others prefer to discuss the topic in a mixed racial setting. Frequently we hear from the latter that they prefer such an environment because they want to learn how people of color feel and what they want White Anglos to do about racism. Perhaps the people fostering mixed racial group discussions are in Resistance and are seeking engagement with all others to discuss racism. However, individuals who say they want to talk in a mixed environment because they do not think White Anglos know anything about racism might be in Passive Acceptance.

In our trainings we have found that a large number of people of color and a smaller number of White Anglos look forward to the opportunity to meet in separate groups to discuss racism. These individuals are likely in Redefinition or Internalization (Stage five). They are likely to understand the benefits of meeting in homogeneous groups—target and dominant—to discuss racial identity and racism. These are examples of typical group conflicts that are actually tied to the stage of identity development which people are in, as opposed to their racial group membership.

Conflicts also occur between people when they are all in the Redefinition stage. Disagreement can emerge as they struggle together to create a new positive racial identity and find that they are not in agreement with one another about how to accomplish this. We see this occur in the separate group discussions on racism we hold during the mediation trainings. Often, as trainees of color discuss the illegitimacy of the racial categories ascribed to their communities by White society, there are different views about the political ramifications of identifying according to these categories. In the discussions among White Anglos in this stage, common topics of debate include: whether there is such a thing as White culture separate from White privilege and whether White pride has a place in the antiracist movement.

The final stage (five) of the RIDT is Internalization, when people look to internalize a new sense of racial identity not based on or in reaction to the assumptions and functions of racism. Having raised their consciousness about their own relationship to racism, people often have an increased appreciation for the experience of targets of all forms of oppression (for example, women, people with disabilities, or lesbians, gays, and bisexuals). An instance of someone moving into Internalization may have been when a man of color commented at the close of one of our trainings that he had done a tremendous amount of work on racism in his own life but had not thought much about sexism. Not until his interaction with other trainees did he begin to realize that he had previously not understood the experiences of women of color and White women. During the training he began to understand some of their experiences with regard to sexism in light of his own experiences with racism. At the end of the training he felt more prepared to respond to both male and female mediation participants.

In summary, each person involved in the mediation is viewing the world through one of the stages of racial identity development (Wing 1998). Therefore it is crucial that mediators understand racial identity development theory so that they fully appreciate the impact of their own lens and others' on the conflict resolution process.

RIDT and Mediation Practice

The use of the RIDT in mediation has to be managed carefully, given the historical expectation in the United States that mediators do not provide education, solve problems *for* participants, or name the participants' reality for them. Since most people expect mediators to be neutral, it would be seen as clearly inappropriate for a mediator to analyze the participants by telling them which stage of racial identity development the mediators thought they were using. While many in the field of conflict resolution recognize that neutrality is a difficult if not impossible task, there has been general consensus that attempting to achieve it is a valued goal.

In this context, how could we best introduce RIDT as a tool for mediator training and intervention? To answer this question, we took a look at the reality of neutrality. We carefully explored the findings in the conflict resolution field and concluded that mediators could not be neutral (Cobb and Rifkin 1991a). Specifically we found that what was asked or not asked, how a mediation session was set up physically, and how the process was facilitated all reflected the mediators' values and levels of consciousness about oppression and social justice. Believing that neutrality was impossible, we went further and explored the notion that mediators ought not be held captive by the idea of neutrality which can obscure the realities of oppression and social injustice (Cobb 1994; Moore 1997).

To illustrate these points, let us look at how the different stages of the RIDT can influence mediator interventions. For example, a mediator who uses an Internalization lens might intervene quite differently from one who sees the world through a Passive Acceptance lens. Consider a mediator in Internalization. She might ask questions that allow for or even encourage participants to speak about their experiences in ways that recognize oppression as it exists in their lives and their relationships. This mediator would be able to see that a participant who is in Active Resistance, for example, could have come to mediation primarily to discuss and express anger about racism and how he has experienced it in relation to the other participant. In contrast, the other participant might be in Passive Acceptance, with a lens that does not reveal any focus on race. This latter participant might not view the relationship or the conflict that brought them into the session as related in any way to racism or racial identity (Wijeyesinghe and Kandel 1997). Using the RIDT, the mediator in this case would have a tool for understanding why the two participants were having difficulty agreeing on what the focus of the conflict was and that an agreement regarding issues of racism would not be likely to emerge at the session. This mediator could also be in a position to understand the need for *each* participant to name, explore, and have validated the story of their experiences according to whatever stage they were in.

Yet a mediator using a lens from Passive Acceptance would probably find it neither easy nor worthwhile to solicit such stories and might lack the tools to understand where both participants were coming from in terms of their approach to the issues of race and racism. This situation speaks to the need not only for RIDT to be taught to mediators but for mediators to attempt to explore what lens *they* function with regarding racial identity. This can help mediators see how their lenses might influence the types of questions they solicit and the ways in which they influence the involvement of each participant in the mediation session (Wing 1997b).

Mediators have the crucial role of assisting participants to share their experiences during a session; and here, specifically, we want to highlight the significance of being able to storytell about the dynamics of oppression, racism, and racial identity in mediation. This is particularly important due to the general discomfort and fear that most White Anglos in this country have about engaging in conversations about race and racism. Given this reality, mediation is empowering as a site where stories regarding race are either allowed to surface and treated as real or are colonized by their suppression (Cobb and Rifkin 1991a; Cobb 1994; Wing 1997b).

As noted in previous research on mediation and storytelling (Cobb and Rifkin 1991a), access to storytelling, to engaging in the discourse of a session is a critical aspect of the mediation process. The ability to tell one's story, utilizing the lens of whichever stage one is functioning in, and having one's words responded to and built upon is a source of power. Therefore, providing access to this storytelling process is a fundamental way in which power is managed and controlled within a mediation. During a session, mediators facilitate access to this vital resource and in this way can either perpetuate or undermine the power imbalances between participants which stem from target or dominant identities.

Since we see the mediator's role fundamentally as facilitating access to story development, it is important to describe the characteristics of the storytelling process and to show how they are interwoven with issues of power and social justice. Mediation research by Cobb and Rifkin (1991b) found that

> not all people share equal access to the narrative process . . . to construct a story that is recognized by the others as coherent. Thus the mediators will necessarily have to adjust their interventions to account for the political nature of narrative interaction.

However, when mediators do not recognize that there is unequal access to the narrative process and do not adjust their interventions accordingly, they can support the maintenance of hegemonic power relationships. Since mediators are rarely trained to view mediation in this light, examinations of actual mediation sessions overwhelmingly find that the dynamics reflecting such power relationships continue to occur and are not interrupted in the session.

The distribution of access to communication influences the participants' ability to engage in a mediation and thus it affects the content outcome, such as an agreement, as well as the quality of their mediation experience. As Cobb and Rifkin (1991b:18) have put it:

> Story facilitation recognizes the mediator as an active participant in the co-construction of the narrative. . . . Although the mediators can attempt to monitor their influence, it must be recognized that mediators, as do the rest of us, legitimize certain stories over others. Thus once the "magic" of mediation is critically examined, it must be

understood as a political process which privileges certain speakers/ disputants over others.

All this must be considered when training mediators so it can be accounted for in their interventions. Mediation must be seen as a political process, requiring not neutrality but rather recognition that each mediator operates from a particular stage of racial identity development that influences their practice. In addition, training needs to promote reflection on how stages of racial identity development influence whose stories about which topics mediators are fostering, summarizing, building upon, asking questions about, and assisting the other participants to understand (Wing 1997b).

Typically, mediators are not trained in the areas mentioned above, being trained instead to attempt to balance power in a session by utilizing symmetry in their interventions: to ask the same questions to each side, to give equal time to each side, and in all other ways to attempt to treat participants equally. We note here that these are common ways of attempting to operationalize the notion of neutrality. However, treating those participants the same who have had asymmetrical experiences regarding oppression, violence, and access to power due to group identity can actually serve to support the needs and expectations of those from a dominant group (Rouhana and Korper 1996). This symmetry of intervention commonly occurs by excluding racial identity and racism from the discussion. Since such discussions are not of concern to most people in Acceptance, mediators do not pursue these concerns. It becomes evident when using this analysis that a symmetrical approach could benefit those belonging to a dominant or higher power group, White Anglos, and exclude and undermine the target or lower power group members, people of color (Bell 1997).

The use of a symmetrical intervention process in mediation can perpetuate silence about racial oppression by not providing a conversational space for stories about racism. Mediators in Acceptance support the maintenance of the structural status quo and consequently the preservation of the dominant group. An example of this is when a mediator does not acknowledge experiences of racism as relevant to a discussion. By such an exclusion participants do not have access to storytelling or agreement building about this topic. This exclusion serves to undermine full participation in the mediation process for the person desiring the discussion involving racism and is in direct contradiction to the goals of those in Resistance, Redefinition, and Internalization. These goals often include gaining more power for those in the target group and increasing the balance of power between the groups. If mediators use lenses from these later stages, their attempts to gather participants' stories and to help them build agreements are more likely to be related to issues of inequality, racism, and power imbalances based on racial identity.

Again, what we are emphasizing here is that it is not possible for a mediator to intervene in a neutral manner. It becomes evident that the degree of the mediator's consciousness and the stage of RID she is in influences her intervention. It guides whether her focus is on providing a symmetrical intervention process which supports the goals of those in Acceptance, or whether her focus is on assisting the participants to meet their storytelling needs given the actual realities of their lives.

Since research has shown that mediation is a political process and that the way a story is facilitated can either empower the participants or disenfranchise them (Cobb 1994; Cobb and Rifkin 1991b; Rouhana and Korper 1996), it will help to examine further the complexities of facilitating storytelling in mediation. This examination will also highlight how story facilitation can provide for the use of the RIDT.

Story Facilitation and RIDT

Mediators could benefit from learning the pragmatics of how to facilitate a storytelling session—a mediation—in ways which do not allow for the domination of one participant's story over another's. In particular, the mediation session should offer a space for the stories involving race and racism. Understanding story facilitation can help provide mediators with tools for specific intervention techniques that make it possible for each participant to tell his story without disenfranchisement. Mediators can then promote access to the resources of storytelling and legitimation through visible and valued participation in the mediation.

There are three features of storytelling that help us understand the pragmatics and politics of mediation: narrative coherence, narrative closure, and narrative interdependence (Cobb 1994). As a story is told in mediation, characters, plot, and relationships are described which the other participant(s) can elaborate on, not respond to, or can contest. The more complete the story is, the less vulnerable it is to critique and attack by another participant, thereby affording it narrative coherence and closure. Stories that resonate more with dominant cultural myths than other narratives "have more stability because the broader culture has already done the 'work' to seal off discursive sites where these meanings can be contested" (Cobb 1994:56). For example, when a stereotype that exists in the dominant culture is perpetuated in a story told in mediation, it has a legacy and is told and heard with greater meaning than merely as part of a participant's story. The cultural stereotypes of the broader society help to seal and legitimize the perceptions of many participants who have not unlearned what they had been taught during Acceptance (Harro 1994; Wing 1998). If a participant's story is not part of a larger story supported by the dominant culture, it can lack this coherence and closure.

The next feature of storytelling is narrative interdependence. When telling their story mediation participants frequently frame the other participant as their victimizer and themselves as the victim. This relationship defines a narrative interdependence that is common in stories of conflict. Cobb (1994:57-58) notes that

> this accounts for the cycles of escalations in which conflicts are enacted. Here narrative theory provides a rationale for third-party intervention in conflicts: Disputants inside of narrative structures reproduce conflict stories as they try to transform them. The resolution of conflict requires the intervention of a third party precisely because the third party can alter persons' discursive positions and, in the process, generate a new pattern of interaction, a new interdependence.

Once again, the mediator plays a crucial role since she manages the access to storytelling. She could, for example, facilitate a discussion which builds on one participant's victimization more than the other participant's. In this way, the mediator assists in the colonization of one participant's story and helps to empower one at the expense of another.

Marginalization and domination are a function of the degree to which a person can self-define in the discourse (Pallai in Cobb 1994) and the degree to which these self-definitions are elaborated upon by others (Cobb 1994). In addition to being marginalized during the discourse of a mediation session, it is important to note that there can be attending material results from being effectively silenced during the mediation process (Wing 1997a). For example, an agreement may not reflect the essential needs of both participants if they have not been able to fully develop their own stories and be understood beyond their role as the victim or the victimizer in the story of the other participant.

The transformation of a participant's role in a story can occur when the interpretation of a story changes, carries new meaning, and is built upon. It is during this process that a new understanding of the past occurs which creates the potential for new roles for each participant in future stories. Mediators can use several methods to assist with such story transformation, including: circular questioning, reframing—looking at other possible interpretations, framing positive connotations of the other participant—and externalizing the conflict as something that is outside the people involved. This understanding of mediation as a storytelling process which mediators facilitate, charges mediators with the role of managing a conflict intervention based on narrative construction, narrative destabilization, and narrative transformation (Cobb 1994).

As stated earlier, mediators need to understand both the larger power dynamics that occur on a macro level in society as they are tied to identity-based oppression, and to attend to the manifestations of these dynamics in a mediation session on a micro level. This is the case whether such manifestations are due solely to oppression or whether micro-level domination is also occurring due to the discursive finesse of an individual (Wing 1998). It is the mediator's responsibility, then, to prevent story colonization through the careful facilitation of story construction which ensures that all participants' narratives are given the opportunity to develop as complete, coherent, and capable of being transformed as well as built upon by others. Let us take an example: a mediator might initiate by asking both a White Anglo participant and a participant of color how race may be related to the relationship or the issues at hand. This could: (1) help to create an environment in which the participants know that topics considered "difficult" to deal with in the culture at large are welcomed as points of discussion within the session; (2) let the participants know that the mediator is aware of the larger stories of race in society and how these stories can and do permeate relationships between people of different races, as well as people of the same race; (3) facilitate the creation of an alternative interpretation or future story, undermining a cycle of blaming; and (4) make a discursive place for the person of color, for example, to discuss a topic not often validated in the stories told outside the room in society at large. This is particularly important since a participant in a mediation session might not even raise the issue of race, concerned that such stories will be unwelcome, and anticipating that the mediation is likely to replicate his experience in the larger culture.

In the illustration above, the mediator's intervention is geared toward providing effective story facilitation for both participants while attempting to prevent story colonization. This intervention must be handled with delicacy since the mediator who asked how race might be related to the mediation could potentially alienate someone in Acceptance. For example, the White Anglo participant might not have viewed race as an issue and could experience the mediator's introduction of it into the conversation as a threat to conflict resolution and to her position in the story under discussion. Viewing the circumstances from an Acceptance lens, perhaps, she might see race as irrelevant and fear that a discussion of it could lead to the participant of color framing her as the victimizer, a role with which she feels she has no connection. The fact that the mediator introduced the issue of race could anger and alienate the White Anglo participant from the mediator and the process.

In order to decrease the chances of such alienation and maximize the possibility of the White Anglo participant sharing a story regarding race, the mediator would undoubtedly utilize features of the mediation process such as private sessions. By meeting with each participant separately the mediator works to create as comfortable a conversational context for exploring these issues and feelings as possible. The White Anglo participant may be responding to an unsolicited question about race. However, her response can be seen as part of her story in the mediation to be explored, understood, and built upon as well.

It is here that our approach departs fundamentally from other mediation practices in the United States as we argue that mediators need to make asymmetrical interventions; that is, by raising questions of race knowing some participants may not share the perspective that it is a relevant topic. However, we remain committed to hearing and legitimating each participant's story and perspective that arises in response to such questions. Therefore, it is also the mediator's job to prevent the colonization of the story of the White Anglo person using the lens of Acceptance in this example.

While we have highlighted how a mediator might be able to effectively make use of RIDT, we acknowledge that some mediation practitioners and participants who expect and value neutrality might find the use of RIDT problematic. However, given our guiding assumption that oppression exists and that it is within a context of oppression that we mediate, we question the choice of mediating without accounting for it. More specifically, if a mediator does not consider the differentials of power *and* the ramifications that oppression might play within a mediation and between the participants, we ask whose interests the mediation serves (Wing 1998)?

As we have mentioned previously, it is quite common for mediators to work hard to balance the power differential between participants during the session. However, these mediator interventions traditionally do not account for the larger societal imbalances of power that exist due to racial group memberships. Additionally, in striving for neutrality mediators typically attempt to balance the power between participants by utilizing symmetrical intervention techniques. However, such interventions favor people from the dominant group, namely, White Anglos, and are likely to exacerbate such imbalances.

Some Implications for Mediation Practice

Clearly, the mediation field would benefit from further research and experimentation with the way mediation processes can more effectively incorporate a social justice approach. A few ways we have explored include training members of many different identity groups for our mediation team, thereby promoting mediation skill development in different communities. We recommend working to ensure that the materials, approach, and design of trainings reflect the different realities and needs of the trainees (Bailey 1997). It has been our hope that by having mediators from many different identity groups and, in particular, by having people of color who are in later stages of the RIDT and are comediating with White Anglos who are allies (also in the later stages), our program can accomplish a number of things. For example, we hope that these mediators' interventions will support storytelling and transformation and prevent story colonization.

In addition, we want participants coming to mediation to be able to work with members of a Multiracial team committed to social justice within the mediation setting.

There are other benefits to having mediators of many different backgrounds available to work in a particular mediation program. When a participant sees someone like himself at the session he may be more likely to trust the process, anticipating that his story may be validated. It can make it possible to hold mediation sessions in the first language of the participants, without requiring translators. A mediation occurring in a participant's first language provides recognition of and validation for her identity and also gives her access to being understood in her own tongue (Moraes 1996).

Ensuring that each participant has the access he needs to storytell and that no one is disenfranchised in the mediation process is a significant challenge for mediators. This challenge is reduced by an understanding of oppression theory, RIDT, and the dynamics of storytelling facilitation. However, more needs to be known to assist mediators in operationalizing tools to make mediation empowering for all participants seeking to engage in this conflict intervention process. In order to explore further how an understanding of oppression dynamics, RIDT, and story facilitation can be utilized in mediation we have constructed a case study for analysis.

Case Study of a Student-Faculty Dispute

The following case is a composite drawn from our experiences mediating conflicts on a variety of college and university campuses.

Tamara, an African American student majoring in psychology at a small liberal arts college, contacted the Mediation Program because she was upset about a grade she had received in a class she had taken. Tamara was an undergraduate honors student and had never received a grade below an A in any course before. In this class, however, she had received a C. She told the coordinator the following story. She had spoken to Professor Murray about her grade and was told that her written work was weak and that her lack of participation in class discussions had contributed to her final grade. The professor reminded her that the course syllabus had clearly explained that the grade would be based on the two assigned papers, worth 80 percent of the grade, and class participation, worth 20 percent. Tamara tried to talk about her discomfort level in the class, which she felt had contributed to her overall performance, but the professor felt that she had graded Tamara fairly. The student had contacted the Mediation Program because she had come to the conclusion that, while she wanted her grade changed, it was even more important for her to be able to tell Professor Murray why she had uncharacteristic trouble in her class and to feel that the professor understood her feelings.

The Mediation Coordinator, a White Anglo woman, contacted Professor Murray, also a White Anglo woman, who told the coordinator the following story. She explained that she was very disturbed about Tamara's performance and had talked to her on several occasions during the semester to find out what was wrong. She said that Tamara had been reluctant and unwilling to really talk to her. After teaching for over a decade she prided herself on having had good relationships with African American students and felt that she had a special commitment to helping them be successful. The situation with Tamara not succeeding in her class was, she explained, unique in her experience and was upsetting. She hesitated to come to a mediation session, claiming that it was her right as a professor to grade as she saw fit. But she agreed to participate when she understood that the grade issue was secondary to Tamara, who hoped to focus on communicating her perspective to the professor. Professor Murray said that she wanted to hear Tamara's concerns and to convey what her own had been.

At one level this is a typical dispute between a student and a professor which most campus-based mediation programs would accept, based on the willingness of the participants to mediate. With a student initiating mediation over a grade complaint, participation would not be assured as many professors feel that grades are not negotiable and that their academic freedom is inviolable. However, in the event that a professor was willing to discuss the relationship or the circumstances surrounding a grade, a case would proceed. In this case study the case did ultimately go forward despite Professor Murray's initial reticence.

The two mediators who facilitated this session were a White Anglo woman who was a faculty member at the college, and an African American woman who was an undergraduate there. Neither of the mediators knew Tamara or Professor Murray. The mediation was structured according to typical mediation practice which the mediators described: first the mediators would give an introduction to this confidential process, each participant would tell her story, a facilitated discussion between them would follow, and the session would conclude with a written or oral agreement, if one was reached. The mediators told the participants that both mediators might have private sessions with each participant and that the mediators periodically would be taking breaks to caucus together.

The mediators asked Tamara if she wanted to begin with her story of what had brought her to mediation. They gave her the opportunity to go first since she was a member of several targeted groups: a young person, a woman, and an African American. While not explaining this to either Tamara or Professor Murray, the mediators wanted to show Tamara right away that she would have access to storytelling in the mediation, in contrast to what many of her experiences in society were likely to have been.

Tamara began her story by explaining that she had been uncomfortable in the class from the very beginning when Professor Murray announced that she had been a civil rights activist and was committed to racial equality. It had seemed to her that the professor was looking directly at Tamara when she spoke about her commitment to fighting racism. While Tamara respected the professor's political perspective and experience, as the only African American student in the class she felt that Professor Murray had expectations of her that made her feel uneasy. Tamara wondered out loud to the mediators if Professor Murray had been seeking her approval. She went on to say that Professor Murray seemed to look at her whenever she talked about African Americans, and had called on her several times asking what her reaction to particular topics being discussed was from a Black perspective. Tamara resented being the "spokesperson" for African Americans and felt she was being stereotyped.

Although she attended class regularly, she became increasingly distracted and unable to concentrate. She agreed that her papers weren't very good but felt that Professor Murray's insensitivity was a major cause of this. Her discomfort became so severe, she stated, that she eventually did not speak at all in class. When she had tried to talk about this with the professor, Tamara had felt unheard and that she was being lectured.

Professor Murray began her story by saying that she was unsettled by Tamara's account. She said that she had been aware that Tamara was unhappy and felt that she directed a lot of comments toward her as a way of getting her involved because she was the only African American student in the class and that she had thought she was being helpful by reaching out to Tamara. She underscored how much she saw herself as "championing" students of color and that she had always been recognized by her colleagues and other students as a particularly sensitive teacher around issues of race. She recounted numerous occasions in which she had reached out to Tamara and discussed Tamara's work with her outside class and how Tamara had been distant and nonengaging. She closed by expressing her concern about the entire situation and again asserted she still felt that she had given Tamara an appropriate grade. At this point the mediators caucused briefly.

The mediators checked in with each other to ensure that they had similar understandings of the two stories. Next, they strategized for the following session. The mediators noted that among the variety of issues raised, both participants indicated an understanding of the reality of racism in society at large. Both the participants acknowledged, albeit in different ways, that racial identity had been a factor in their interactions. The mediators noticed that there was a real difference between their perceptions in that Tamara focused on the manifestation of racism within her classroom experience and her interactions with the professor, while Professor Murray did not seem to view racism as a factor in their relationship or in the classroom. The mediators noted that both participants had concerns related to racial identity that they had each raised in their stories. Then the mediators talked about how to help facilitate further storytelling about this.

The mediators then discussed how RIDT might apply and which strategic interventions they would pursue. They speculated that Tamara might be looking at this situation with a lens from the Resistance stage. They also noted the additional power imbalance due to Tamara's student status and Professor Murray's status as faculty. They noted that they needed to make sure that Tamara's story was legitimized, at least by the mediators and ideally by Professor Murray as well. They then speculated about what lens the professor might be using. It appeared to them that she had used the lens of Resistance in her understanding of dynamics in society and, perhaps, she had been using a Passive Acceptance lens in her classroom. The mediators also acknowledged the same need to legitimize the professor's story and hoped that eventually Tamara might understand Professor Murray's intentions and experiences, in this way also legitimizing the professor's story. Drawing on their oppression training, the mediators wondered how they could help Professor Murray understand Tamara's experience through the lens that the professor used to understand racism in society at large. This focus is an example of how an understanding of oppression theory and RIDT can lead mediators to make an asymmetrical intervention.

Together both mediators met with each participant separately and asked them to delve more deeply into their stories. The mediators then asked each participant questions about their understandings of the other's experiences, perceptions, and intentions. Because the mediators wanted to help Professor Murray see that Tamara viewed her experiences in the classroom similarly to the way the professor, herself, viewed racism in society at large, they asked her the following question. The African American mediator addressed Professor Murray, saying, "It seems that both of you share an understanding of what behaviors took place in your class. But it seems that Tamara did not experience it the same way that you intended her to." The White Anglo mediator then said: "Tamara experienced a sense of isolation and deep discomfort in class even though you made it clear today that you intended the opposite—to include her and to encourage her participation. When you asked her to provide the 'Black perspective,' she has said that made her feel stereotyped. Given the disparity between your intentions and what you have learned were her experiences, what are you thinking now?" Professor Murray thought briefly and then expressed her hope that she would never again single out, even unintentionally as in this case, a student based on race. At this moment she turned to the African American mediator and said, "What should I do to never offend another African American in class again?" In response, the White Anglo mediator said, "It's clear that you've understood Tamara's experience and that you want all your students to feel welcome in your classes. And one of the things that you mentioned that you do not want to replicate is asking an African American to speak for all others in their racial group." After a pregnant pause, the professor exclaimed, "Oh, no! I guess I did it again by asking you [looking at the African American mediator] to tell me how not to offend any other African American student in the future." At this moment the professor commented that she planned to think some more about this.

When the mediators met with Tamara they shared with her Professor Murray's stated intentions and the professor's understanding of how her classroom behaviors affected Tamara. They followed this by asking her what she was thinking at this juncture. Tamara indicated that she could now see that the professor had wanted to encourage her to participate and had wanted her to feel welcome in the class. She also reiterated how offended she had been based on her experience in the class, but that she now felt ready to accept the professor's story of her intentions.

The session came to a close with all four present. Tamara and Professor Murray expressed their new understandings to one another and although the grade was not changed, both indicated that they felt pleased about what had transpired in the mediation. Tamara indicated that she was relieved to have been able to express herself and be understood by her professor. (The mediators later noted to each other that this was the first time in the mediation that Tamara had referred to Professor Murray as "my professor.") Professor Murray stated that she had found the mediation useful and that she had a lingering doubt about her decision not to change the grade, something she thought she might revisit after the mediation.

Case Analysis

As we reflect on the case, we can see the characteristics of storytelling taking place: narrative closure, narrative cohesion, narrative interdependence, and the moves that the mediators made to assist in story legitimation and story transformation. For example, when Tamara and the professor spoke about their experiences with each other they framed the other as having been in the wrong and framed themselves as mistreated or misunderstood. This demonstrates the narrative interdependence present in their stories. The mediators worked to show an understanding for each of their perspectives and also worked against the narrative coherence and closure that was likely to support the professor's story regarding the role race had played as opposed to the lack of narrative coherence and closure that was likely to occur regarding race in Tamara's story. They accomplished this by keeping Tamara's narrative of her experiences related to race and racism in the classroom alive. They assisted both participants to fully explore their own narratives and each other's, which led to mutual story legitimation and the building on each of their stories by both the mediators and the other participant.

This process led to story transformation as Tamara and Professor Murray altered the role the other had played in their discourse. For example, this occurred when Tamara began to refer to Professor Murray as "my professor." Potentially, such story transformation in discourse as occurred in this mediation could lead to material changes in the future. In this case, although Professor Murray still maintained the power to refuse to change Tamara's grade, she made it clear that given her new perspective, she would be seriously considering changing it. In addition, the professor mentioned her commitment to use her new understanding in future classes to ensure that she did not ask students of color to speak for their racial group. Should that materialize in the future, the mediation, based on the story transformation which occurred, would have contributed to material changes.

This case illustrates that mediators trained in the dynamics of oppression and racial identity development theory understand that these factors influence all present in a session. As a consequence of infusing mediation training with social justice theory and storytelling techniques, mediators have more tools to facilitate problem solving, relationship building, and conflict resolution. In the case we have described the mediators made strategic interventions based on explicit discussions in their caucus about how racial group membership and identity development affected the conflict. While these issues may not be directly addressed in every mediation case, the strategic moves and questions that mediators with RIDT training pursue depend on the stories told, consciousness of racial group membership, identity development, and the dynamics of oppression.

Conclusion: Racial Identity Development Theory and Mediation Practice

The cultivation and exploration of the aspects of the stories involving race is unusual in the field of mediation. Even when participants themselves raise an identity issue, mediators generally feel unprepared to manage the discussion. There are a number of reasons for this: mediators are wary of violating neutrality which they believe would occur by discussing a topic with which at least one of the participants may not feel comfortable; they are not trained to facilitate conversations about race which is a controversial topic in this country; and they are commonly trained to work with the participants to narrow the topics discussed down as much as possible for the purpose of agreement building.

Therefore, the typical approach to mediation (in which issues of race, racism, and racial identity are less likely to be raised and discussed) perpetuates the imposed silence that exists on these topics in our society. In other words, story closure and cohesion favor the individual from the dominant group, White Anglos. Since the story in society which predominates reflects the lens of Acceptance, racism is viewed by many mediators as not an issue and they view the relationship interactions between the participants in the mediation as occurring only on an individual level. If the framework of Acceptance is allowed to remain the more powerful story in mediation, then the participant describing her personal story through the lens of Acceptance finds it easier to have her story legitimated than the participant using a different lens. To counter this we suggest that mediators enter a mediation with a carefully framed set of assumptions about racial identity and conflict such as we have explored in this chapter. This will allow mediators to raise questions which explicitly explore the role of race in the experiences and relationships of the participants. And as we have already explored, this can prevent a story about race from being colonized. In the process, it can provide further access for all participants to more fully engage with each others' stories.

Over the last several decades mediation has become an increasingly popular form of dispute resolution in the United States, offering an expedient and often successful alternative to litigation and claiming the ability to resolve underlying issues (Fisher and Ury 1981), transform relationships and society (Bush and Folger 1994), empower disputants (Davis 1989), and build stronger communities (Shonholtz 1984). However, social justice advocates have asked whether mediation can fully meet these expectations as long as its practice is based on neutrality. We believe these expectations can be more fully met by focusing more explicitly on the complexities of social identity. We wish to make mediation a social justice practice, a practice which understands that social identity is central to conflict and its facilitation in relationships and communities. However, there are challenges in construing mediation as a social justice practice.

These challenges arise from the fact that despite the existence of areas in which the traditional rhetoric of mediation and social justice overlap, their underlying values are, in many ways, at odds. For example, while both fields express an interest in empowerment, inclusion, and balancing power there are core conceptual differences between the two. Mediation in the United States is driven by the ideology of neutrality; social justice is value-driven. Mediation focuses on the micro level of specific relationships; social justice focuses on a macro-level structural analysis. Mediation seeks conflict resolution between participants; social justice seeks social change, which inevitably requires conflict engagement. Mediation typically focuses on the needs of the participants; social justice focuses primarily on the rights of groups (Wing 1996). Yet despite the significant differences between these two fields, we have found some theory from each helpful in bridging the paradigmatic differences. We have used theories of oppression and racial and social identity development (Hardiman and Jackson 1997) from the social justice field and narrative theory (Cobb and Rifkin 1991a) and symmetrical intervention theory (Rouhana and Korper 1996) from the mediation field.

Our challenge has been to use theory from both fields in the service of a social justice approach to mediation and to explore through mediation practice what works, for whom, and why. We see this social justice approach to mediation as a work in progress and we hope others from both fields will join us in further exploration. Additional research is needed to explore more concretely how to operationalize the theories behind the approaches we have discussed. RIDT and narrative theory can offer a new perspective to mediation practitioners. However, the mediation field is driven by intervention practice and until theory is grounded in well-defined techniques, mediators— even those welcoming the new approach—will be hard-pressed to change their intervention styles (Rifkin 1994).

Therefore, continued research is needed to expand the understanding of how oppression and racial identity development influence mediator intervention, the participation of those utilizing mediation services, and specifically what techniques should be used to account for it. This is a particularly important endeavor as our society engages in the healthy reexamination of racial identity, recognizing the complexities of its social construction in a society structured by oppression and increasingly made up of Multiracial and Multicultural families, schools, and workplaces. This work to reexamine racial identity development theory and to integrate its use in the practice of mediation is an exciting process which is only in its infancy.

NOTES

1. This program was designed by the Biracial team of Leah Wing, Janet Rifkin, and Martha Wharton in 1993, and has benefitted from the Multiracial team efforts of Richard Ford, Pilar Hernandez, Deepika Marya, and Vilmarie Sanchez in the years since then.

2. While we recognize that oppression dynamics within a society are tied to historical and material conditions that transcend national boundaries, for the purposes of this chapter we have chosen to focus on the present domestic U.S. context.

REFERENCES

Bailey, Deborah L. 1997. "Life in the Intersection: Race/Ethnic Relations and Conflict Resolution." *The Fourth R* 77 (May, June, July):3–4,18–19.

Bell, Lee Anne. 1997. "Theoretical Foundations for Social Justice Education." Pp.3–15 in *Teaching for Diversity and Social Justice*, ed. M. Adams, L. A. Bell, and P. Griffin. New York: Routledge.

Bush, Robert A. Baruch, and Joseph P. Folger. 1994. *The Promise of Mediation: Responding to Conflict through Empowerment and Recognition*. San Francisco: Jossey-Bass.

Cobb, Sara. 1994. "A Narrative Perspective on Mediation: Toward the Materialization of the 'Storytelling' Metaphor." Pp. 48–63 in *New Directions in Mediation: Communication Research and Perspectives*, ed. J. P. Folger and T. S. Jones. Thousand Oaks, Calif.: Sage.

Cobb, Sara, and Janet Rifkin. 1991a. "Practice and Paradox: Deconstructing Neutrality in Mediation." *Journal of Social Inquiry* 16:201–227.

———. 1991b. *The Social Construction of Neutrality*. Washington, D.C.: The Fund for Research on Dispute Resolution.

Davis, Albie. 1989. "The Logic behind the Magic of Mediation." *Negotiation Journal* 5(1):17–24.

Fisher, Roger, and William Ury. 1981. *Getting to Yes: Negotiating Agreement without Giving In*. Boston: Houghton Mifflin.

Hardiman, Rita, and Bailey W. Jackson. 1992. "Racial Identity Development: Understanding Racial Dynamics in College Classrooms and on Campus." Pp. 21–37 in *Promoting Diversity in College Classrooms: Innovative Responses for the Curriculum, Faculty, and Institutions*, ed. M. Adams. San Francisco: Jossey-Bass.

———. 1997. "Conceptual Foundations for Social Justice Courses." Pp. 16–29 in *Teaching for Diversity and Social Justice: A Sourcebook*, ed. M. Adams, L. A. Bell, and P. Griffin. New York: Routledge.

Harro, Roberta. 1994. "Cycle of Socialization." P. 52 in *Social Diversity and Social Justice: Selected Readings*, ed. M. Adams, P. Brigham, P. Dalpes, and L. Marchesani. Dubuque, Iowa: Kendall/Hunt Publishing.

Moore, Pamela. 1997. "Conflict Resolution and Anti-Bias Education: Connections and Boundaries." *The Fourth R* 77 (May, June, July): 1, 10, 12–14.

Moraes, Marcia. 1996. *Bilingual Education: A Dialogue with the Bakhtin Circle*. Albany, N.Y.: State University of New York Press.

Rawls, John. 1971. *A Theory of Justice*. Cambridge: Harvard University Press.

Rifkin, Janet. 1994. "The Practitioner's Dilemma." Pp. 204–208 in *New Directions in Mediation: Communication Research and Perspectives*, ed. J. P. Folger and T. S. Jones. Thousand Oaks, Calif.: Sage.

Rouhana, Nadim R., and Susan H. Korper. 1996. "Case Analysis: Dealing with the Dilemmas Posed by Power Asymmetry in Intergroup Conflict." *Negotiation Journal* (October):353–366.

Shonholtz, Ray. 1984. "Neighborhood Justice Systems: Work, Structure, and Guiding Principles." *Mediation Quarterly* 5:3–30.

Susskind, Lawrence, and Jeffrey Cruikshank. 1987. *Breaking the Impasse: Consensual Approaches to Resolving Public Disputes*. New York: Basic Books.

Wijeyesinghe, Charmaine L., and Andrea C. Kandel. 1997. "The Role of Social Group Membership and Identity Development in Conflict Resolution and Anti-Bias Education." *The Fourth R* 77 (May, June, July):5–6, 15–17.

Wing, Leah. 1996. "Multi-Cultural Mediation in Education: A New Approach to Conflicts Involving Difference and Dominance." *SPIDR News* 20 (summer/fall):13.

———. 1997a. "Multicultural Mediation in Education." *Globe* (spring):1–2.

———. 1997b. "Mediation and Social Justice in an Educational Community." *The Fourth R* 77 (May, June, July):20–21.

———. October 1998. "Multicultural Mediation: A New Approach to Conflict involving Difference and Dominance." Presentation at the Society of Professionals in Dispute Resolution, 26th Annual International Conference, Portland, Oregon. Available on tape.

Chapter 9

Core Processes of Racial Identity Development

Maurianne Adams

What we are looking at here is *not* an *ethnic* identification or culture, but an awareness of shared experience, suffering and struggles against the barriers of racial division. These collective experiences, survival tales and grievances form the basis of a historical consciousness—a group's recognition of what it has witnessed and what it can anticipate in the near future.

—Marable 1995:187

While writing this chapter, I was coteaching a course on Blacks and Jews in the United States. My coinstructor and many of our students identify themselves as Black, but others who "look" Black and who grew up in Chicago, New York, or Boston prefer ethnic designations such as Afro-Caribbean, West Indian, Jamaican, or Haitian. Their complicated racial and ethnic lineages include parents or grandparents not born in the United States, and their family trees include Blacks, Whites, Asians, and indigenous peoples of the Americas. The students disagree with each other over the terms *race* or *ethnicity* to describe their own self-definitions, but uniformly reject the U.S.-based ethnicity of African American. They are children of the African Diaspora who describe their cultures in different ways but agree on their experiences of racism in the United States and its impact on them and on their families.

I am the product of another dispersed and "mixed" people, for whom the terms *race* and *ethnicity* as well as *religion* and *nationality* are similarly problematic. If Jews constitute a *race*, then how do we square the view that today's American Jews are racially privileged as "White" (although such a statement ignores the numerous Black Jews of the Americas), with the fact that a generation ago we as European Jews were persecuted as non-Aryans? We have intermarried among Europeans, Africans, and Arabs, producing offspring who look (racially) like other Europeans or Africans or Arabs but who are known to ourselves and our neighbors as Jews. The *ethnic* designation of Jewish Americans (parallel to African, Irish, and Italian Americans) obscures our own *ethnic* subdivisions among Sephardic, Ashkenazi, and Mizrachi Jews. The notion of Jews as a *religious* group is challenged by nonprofessing Jews who identify "culturally" as Jews, and by the range of religious beliefs and practices that separate our Hasidic from our Reform congregations. Jewish *national origins* include Cuba, Iran, Morocco, France, and Russia, and as American Jews we are *nationally* distinct from Israeli Jews.

Yet the social psychologist Kurt Lewin (in 1941) could claim convincingly that our Jewish identity crosses national boundaries through an "interdependence of fate" grounded in our shared (and recurrent) historical experience of both danger and well-being:[1]

> [E]very individual American Jew depends in a specific way on the social status that Jews as a group have in the more inclusive community of the United States. In case Hitler should win the war, this special interdependence of fate will become the most important determining factor in the life of every single Jew. If Hitler should lose, this interdependence will still be one of the dominant factors for the lives of our children. (1941:222–223)

Lewin noted a similarly shared interdependence of fate in the historical experience of Black Americans, an insight taken up by later writers on Black identity (Cross 1991). Marable's phrase, "a group's recognition of what it has witnessed and what it can anticipate"—used in the epigraph to this chapter—can be read in the same vein. This interdependence of fate (or "historical consciousness," as Marable calls it) grows out of a group's shared and acknowledged experience of social inequality and oppression, the salience of which hardly rests on whether race or ethnicity is the more accurate term to explain the visibility that allows for persecution based on difference.

The goal of this chapter is to identify and describe generic processes of identity development across various racial and ethnic groups. This task is not helped by the unreliable, confusing, and interchangeable ways in which *race* and *ethnicity* have been used, as illustrated by several recent titles: *Ethnic Identity* (Bernal and Knight 1993), *Race, Ethnicity, and Self* (Salett and Koslow 1994), *Racial and Ethnic Identity* (Harris, Blue, and Griffith 1995). It may well be that the decision to describe oneself and one's group racially or ethnically is in itself a statement about identity. However, I find it more useful in this chapter to suggest that the term *race* be considered a *panethnic* social category based on presumed "racial" attributes that have emerged, in this country at least, out of legal and political constructions of group inequality still generally unquestioned in popular usage.[2]

According to this view, a three hundred-year historical process of "racial construction" in the American colonies and then in federal and state systems resulted in hierarchically structured social, political, and economic relations among *ethnically* and *nationally* diverse peoples of European ancestry and *ethnically, nationally,* and *tribally* diverse peoples of African, Asian, Latino, and American Indian ancestry (Banks and Eberhardt 1998; Haney López 1996; Choney, Berryhill-Paapke, Robbins 1995; Torres and Ngin 1995; Omi and Winant 1986).[3]

For obvious historical reasons, *race* in the United States has been associated with cultural, material, physical, and linguistic differences which need not imply inequality of social status. Used in this sense, *race* is often indistinguishable from *ethnicity* as a group category. But *race* has also been perceived through an ideology of superiority or inferiority used to justify unequal educational and occupational opportunities, as well as segregated residential communities and public spaces. This second set of meanings clearly involves *racism*, understood as a "system of advantage based upon race" (Tatum 1997; Wellman 1977) that uses scientifically discredited "biological features to make social distinctions" (Dobbins and Skillings 1991:41; Montagu 1997; Smedley 1993; Spickard 1992; Van den Berghe 1967).

Ethnicity refers more neutrally to the lifestyles, value orientations, languages, customs, beliefs, and habits by which a people who have lived and interacted together over generations are likely to differ from their neighbors (Smedley 1993:29). It refers to a people's *culture* more than to their *physical* characteristics. Yet peoples of African,

Asian, Latino, and Native American heritage who maintained ethnically distinct communities in the United States were not only "lumped" racially by their Anglo neighbors, but were also racially categorized as non-White through processes of law, public policy, and immigration status (Haney López 1996; Torres and Ngin 1995; Omi and Winant 1986; Takaki 1993). What actually developed was a pattern of citizenship and suffrage which drew a sharp distinction between ethnicity and race, and subsumed ethnicity to race on the basis of perceived physical characteristics of sameness or difference.[4]

This historical explanation provides my frame of reference for understanding some of the core generic processes of racial identity development that appear to operate similarly for otherwise distinctive racial and ethnic communities. The racial identity development processes that I stress in this chapter stem from similar historical experiences of group subjugation undergone by various ethnic groups who had been officially designated as non-White. These culturally subordinated and economically marginalized ethnic communities have struggled to forge their own positive American identity against presumptions of their racial inferiority. In this process, the dimensions of group identity expressive of cultural distinctiveness cannot always be disentangled from the dimensions affected or shaped by group resistance to inequality and oppression. As a result, culture and social status remain closely intertwined and analytically indistinguishable. "Not only [do] Black Americans constitute a distinct cultural group, but also their cultural group has experienced a history of systemic oppression as a racial minority. Therefore their individual identities as Blacks and as Americans are affected both by Black culture and by American racism" (Hardiman and Jackson 1992:22).

The pioneer analyses of racial identity development (Sherif and Sherif 1970; Thomas 1971; Cross 1971; Hall, Freedle, and Cross 1972; Jackson 1976) were written in the aftermath of the Black civil rights struggle and in the context of Black Power. These authors were interested in understanding and transforming the individual and social systems that supported racial discrimination and oppression. Based upon the experiences of Black Americans during the 1960s and 1970s, they described dramatic transformations in *racial* identity from internalized subordination into a liberated valuing of Blackness. More recent accounts of identity development among peoples of Asian ancestry (Gupta 1997; Spickard 1997; Sodowsky, Kwan, and Pannu 1995) or

Latin American descent (Rivera-Santiago 1996; Casas and Pytluk 1995; Hurtado, Gurin, and Peng 1994; Keefe 1992) have tended to substitute *ethnic* terminology to call attention to differences grounded in culture and language rather than race as sites of internalized domination and subordination. Ethnicity also highlights panethnic issues of colonized or immigrant status and contests the Black/White paradigm associated with *race* in the United States. Recent writings on *racial* identity development have also focused increasingly on the numerous multidimensional sources of social and cultural variability among Black identity profiles, based on factors such as class, gender, immigrant status, sexual orientation, or religious belief (Cross and Fhagen-Smith, this volume; Cross, Strauss, and Fhagen-Smith 1999; Greene 1997; Bodkin 1996; Reynolds and Pope 1991).

In what follows, I extricate from the foundational Black identity development models the core features of racial and ethnic identity development that appear to have been shaped by structural hierarchies of domination and subordination in the larger social system. I then differentiate them from idiosyncratic features that appear to be culturally or individually distinctive.[5] I argue that the core processes of racial identity development affect racially subordinated and targeted groups in equivalent ways, although these processes should not be confused with elements of cultural *content* that may be unique to specific racial and ethnic groups.

However, as a caution against overgeneralization, it is critical to balance an analysis of core generic features with an appreciation of the considerable variability among individuals within groups as well as the differences between groups. Variability can be found in historical context, cultural content, social and occupational roles, multidimensional and interacting social identities or agent and target social statuses, and individual dimensions of personality and beliefs. In this chapter, the formative Black identity developmentalists of the 1970s are seen in the historical context of 1960s political activism and social ferment. Similarly, writers on Asian, Latino, or American Indian identity development stress the cultural and historical variability among ethnic groups, as illustrated by the distinctive legacies of Korean and Japanese Americans, or the different racial ascriptions for Cuban Americans and Puerto Ricans, or the tribal affiliations of American Indians. These differences place outer limits on our ability to generalize from one identity group to another and compound the difficulty of extracting common principles from complex and sometimes conflicting racial and ethnic identity experiences.

In this chapter, I refer to racial and ethnic identity models using their own preferred terminology, while acknowledging the lack of agreement and vigorous disputes that sometimes surround preferred usage. Part I of this chapter presents foundational *Black* racial identity development models along with their derivatives and summarizes a set of core principles drawn from these works. Selected Asian and Latino *ethnic* identity development models appear in Part II, with the more generic models of panethnic or panracial development discussed in Part III. In Part IV I review the core generic racial and ethnic identity development processes and make the case for extending their application to other social categories such as gender and sexual orientation. This case is made insofar as these categories are similarly marked by a distinctive group historical consciousness and sense of interdependence ("we-ness") shaped in part by similar experiences of unequal social status, domination, and subordination.

I: Models of Black Identity Development

Foundational Models of the 1970s

The Black identity theorists writing in the 1970s articulated remarkably similar developmental models "conceived of independently and almost simultaneously" (Jackson 1976:159). Jackson, working as an educator and trainer in the humanistic education tradition, developed his Black Identity Development (BID) model primarily as a tool for teachers, counselors, and group leaders who sought "a better understanding of Black identity development based on a positive perspective rather than a cultural- or psychological-deficit perspective" (Jackson 1976:158). During the same period, Cross, then a doctoral student in psychology, described the Negro-to-Black conversion experience (which he termed *Nigrescence* to highlight the process of "becoming Black") as the expression of a positive, transformed Black identity and as the stimulus for a psychology of Black liberation (1971).

A contemporaneous essay by the social psychologists Sherif and Sherif (1970), "Black Unrest as a Social Movement toward an Emerging Self-Identity," placed the emergent Black consciousness directly within the historical context and political activism of the 1960s. Echoing such influential writers as Fanon (1963), Memmi (1965), and Freire (1970), the Sherifs described Black consciousness as "the most effective vehicle for change of attitudes and self identity" among a long-suppressed and dissatisfied people (Sherif and Sherif 1970:42) and the precondition for a broadly based liberation movement (Hall, Freedle, and Cross 1972). They noted that there were two overarching themes within the Black identity movement, namely, a turning away from dominant White values and standards ("the dissociation from those white standards, institutions and values that define black men as inferior") and an affirmation of non-White reference points ("turning towards other non-white peoples in different parts of the world especially in Africa and looking elsewhere for values to replace those they have rejected" (Sherif and Sherif 1970:48–49). For Cross in the 1970s, these two interconnected Black identity development processes—"rejection of white standards, and a search for a new reference"—promised to promote "psychological liberation under conditions of oppression" (1971:13).

Core Generic Features of the Jackson Model

During the decades that followed, several core processes have come to characterize foundational racial identity development models and to chart "the journey from an identity in which racism and domination are internalized to an identity that is affirming and liberated from racism" (Hardiman and Jackson 1992:23). The first core process is *transformed consciousness*, by which the Black person who has earlier accepted and conformed to White standards, now actively rejects them and redirects his or her attention to the values, beliefs, and culture of other Black people. This transformation is stimulated by a series of contradictions to his or her current worldview that enables the Black person to recognize and challenge his or her internalization of the dominant White racial order. Further experiences and contradictions lead to a second dynamic process of *redefinition* in which the Black person explores the possibilities for a self-affirming Black identity, oriented away from the hegemony of the dominant White order and toward a positive engagement with what it means to be Black.[6]

A third core process can be described as the *parallel developmental tasks* experienced across both dominant (agent) and subordinate (target) identity statuses in White and Black identity development respectively, as well as among people of similarly targeted ethnicities. Thus, Jackson's account of the developmental tasks confronted by Black Americans on their journey from the "Acceptance" of White hegemony to their "Internalization" of a new Black identity has been mirrored in Hardiman's model of White identity development (1994; Hardiman and Jackson 1992). Helms, whose models of White and Black identity development differ from those of Hardiman and Jackson, describes these parallel developmental tasks in a similar vein: "the general developmental issue for Whites is abandonment of entitlement [internalized domination], whereas the general developmental issue for people of color is surmounting internalized racism [internalized subordination] in its various manifestations" (1995:184, my brackets; see also Helms 1990). *Parallel developmental tasks* also describes the adaptation of Jackson's Black identity model for Asian racial identity development (Kim 1981, this volume) as well as for generic racial identity development (Atkinson, Morten, and Sue 1979, 1998).[7]

Two further core processes emerge from the recent work of Cross and will be taken up in the next section. In this section, however, it is important to observe that Hardiman and Jackson extend the implications of parallel developmental tasks among Blacks and Whites to suggest global stages applicable to other stigmatized or privileged identity groups within a generic analysis of social oppression (1997). Hardiman and Jackson elaborate their analysis of racial identity development within a broad conceptual model of oppression. They describe oppression as a set of self-perpetuating structures of domination and subordination held in place by the power of social institutions and the collusion of individual agents and targets. Their multilayered view of the relationship between an oppressive social order and the dynamics of racial identity development is that "oppression affects the identity development of targets and agents as they are socialized into dominant or subordinate social groups," and thus racial identity development involves the directionality "of targets and agents as participants in oppression and liberation who are capable of change" (1997:22–23). In this, they propose a generic model of racial identity development for theorists and researchers working within an oppression-liberation paradigm.[8]

Kim (1981) draws upon this paradigm in her account of the panethnic identity development of Asian Americans. She emphasizes the cumulative impact of anti-Asian racism on Asian Americans whose families, neighborhoods, and social and religious institutions had taught them positive ethnic identity during childhood. In Kim's model, "ethnic awareness" (the first of her stage descriptors) provides an ethnic anchor in childhood for Asian Americans. Kim describes how her informants' early pride in their Asian ethnicity is gradually eroded by "White Identification" (her next stage) that results from their interactions with White peers, their exposure to White cultural hegemony, and their unremitting experiences of racial prejudice which they internalize as negativity about their Asian physical characteristics. Kim's "White Identification" stage presents developmental tasks that are parallel to those in Jackson's "Acceptance" stage.

Kim also calls attention to sources of variability within the social contexts for Asian identity development, such as the differential long-term impacts of growing up in predominantly White-ethnic or racially mixed or predominantly Asian American communities. She notes the role of historical context in the "redirection to an Asian American consciousness" (Kim's fourth stage) which for her informants is specifically rooted in their activism in the Black civil rights movement during the 1960s and 1970s. Their activism on behalf of Black civil rights sets in motion a sociopolitical awakening that they ultimately apply to their own Asian American self-identity. In this case, the explicit "ethnic awareness" starting point of Asian American racial identity development and the specific historical conditions which stimulate "redirection to an Asian American consciousness" are instances of cultural and historical variability that help guard against overgeneralizing the similarities between Asian American and Black American identity development processes.

Nonetheless, like Jackson, Kim describes a developmental process in which a targeted racial group undergoes transformation from internalized racism to a redefined, positive racial identity. And like the Sherifs, Kim notes the historical significance of the Black civil rights movement for the transformations she describes. And finally, again like Jackson, she pays attention to the complex interactions of the culturally distinctive features of Asian American ethnic communities with the systemic oppression they face as members of a racially subordinated panethnic group.

Recent Elaborations of the Cross Model

Over the years Cross has focused inward upon the striking variability among Black identity profiles rather than outward upon parallel tasks of racial identity development among targeted ethnic groups. His attention has been drawn more to the interaction of *Nigrescence* (his term for the specific conversion process of becoming Black) with other dimensions of identity development among Black Americans, and less to the extension of core racial identity development processes to other agent or target groups. Cross distinguished *personal identity* from *reference group orientation* (Cross 1985, 1991) and demonstrated that Blacks who have achieved *Nigrescence* may nonetheless consider their Black identity salient in varying degrees and also maintain different racial ideologies such as Black nationalism, multiculturalism, or Biracial African American identity (1985; Cross, Strauss, and Fhagen-Smith 1999; Cross and Fhagen-Smith, this volume).

Despite this emphasis on accounting for variability within specific Black identity profiles—based upon dimensions such as socialization, other salient social identities, self-esteem, general personality, and ideological belief systems—Cross nonetheless identifies core identity processes in his analysis that seem to be generalizable to other targeted identity groups. Cross treats *Nigrescence* as distinct from other potentially salient dimensions of social identity (such as gender, religion, or sexual orientation) and also as distinct from other generic or core processes of ego identity development (Cross and Fhagen-Smith 1996 and this volume). It is difficult to overestimate the importance of this two-pronged distinction between *Nigrescence* and other dimensions of social identity on the one hand, and between social and ego identity development processes on the other, for clarifying muddy identity constructs within the social psychology and developmental literatures (for the many conceptual problems and semantic confusions, see Gleason 1983 and Hoare 1991).[9]

Cross and his coauthor Fhagen-Smith do not believe that racial identity development and ego identity development are one and the same phenomenon, although both phenomena are likely to evolve across the life span and to interact during adolescence when identity dilemmas are understood to be especially acute (see Cross and Fhagen-Smith

1996; Cross, Strauss, and Fhagen-Smith 1999; Cross and Fhagen-Smith, this volume). A Black person's *Nigrescence* is determined by his or her having gone through a specific encounter and redirection of racial identity (that is, a process of *Nigrescence*) rather than by a foreclosed, diffused moratorium or achieved dimensions of ego identity (that is, the processes of ego identity development common to all groups) (Cross and Fhagen-Smith 1996:120 and this volume).

Having argued that they "in no way" believe that "the search for the link between Nigrescence theory and generic models of human [ego] development should be abandoned" (1996:118 and this volume), Cross and Fhagen-Smith intertwine *Nigrescence*, which is *"not a generic* model" and which reveals nuances *"unique* to the experiences of Black people," with an Eriksonian map for "the unfolding of any Black person's [ego] identity from one status to the next, independent of any [*Nigrescence*] content of that identity" (1996:111, 121, my italics and brackets). Their acknowledgment that Cross's model of *Nigrescence* and Jackson's model of Black Identity Development have proven foundational for Asian American, feminist, and gay and lesbian models of identity development (1996:111) suggests that in Cross's view, generic developmental processes (dimensions of social and of ego identity), as well as cultural factors unique to specific groups may be almost inextricably intertwined. The comprehensive view offered by Cross and Fhagen-Smith in this volume illustrates the complex interplay of the dimensions of social identity (including but not limited to *Nigrescence*), of ego identity (taken as a human "generic"), and of unique individual factors such as socialization, temperament, and beliefs.

Nonetheless, core generic processes do surface in Cross's substantially revised model (Cross, Strauss, and Fhagen-Smith 1999 and this volume). First, Cross retains the two features that characterized his early foundational *Nigrescence* model and the early work of Jackson, namely *transformed consciousness* and *redefinition*, although now substantially modified by many sources of variability. Second, in their more recent life span approach to variability among Black identity profiles, Cross and Fhagen-Smith note "the dual themes of identity development and identity variability" (1996:121) characterized by sequences, recycling, and interaction of *Nigrescence* stages with ego identity sectors across the lifespan (Cross and Fhagen-Smith 1996 and this volume). I see this as a core generic developmental process and term it *interactions between racial and ego identity processes*. They also attend to the role played by what I consider to be core *racial identity functions* (which they specifically identify as buffering, bonding, bridging, code switching, and individualism)(Cross, Strauss, and Fhagen-Smith 1999; Cross and Fhagen-Smith, this volume).

Summary

Briefly to recapitulate and before going on to a discussion of selected panethnic identity development models: I am identifying five core generic processes grounded in the racial identity development models of Jackson and Cross. The first two are processes of Black identity development applicable to other racially targeted as well as agent identities:

- transformed consciousness,
- redefinition.

The third,

- parallel developmental tasks,

refers to the parallel processes of Black and White target and agent identity development conceptualized within a general oppression-liberation paradigm (Hardiman and Jackson 1997; Hardiman 1982, 1994; Helms 1990, 1995). It is also taken to refer to the parallel processes of Black, Asian American, and other targeted ethnic identity development (Kim 1981).

The fourth and fifth generalizable features include the interactions of *Nigrescence* with lifespan sectors of ego identity, and the functions of buffering, bonding, bridging, code switching, and individualism served by racial identity.

These last two I term

- *interactions between racial and ego identity processes,*
- racial identity functions.

Meanwhile, it is critical to temper these core generic processes with a caution grounded in the many areas of variability within any one racial or ethnic profile, as well as the substantial differences that exist between similarly situated racial and ethnic groups.

II: Models of Ethnic Identity Development

Since this chapter cannot presume to represent the range and complexity of current writings on ethnic identity development, I limit my focus here to instances drawn from models of Asian American and Latino ethnic identities that seem best to illustrate or elaborate the core generic processes noted above.

I have already described how Kim's model of Asian American identity development adapts Jackson's approach by renaming the "ethnic awareness" stage as its developmental starting point and acknowledging the historical impact of the civil rights movement on the panethnic awareness of her Asian American subjects. Kim modifies the model of Black identity development to represent more accurately the identity processes experienced by a specific cultural and historical cohort of Asian Americans. She also delineates their conflicts with internalized White racism as they create a new panethnic Asian American identity. Kim writes within the intellectual framework of Racial Identity Development (Hardiman and Jackson 1997, 1992; Jackson 1976; Hardiman 1994) which combines principles of developmental and social psychology with a sociological approach to the dynamics of systemic oppression.

Whereas Kim interweaves ethnic awareness with the impact of racism upon the construction of a panethnic Asian American identity, other theorists work within different conceptual frameworks (Root 1997; Gupta 1997; Spickard 1997; Sodowsky, Kwan, and Pannu 1995). These writers take ethnicity as their operative term, to signify the primacy of culture, religion, and language, while acknowledging "*unfortunately*, the fact that race has assumed a synonymity with ethnicity and culture in this country" (Root 1997:29, my italics). A recurrent theme in the ethnic identity literature is the reassertion of ethnic pride in the face of historic legacies of racism. Examples include the "double identity" experienced by Nisei children who may feel and speak Japanese at home, while learning to be American and use English at school (Takaki 1989:212–230); this suggests the "double consciousness" described by W. E. B. Du Bois speaking as an African American. Other layers of cultural complexity emerge with multiple targeted social identities (Root 2000), such as gay Latino adolescents who feel marginalized by both the gay and Latino communities (Casas and Pytluk 1995; for Asian American and African American parallels, see Chan 1995, 1989; Lachine 1989; Bodkin 1996) or Ambrosian children whose status may be marginalized by both the White and Asian communities (Root 1997:30–31; Gupta 1997; Spickard 1997; Alexander 1994).

Like Asian American identity, Latino identity is a panethnic product of the struggles shared by various Spanish-speaking ethnic and racial groups born of different national and cultural traditions, who have nonetheless organized to maintain their panethnicity and linguistic culture against the encroachments of Anglo hegemony and English-only practices (Barrera 1997; Santos 1997; Lopez and Espiritu [1990] 1997; Arce 1981; Estrada et al. 1981). In her intergenerational study of Mexicans, Mexican Americans, and Chicanos (each presented as a generationally distinctive ethnic entity), Aida Hurtado and coauthors (Hurtado, Gurin, and Peng 1994) describe the impact upon identity of pervasive negative stereotypes and daily hostilities experienced by immigrant Mexicans and their Mexican American children. By the second U.S.-born generation, political activism and transformed consciousness come together to form a new *Chicano* panethnic identity, redefined from an insult into a term of pride and defiance, and similar in transformative effect to Black Pride and Black Power.

Chicano identity development also includes unique dimensions of colonial, ethnic, and class status. However, like the other racial identities, it critiques the dominant culture which leads to transformed consciousness and a redefined and cohesive panethnic identity. This identity is based upon the cleansing of internalized subordination and redirection toward specific ingredients of Mexican culture and language. In this sense, the processes underlying Chicano identity development can be said to parallel those of Black identity as described by Jackson and Cross, and Asian American identity as described by Kim. Similar processes appear in the development of a panethnic Latino identity out of grassroots organizing that crosses but also coexists with the "more core national-origin ethnicities" of Puerto Ricans and Chicanos in American cities (Santos 1997:213; Lopez and Espiritu [1990] 1997).

The new Chicano panethnic identity emerges as "a new sense of self that [is] neither oriented to Mexico nor an assimilated American" (Hurtado, Gurin, and Peng 1994:132–133; also see Alvarez 1973). It is a historically specific and culturally unique "emergent reaction to the situation in the receiving country" based upon a shared but contested history of discrimination, exclusion, negative labeling, and stereotypes (Hurtado, Gurin, and Peng 1994:148). In a manner similar to Hayes-Bautista's (1974) "dis-assimilation" construct, Chicano identity evolves out of an awareness of group-based discrimination that "is more, not less, widespread the longer persons of Mexican descent have lived in the United States" (Hurtado, Gurin, and Peng 1994:149).

Hurtado and her coauthors (Hurtado 1997; Hurtado, Gurin, and Peng 1994) arrive at their analysis of Chicano identity from a framework that is distinct from, although compatible with, the racial identity development tradition of Cross and Jackson, Hardiman and Kim. They use Social Identity Theory (Hogg 1995; Abrams 1992; Abrams and Hogg 1990; Tajfel 1978, 1981; Tajfel and Turner 1979) which, like the Hardiman-Jackson oppression-liberation paradigm (1997), describes the macrodynamics that maintain intergroup relations of domination and subordination. However, unlike Jackson they do not use a developmental model to examine the microprocesses of racial identity transformations in the development of the individual.[10]

Within the larger social hierarchy highlighted by Social Identity Theory, the macrodynamics of unequal group interaction include social categorization (the tendency to categorize people into distinctive social groups), social comparison (the tendency to perceive, evaluate, and rank socially categorized groups relative to each other), and psychological work (the tendency to desire and work toward a positive sense of distinctiveness and self-worth). This conceptual framework leads Hurtado and her coauthors to observe that these racial identities most likely to prove "most problematic for a sense of positive distinctiveness—ones that are disparaged, memberships that have to be negotiated frequently because they are visible to others, ones that have become politicized by social movements" are the very identities people are likely to pay most attention to and that are most likely to have salience across social interactions (Hurtado, Gurin, and Peng 1994:132). They are of course the targeted racial identities also described in the models of Jackson, Cross, and Kim.

Hurtado and Gurin (1995) analyze the processes by which Chicano identity became politicized during the late 1960s and 1970s, focusing especially upon ways in which members of subordinated groups managed to achieve positive distinctiveness. One strategy highlighted in their work involves transforming the terms of comparison with the dominant group from negative to positive: "Political consciousness arises as members reinterpret and affirm the previously denigrated identity. This new consciousness also provides motivation for collective action to change group inequalities" (Hurtado and Gurin 1995:93). This seems another way of expressing the core generic processes of *transformed consciousness* and *redefinition*; it also parallels "decolonization" (Fanon 1963; Memmi 1965), "identity transformation" (Hall, Freedle, and Cross 1972), and "dis-assimilation" (Hayes-Bautista 1974). Early on the Sherifs (1970) had noted that this process was characteristic of the Black social movements. The Sherifs (1970), with Tajfel (1978), were among the originating theorists of Social Identity Theory.

Other ethnic identity theorists, working outside the Social Identity Theory and the Racial Identity Development traditions, focus attention upon the historical struggles and processes that give rise to Latino identity as a panethnic label for otherwise ethnically diverse peoples of Mexican, Cuban, and Puerto Rican descent, all of whom nonetheless understand themselves to be similarly situated as colonized, stigmatized, "dually identified" peoples within the United States. Rivera-Santiago (1996), for example, examines both the consciousness of oppression that stimulates personal and social movements toward transformation and redefinition, and the acculturation processes that give rise to bicultural Latino self-definitions. These bicultural variables include factors such as degree of bilingual or monolingualism; mode of family affiliation, and school, neighborhood, and work acculturation; and repertoires of cultural values that enable the Latino person to function effectively in the two adjacent Spanish- and English-speaking cultures.

For example, an immigrant Mexican woman might incorporate what she understands to be an Anglo gender role in the workplace while maintaining her traditional role at home with her family, while her more Americanized daughter, who identifies herself as Latina, might embrace a feminist identity that is consistent across the contexts of home, work, and school (Casas and Pytluk 1995). This approach ("acculturation") differs in important ways from a developmental approach that might hypothesize the experiences and contradictions, transitions and stages that would characterize the changes over time in the racial identities of such a woman and her daughter.

The challenges inherent in various bi- or multicultural identities are readily apparent in discussions of colonized and/or immigrant communities, whether of Latino, African, Asian American, Asian Indian American, or American Indian descent, and on the basis of gender oppression, social status, and economic class, racism, and language. For example, a young Indian American woman may define herself as 100 percent American and 100 percent Asian Indian, while her best friend may feel forced to make choices between her family's religious beliefs and cultural values and those of the dominant Anglo culture (Sodowsky, Kwan, and Pannu 1995). An African American woman may feel alienated both by the sexism she experiences in the Black community and the racism she experiences among White feminists (Reynolds and Pope 1991).

There is a prevailing emphasis in current social identity discourse on the uniqueness of specific racial and ethnic group experiences, and on the multidimensionality of their interactions—whether multiethnic and multiracial, or among the different internal dimensions of social identity. This emphasis encourages the development and parochialism of "identity development models that are specific to each group, resulting in as many identity development models as there are ethnic and racial groups" (Cross and Fhagen-Smith 1996:109). Thus despite the understandable recent tendency to emphasize uniqueness, variability, multidimensionality, and cultural specificity at the expense of across-group commonalities, a few panethnic and panracial theorists have focused attention upon core developmental processes they consider to be generic for racially targeted ethnic groups. It is to these explicitly panethnic and panracial models that I now turn.

III: Generic Models of Panethnic or Panracial Identity

Jean Phinney's Model of Ethnic Identity is one of the more widely cited research-based panethnic identity development models in the social psychology literature (1996a, 1996b; 1993, 1991, 1989) and is discussed elsewhere in this volume (chapter by Cross and Fhagen-Smith). It presents racial identity development stages (derived from Cross) in the context of ego identity development statuses (derived from Erikson 1968, 1956; Marcia et al. 1993; Marcia 1966). Phinney's research subjects are primarily adolescents and young adults for whom identity issues are especially salient, and who, if they also identify as members of targeted ethnic groups, are more likely than not to focus on ethnic identity issues during adolescence (Aries and Moorehead 1989). But this is not to say that the two dimensions constitute one and the same thing, or that foreclosed, diffused moratorium or achieved adolescent ego identity statuses necessarily correspond in a one-to-one relationship to stages of racial identity development (see Cross and Fhagen-Smith 1996 and this volume, and note 9 above).

Recently, Phinney has suggested that ego identity statuses and racial identity stages may develop in tandem rather than unidimensionally: "ethnic identity shows a developmental sequence *similar to* that identified for ego identity" (Phinney et al. 1994:169, my emphasis). In this looser formulation of their interrelationship, her position appears closer to that of racial identity theorists such as Cross and Helms, although Helms takes strong issue with Phinney on definitional issues of race versus ethnicity. Phinney asks, "When We Talk about American Ethnic Groups, What Do We Mean?" (1996a) and answers that we do *not* mean race "because of the wide disagreement on its meanings and usage for psychology" (1996a:918). *Ethnicity* can refer equivalently to "both race and culture of origin," meaning both the subjective sense of ethnic identity and "experiences associated with minority status, including powerlessness, discrimination, and prejudice" (1996a:919).

Not surprisingly, Helms counter argues that "Race Is Not Ethnicity" and that ethnicity has "no real meaning apart from its status as a proxy for racial classification or immigrant status" (Helms and Talleyrand 1997:1246). Calling *race* by any other name "does not change its sociopolitical implications" nor does it change its significance for people who survive "in environments that differentially value or devalue their ascribed racial characteristics" (Helms 1994:298). Similar points have been made by other researchers about the impact of racism on Asian Americans (Takaki 1989; Kim 1981) and Latinos (Darder, Torres, and Gutiérrez 1997; Nieto 1996; Arce 1981; Estrada et al. 1981). It is interesting in this regard that Phinney uses the language "ethnic groups of color" (1996a:923) to illuminate the prejudice, discrimination, and exploitation, that is, the *racism* that African, Asian, Native American and Latino communities encounter.

The semantic issues at stake here are not trivial and appear irreconcilable (most recently, see Spickard and Burroughs 2000, Pierce 2000).

Helms stresses the importance of *racial* group membership as a core dimension of identity development because of "th[is] country's emphasis on racial markers" (1994:286). She urges a *panracial* approach, based on her view that "the *process* by which identity development occurs is similar across racial groups" despite differences of *content* based on relative sociopolitical power as well as "perceived race" (1994:286). Thus, all Americans experience processes of racial identity development based on their location relative to each other in the racial hierarchy and based on their "differential socialization due to racial (rather than ethnic) classification as well as differential reactions to that socialization" (Helms 1995:183).

It follows that Helms's model emphasizes parallel developmental tasks. For peoples of color, the central developmental task is to overcome internalized racial subordination and redefine "an identity with its roots in the culture and sociopolitical experiences of their socially ascribed racial group," whereas for Whites the central tasks are "the recognition and abandonment of internalized White privilege and the creation of a nonracist, self-defining White identity" (Helms 1994:301; 1995:184, 189). Helms's account resembles the parallel developmental tasks for Whites and Blacks detailed in the work of Hardiman and Jackson (1992; Hardiman 1994).

There are other explicitly *panracial* or *panethnic* identity development models that follow the foundational Black identity development models described earlier (Cross 1971; Jackson 1976). These multigroup models take the view, similar to Helms's, that "the once biological and now social meanings and beliefs associated with racial group membership supersede ethnic group membership"; that persons from diverse ethnic groups share similar patterns of "racial, ethnic, and/or cultural oppression"; and that decades of political activism have led to the emergence of "cultural oppression as the common unifying force" (Casas and Pytluk 1995:164, 165; Sue 1990). This, for example, is the perspective taken by the Minority Identity Development Model (Atkinson, Morten, and Sue 1979, 1998) which adapts the processes of Black identity development "to other minority groups, due to their shared experience of oppression" (1979:193).

The result is an avowedly generic panracial model based upon five relatively simplified stages of development that "oppressed people may experience as they come to understand themselves in terms of their own minority culture, the dominant culture, and the oppressive relationship" between them (Atkinson, Morten, and Sue 1979:194). This model has been recently recast (Atkinson, Morten, and Sue 1998) as a multidimensional framework that takes into account some of the complexities and contradictions of various targeted racial and ethnic identities.

IV: Core Developmental Processes

I am proposing an approach to racial and ethnic identity development that identifies core generic developmental processes while also acknowledging sources of variability within and between groups and individuals. These core processes arguably hold true across racial and ethnic identity groups based on their similar experiences of domination or subordination in an unequal social hierarchy. Several of these processes derive specifically from the race-based subjugation experienced by non-White peoples of various ethnicities in the United States. *Transformed consciousness* and *redefinition* are two terms that help capture the core generic processes by which members of subordinated groups affirm their own identity against cultural imperialism and social exploitation by the dominant cultures. These processes point to the *parallel developmental tasks* for members of both dominant and subordinate groups, which have to do with establishing new identities not based on internalized domination or internalized subordination. As one imagines a society without racism and without ethnocentrism, one can also imagine racial and ethnic identity development processes under different historical conditions that are directed toward new, as yet unknown, developmental goals.

These first three core generic processes, derived primarily from the work of Jackson, have sharpened the awareness of other writers toward the levels at which "individuals play a variety of roles in a multilayered and dynamic script" based upon their "dominant and subordinate social roles" across an array of agent or target social identities (Hardiman and Jackson 1997:16). The fourth and fifth processes, derived from Cross, are psychological. They describe *the interactions between racial and ego identity processes,* and *the racial identity functions* of bonding, buffering, bridging, code switching, and individualism.

Each of these five core generic developmental processes, along with the concomitant constraints of historical context and cultural and individual variability, may be extended beyond the discussion of race and ethnicity in this chapter and applied to other dimensions of social identity such as gender, class, and sexuality. The likelihood of such beyond-race generalizability has been predicted by Hardiman and Jackson (1997) and is also assumed by Social Identity theorists. As of this writing, adaptations of these generic processes appear in the literature on feminist identity development (Bargad and Hyde 1991; McNamara and Rickard 1989; Gurin and Markus 1989; Gurin and Townsend 1986; Downing and Roush 1985; Sherif 1982); on sexual identity development (Cox and Gallois 1996; Cass 1996, 1984; D'Augelli 1994; Sophie 1985–86); on class (Russell 1996); and on the interactions between them (Frable 1997). Most recently Root (2000: 211) has identified similarities across racial identity models that overlap with what I identify here (2000:211–216). Further research will be needed to test these areas of generalizability.

In my view, the explicitly panethnic and panracial identity development models reviewed in this chapter (Phinney 1993, 1996a, 1996b; Atkinson, Morten, and Sue 1998) are limited by their emphasis on across-group generalizability at the expense of variability within specific cultural groups and individual profiles. If sufficient attention is paid to and research conducted on these factors, might we someday be able to disentangle the core generic dimensions of social identity development from their unique or idiosyncratic historical or cultural features? The answer, I believe, is yes.

Patricia Hill Collins (1991, 1993) has argued for "new categories of analysis that are inclusive of race, class, and gender as distinctive yet interlocking structures of oppression" (1993:26), an argument that should be extended to other domains of social identity. She illustrates the coordination of multiple and sometimes contradictory agent/target identities in her everyday experience as college professor and mother, as employer and employee, as African American and female. The endeavor to coordinate multiple identities is especially enticing if one can also theorize a cluster of core generic developmental processes that characterize each of these multidimensional aspects of a person's composite identity.

Not only do race, class, and gender each constitute social categories that are analytically separate yet coordinated in everyday experience; race, class, and gender are similarly characterized by social hierarchies of domination and subordination. Specific analyses of race, class, and gender would then combine elements of individual, cultural, and historical variability with core generic processes derived from stratification and inequality. As Collins writes, to coordinate these categories of social experience without distorting them, one must maintain a "tension between the *specificity* needed to study the workings of race, class, and gender" and the *"generalizations* about these systems created by cross-cultural and transhistorical research (1991:224, my italics).

Race and ethnicity are likely to remain significant cultural forces that shape American life, organize social relationships, and anchor personal as well as group identity, meaning making, and orientation. Racism and ethnocentrism are also likely to continue to affect identity development for all persons born in as well as immigrating to the United States. It is arguable that for the foreseeable future racial and ethnic identity development will be characterized by core generic processes described in the foundational racial identity models, according to which members of devalued communities transform their consciousness of themselves and redefine their terms of negative social comparison through reaffirmations of pride and empowerment. The personal and social transformations inherent in racial identity development as we understand them today are likely to remain, as they have in the past, the preconditions for activism and social change in the future.

NOTES

1. Cross considers Lewin's influence on early conceptions of Black identity in his chapter "Landmark Studies of Negro Identity" (*Shades of Black* [1991]). For the question, "Who is a Jew?" see Petersen (1997), Hartman and Hartman (1999), and Spickard and Burroughs (2000:2) who locate Jewish identity in the belief more than the fact of common descent. Concerning the specific racial context of the United States, Kaye/Kantrowitz observes that "*Jewish* is both a distinct category and an overlapping one. . . . The problem is a polarization of white and color that excludes us. We need a more complex vision of the structure of racism . . . [and] the process of 'whitening'" (1996:125).

2. Lopez and Espiritu define *panethnicity* as "the development of bridging organizations and solidarities among subgroups of ethnic collectivities that are often seen as homogeneous by outsiders" ([1990] 1997:195). They also

note that "when subgroups 'look alike' from the perspective of the outside, they experience a powerful force for panethnic solidarity" ([1990] 1997:199). This involves "the discovery by a group of people that they constitute a category in the minds of others that has not previously existed in their own system of classification" and "that they had not previously recognized as including themselves" (Cornell 2000:98). Takaki (1989) describes Japanese and Filipino immigrants' efforts to preserve their ethnic cultures in the face of the Anglo majority's attributions of racial homogeneity based on skin color, physiognomy, and accented speech. "Racial lumping" is the term for this phenomenon used by Lopez and Espiritu ([1990] 1997:199).

3. American cultural historians have described how White ethnics of European descent assimilated and exchanged their ethnically distinctive cultural and linguistic practices for a newly forged "American," "White," and English-speaking identity (Spickard and Burroughs 2000; Clark and O'Donnell 1999; Brodkin 1998; Ignatiev 1995; Roediger 1991), whereas Americans of African, Asian, Latino, and Native ancestry understood that "No matter how much like us you are, you will remain apart" (Steinberg 1989:42; Takaki 1993). Not only did White Europeans generally enter the American racial hierarchy on a higher rung than that occupied by Black Americans whether slave or free, but they also maintained their superior position over people of Asian or Latino ethnicities who entered as immigrants or were colonized by the southward and westward expansions of U.S. borders during the nineteenth century. Omi and Winant use the term *"racialization* to signify this extension of racial meaning to previously racially unclassified relationships" (1986:64). They include the evolution of the racial category "Black" coincident with race-based slavery for Africans whose original group affiliations were Ibo, Yoruba, or Fulani (1986:64; Spickard and Burroughs 2000). Torres and Ngin (1995) find these concepts useful in understanding the extension of "racial meaning" to non-European native, colonized, and/or immigrant groups whose initial understandings of themselves were ethnic, not racial. But see Cornell (2000), Choney, Berryhill-Paapke, and Robbins (1995), and Herring (1994) for the distinction between tribal and racial identity made by some American Indian peoples.

4. Rodriguez (1989) illustrates the conceptual difficulty:

Puerto Ricans were both an ethnic group and more than one racial group. Within the U.S. perspective, Puerto Ricans, racially speaking, belonged to both groups; however, ethnically they belonged to neither. . . . Puerto Ricans were White and Black; Puerto Ricans were neither White nor Black. . . . This apparent contradiction can best be understood through an examination of the contrasting racial ambiences and histories of the United States and Puerto Rico at the time of the "great migration."(Quoted in Falcón 1995:197–198)

The historical complexities of "racial formation" described in note 3 are also played out in changing racial (religious) designations for Jews, Irish Catholics, and Indian Hindu and Muslim immigrants.

5. I use the terms *domination* and *subordination* as introduced by Miller (1976) and elaborated by Hardiman and Jackson (1992, 1997). For internalized domination and subordination, see Lipsky (1977) and Hardiman and Jackson (1992, 1997).

6. Cross highlights this transformation (which he calls a "Negro-to-Black" conversion) by naming the first two stages of his *Nigrescence* model "Pre-Encounter" and "Encounter." Jackson, somewhat differently, emphasizes the "transitions" by which a person enters or exits each racial identity developmental stage. These transitions occur as a person's stage-related worldview becomes "illogical, or contradicted by new experiences and information" (Jackson, this volume).

7. For a reader familiar with Erikson's model of ego identity development (1956, 1968), much of the language in this discussion will have special resonance. Jackson and Cross emphasize the formative influence on their early models of Fanon (1963), Memmi (1965), and Freire (1970) in helping them conceptualize racial identity conversion, redirection, and transformation in the context of White hegemonic social structures. Erikson would not have helped them distinguish between various dimensions of identity such as ego identity and social identity, or between the various dimensions of social identity such as racial and sexual identity. In addition, the impact upon one's social identity posed by pervasive and cumulative experiences of domination and subordination in one's racial environment is not adequately elaborated in Erikson's account of ego identity (except for his problematic but also intriguing discussions of "negative identity" among Blacks in 1956 and 1968).

Yet Erikson's notions of "identity" and "development" were much in the air (Gleason 1983; Hoare 1991) and they were in need of elaboration from precisely the perspective that racial identity developmentalists and Social Identity Theorists have since provided. Racial identity developmentalists such as Kim (1981), Hardiman (1982), Cross (Cross and Fhagan-Smith 1996 and this volume; Cross, Strauss, and Fhagen-Smith 1999), and Phinney (1989, 1991, 1993, 1996a, 1996b) discuss the place of the ego identity construct in their own constructions of racial identity. Tatum (1999) notes that it was Erikson "who introduced the notion that the social, cultural, and historical context *is the ground in which individual identity is embedded*" (59, my italics) and quotes the following statement: "We deal with a process 'located' *in the core of the individual* and yet also *in the core of his* [or her] *communal culture* . . . by which the individual judges [her or] himself in the light of what he perceives to be the way in which others judge him in comparison to themselves and to a typology significant to them" (quoted from 1968:22, Erikson's italics).

8. I have found the following accounts of the oppression-liberation paradigm especially helpful: Bell (1997), Hardiman and Jackson (1997), and Young (1990). Two of Young's five criteria of oppression, *marginalization* and *cultural imperialism*, match the situation of target identity statuses.

9. Other theorists have overstated the interactions that may occur within adolescence between racial identity development and the "identity crisis" (as introduced by Erikson 1968; Marcia 1966: Marcia et al. 1993) as if to construe these two processes within one and the same phenomenon (Phinney 1991, 1993; Phinney et al. 1994; Aries and Moorehead 1989; see Cross and Fhagen-Smith 1996 and this volume). The coordination (discussed in Part III below) of domains of social identity (such as race, gender, or sexual orientation) and ego identity developmental processes from within different domains of the self is not much discussed in the ego identity literature, but does appear in substantial discussions by Tajfel (1982), Hogg and Abrams (1988), Cross (1991), Abrams (1992), Liebkind (1992), and Turner et al. (1994), Hurtado (1996), Tatum (1997:18-28), Jackson and Smith (1999). A handbook on ego identity (Marcia et al. 1993) has entries on gender identity but nothing in the contents or the index on ethnic or racial identity.

10. "Social identity theory is framed by an assumption that society is hierarchically structured into different social groups that stand in power and status relations to one another" (Hogg 1995:555). These groups provide members with a social identity, which involves one's self-conception as a group member: "'the individual's knowledge that he/she belongs to certain social groups together with some emotional and value significance to him/he · of the group membership" (Tajfel 1972, quoted in Abrams 1992:58; see Tajfel 1981; Abrams and Hogg 1990; Hogg 1995; Jackson and Smith 1999).

REFERENCES

Abrams, Dominic. 1992. "Processes of Social Identification." Pp. 57–99 in *Social Psychology of Identity and the Self Concept*, ed. G. M. Breakwell. London: Surrey University Press.

Abrams, Dominic, and Michael A. Hogg, eds. 1990. *Social Identity Theory: Constructive and Critical Advances*. New York: Springer-Verlag.

Alexander, Sarah. 1994. "Vietnamese Amerasians: Dilemmas of Individual Identity and Family Cohesion." Pp. 198–216 in *Race, Ethnicity and Self: Identity in Multicultural Perspective*, ed. E. P. Salett and D. R. Koslow. Washington, D.C.: National MultiCultural Institute.

Alvarez, Rodolfo. 1973. "The Psycho-Historical and Socioeconomic Development of the Chicano Community in the United States." *Social Science Quarterly* 53:920–942.

Arce, Carlos H. 1981. "A Reconsideration of Chicano Culture and Identity." *Daedalus* 110(2):177–191.

Aries, Elizabeth, and Kimberley Moorehead. 1989. "The Importance of Ethnicity in the Development of Identity of Black Adolescents." *Psychological Reports* 65:75–82.

Atkinson, Donald R., George Morten, and Derald Wing Sue. 1979. *Counseling American Minorities: A Cross-Cultural Perspective.* Dubuque, Iowa: William C. Brown.

———. 1998. *Counseling American Minorities: A Cross-Cultural Perspective.* 5th ed. Boston: McGraw Hill.

Banks, R. Richard, and Jennifer L. Eberhardt. 1998. "Social Psychological Processes and the Legal Bases of Racial Categorization." Pp. 54–75 in *Confronting Racism: The Problem and the Response*, ed. J. L. Eberhardt and S. T Fiske. Thousand Oaks, Calif.: Sage.

Bargad, Adena, and Janet Shibley Hyde. 1991. "Women's Studies: A Study of Feminist Identity Development in Women." *Psychology of Women Quarterly* 15:181–201.

Barrera, Mario. 1997. "A Theory of Racial Inequality." Pp. 3–44 in *Latinos and Education: A Critical Reader*, ed. A. Darder, R. D. Torres, and H. Gutiérrez. New York: Routledge.

Bell, Lee Anne. 1997. "Theoretical Foundations for Social Justice Education." Pp. 3–15 in *Teaching for Diversity and Social Justice: A Sourcebook*, ed. M. Adams, L. A. Bell, and P. Griffin. New York: Routledge.

Bernal, Martha E., and George P. Knight, eds. 1993. *Ethnic Identity: Formation and Transmission among Hispanics and Other Minorities.* Albany: State University of New York Press.

Bodkin, Keith. 1996. *One More River to Cross: Black and Gay in America.* New York: Doubleday Anchor.

Brodkin, Karen. 1998. *How Jews Became White Folks and What That Says about Race in America.* New Brunswick, N.J.: Rutgers University Press.

Casas, J. Manuel, and Scott D. Pytluk. 1995. "Hispanic Identity Development: Implications for Research and Practice." Pp. 155–180 in *Handbook of Multicultural Counseling*, ed. J. G. Ponterotto, J. M. Casas, L. A. Suzuki, and C. M. Alexander. Thousand Oaks, Calif.: Sage.

Cass, Vivienne C. 1984. "Homosexual Identity Formation: Testing a Theoretical Model." *Journal of Sex Research* 20(2):143–167.

———. 1996. "Sexual Orientation Identity Formation: A Western Phenomenon." Pp. 227–251 in *Textbook of Homosexuality and Mental Health*, ed. R. P. Cabaj and T. S. Stein. Washington, D.C.: American Psychiatric Press.

Chan, Connie S. 1989. "Issues of Identity Development among Asian-American Lesbians and Gay Men." *Journal of Counseling and Development* 68 (September/October):16–20.

———. 1995. "Issues of Sexual Identity in an Ethnic Minority: The Case of Chinese American Lesbians, Gay Men, and Bisexual People." Pp. 87–101 in *Lesbian, Gay, and Bisexual Identities over the Linesman: Psychological Perspectives*, ed. A. R. D'Augelli and C. J. Patterson. New York: Oxford University Press.

Choney, Sandra K., Elisa Berryhill-Paapke, and Rockey R. Robbins. 1995. "The Acculturation of American Indians: Developing Frameworks for Research and Practice." Pp. 73–92 in *Handbook of Multicultural Counseling*, ed. J. G. Ponterotto, J. M. Casas, L. A. Suzuki, and C. M. Alexander. Thousand Oaks, Calif.: Sage.

Clark, Christine, and James O'Donnell, eds. 1999. *Becoming and Unbecoming White: Owning and Disowning a Racial Identity*. Westport, Conn.: Bergin and Garvey.

Collins, Patricia Hill. 1991. *Black Feminist Thought: Knowledge, Consciousness, and the Politics of Empowerment*. New York: Routledge.

———. 1993. "Toward a New Vision: Race, Class, and Gender as Categories of Analysis and Connection." *Race, Sex and Class* 1(1):25–45.

Cornell, Stephen. 2000. "Discovered Identities and American Indian Supratribalism." Pp. 98–123 in *We Are a People: Narrative and Multiplicity in Constructing Ethnic Identity*, ed. P. Spickard and W. J. Burroughs. Philadelphia: Temple University Press.

Cox, Stephen, and Cynthia Gallois. 1996. "Gay and Lesbian Identity Development: A Social Identity Approach." *Journal of Homosexuality* 30(4):1–30.

Cross, William E., Jr. 1971. "The Negro-to-Black Conversion Experience: Toward a Psychology of Black Liberation." *Black World* 20(9):13–27.

———. 1985. "Black Identity: Rediscovering the distinction between Personal identity and Reference Group Orientation." Pp. 155–171 in *Beginnings: The Social And Affective Development of Black Children*, ed. M. B. Spencer, G. K. Brookins, and W. R. Allen. Hillsdale, N.J.: Lawrence Erlbaum.

———. 1991. *Shades of Black: Diversity in African-American Identity*. Philadelphia: Temple University Press.

Cross, William E., Jr., and Peony Fhagen-Smith. 1996. "Nigrescence and Ego Identity Development: Accounting for Differential Black Identity Patterns." Pp. 108–123 in *Counseling Across Cultures*, ed. P. B. Pedersen, J. G. Draguns, W. J. Lonner, and J. E. Trimble. Thousand Oaks, Calif.: Sage.

Cross, William E., Jr., Linda Strauss, and Peony Fhagen-Smith. 1999. "African American Identity Development across the Life Span: Educational Implications." Pp. 29–47 in *Racial and Ethnic Identity in School Practices: Aspects of Human Development*, ed. R. H. Sheets and E. R. Hollins. Hillsdale, N.J.: Lawrence Erlbaum.

Darder, Antonia, Rodolfo D. Torres, and Henry Gutiérrez, eds. 1997. *Latinos and Education: A Critical Reader*. New York: Routledge.

D'Augelli, Anthony R. 1994. "Identity Development and Sexual Orientation: Toward a Model of Lesbian, Gay, and Bisexual Development." Pp. 312–333 in *Human Diversity: Perspectives on People in Context*, ed. E. J. Trickett, R. J. Watts, and D. Birman. San Francisco: Jossey-Bass.

Dobbins, James E., and Judith H. Skillings. 1991. "The Utility of Race Labeling in Understanding Cultural Identity: A Conceptual Tool for the Social Science Practitioner." *Journal of Counseling and Development* 70(1):37–44.

Downing, Nancy E., and Kristin L. Roush. 1985. "From Passive Acceptance to Active Commitment: A Model of Feminist Identity Development for Women." *Counseling Psychologist* 13(4):695–709.

Erikson, Erik H. 1956. "The Problem of Ego Identity." *Journal of the American Psychoanalytic Association* 4:56–121.

———. 1968. *Identity: Youth and Crisis*. New York: W. W. Norton.

Estrada, Leobardo F., F. Chris Garcia, Reynaldo F. Macías, and Lionel Maldonado. 1981. "Chicanos in the United States: A History of Exploitation and Resistance." *Daedalus* 110(2):103–131.

Falcón, Angelo. 1995. "Puerto Ricans and the Politics of Racial Identity." Pp. 193–207 in *Racial and Ethnic Identity: Psychological Development and Creative Expression*, ed. H. W. Harris, H. C. Blue, and E. E. H. Griffith. New York: Routledge.

Fanon, Frantz. 1963. *The Wretched of the Earth*. New York: Grove.

Frable, Deborah E. S. 1997. "Gender, Racial, Ethnic, Sexual, and Class Identities." *Annual Review of Psychology* 48:139–162.

Freire, Paulo. 1970. *Pedagogy of the Oppressed*. New York: Seabury.

Gleason, Phillip. 1983. "Identifying Identity: A Semantic History." *Journal of American History* 69(4):910–931.

Greene, Beverly, ed. 1997. *Ethnic and Cultural Diversity among Lesbians and Gay Men*. Thousand Oaks, Calif.: Sage.

Gupta, Monisha Das. 1997. "'What Is Indian about You?' A Gendered, Transnational Approach to Ethnicity." *Gender and Society* 11(5):572–596.

Gurin, Patricia, and Hazel Markus. 1989. "Cognitive Consequences of Gender Identity." Pp. 152–172 in *The Social Identity of Women*, ed. S. Skevington and D. Baker. Thousand Oaks, Calif.: Sage.

Gurin, Patricia, and Aloen Townsend. 1986. "Properties of Gender Identity and Their Implications for Gender Consciousness." *British Journal of Social Psychology* 25(2):139–148.

Hall, William S., Roy Freedle, and William E. Cross, Jr. 1972. "Stages in the Development of Black Awareness: An Exploratory Investigation." Pp. 156–165 in *Black Psychology*, ed. R. L. Jones. New York: Harper and Row.

Haney López, Ian F. 1996. *White by Law: The Legal Construction of Race*. New York: New York University Press.

Hardiman, Rita. 1982. "White Identity Development: A Process Oriented

Model for Describing the Racial Consciousness of White Americans." Doctoral dissertation, Department of Education, University of Massachusetts, Amherst.

———. 1994. "White Identity Development in the United States." Pp. 117–140 in *Race, Ethnicity, and Self: Identity in Multicultural Perspective*, ed. E. P. Salett, and D. R. Koslow. Washington, D.C.: National MultiCultural Institute.

Hardiman, Rita, and Bailey W. Jackson. 1992. "Racial Identity Development: Understanding Racial Dynamics in College Classrooms and on Campus." Pp. 21–37 in *Promoting Diversity in College Classrooms: Innovative Responses for the Curriculum, Faculty, and Institutions*, ed. M. Adams. San Francisco: Jossey-Bass.

———. 1997. "Conceptual Foundations for Social Justice Courses." Pp. 16–29 in *Teaching for Diversity and Social Justice: A Sourcebook*, ed. M. Adams, L. A. Bell, and P. Griffin. New York: Routledge.

Harris, Herbert W., Howard C. Blue, and Ezra E. H. Griffith, eds. 1995. *Racial and Ethnic Identity: Psychological Development and Creative Expression*. New York: Routledge.

Hartman, Harriet, and Moshe Hartman. 1999. "Jewish Identity, Denomination, and Denominational Mobility." *Social Identities* 5(3):279–311.

Hayes-Bautista, David E. 1974. "Becoming Chicano: A 'Dis-Assimilation' Theory of Transformation of Ethnic Identity." Doctoral dissertation, Department of Sociology, University of California, San Francisco.

Helms, Janet E. 1990. *Black and White Racial Identity: Theory, Research, and Practice*. New York: Greenwood Press.

———. 1994. "The Conceptualization of Racial Identity and Other 'Racial' Constructs." Pp. 285–311 in *Human Diversity: Perspectives on People in Context*, ed. E. J. Trickett, R. J. Watts, and D. Birman. San Francisco: Jossey-Bass.

———. 1995. "An Update of Helms's White and People of Color Racial Identity Models." Pp. 181–198 in *Handbook of Multicultural Counseling*, ed. J. G. Ponterotto, J. M. Casas, L. A. Suzuki, and C. M. Alexander. Thousand Oaks, Calif.: Sage.

Helms, Janet E., and Regine M. Talleyrand. 1997. "Race Is Not Ethnicity." *American Psychologist* 52(11):1246–1247.

Herring, Roger. 1994. "Native American Indian Identity: A People of Many Peoples." Pp. 170–197 in *Race, Ethnicity, and Self: Identity in Multicultural Perspective*, ed. E. P. Salett and D. R. Koslow. Washington, D.C.: National MultiCultural Institute.

Hoare, Carol H. 1991. "Psychosocial Identity Development and Cultural Others." *Journal of Counseling and Development* 70:45–53.

Hogg, Michael A. 1995. "Social Identity Theory." Pp. 555–560 in *The Blackwell Encyclopedia of Social Psychology*, ed. A. S. R. Manstead and M. Hewstone. London: Blackwell.

Hogg, Michael A., and Dominic Abrams. 1988. *Social Identifications: A Social Psychology of Intergroup Relations and Group Processes.* New York: Routledge.

Hurtado, Aida. 1996. "Strategic Suspensions: Feminists of Color Theorize the Production of Knowledge." Pp. 372–392 in *Knowledge, Difference, and Power: Essays Inspired by Women's Ways of Knowing*, ed. N. R. Goldberger, J. M. Tarule, B. M. Clinchy, and M. F. Belenky. New York: Basic Books.

———. 1997. "Understanding Multiple Group Identities: Inserting Women into Cultural Transformations." *Journal of Social Issues* 53(2):299–328.

Hurtado, Aida, and Patricia Gurin. 1995. "Ethnic Identity and Bilingualism Attitudes." Pp. 89–103 in *Hispanic Psychology: Critical Issues in Theory and Research*, ed. A. M. Padilla. Thousand Oaks, Calif.: Sage.

Hurtado, Aida, Patricia Gurin, and Timothy Peng. 1994. "Social Identities—A Framework for Studying the Adaptations of Immigrants and Ethnics: The Adaptations of Mexicans to the United States." *Social Problems* 41(1):129–151.

Ignatiev, Noel. 1995. *How the Irish Became White.* New York: Routledge.

Jackson, Bailey W. 1976. "Black Identity Development." Pp. 158–164 in *Urban, Social, and Educational Issues*, ed. L. H. Golubchick and B. Persky. Dubuque, Iowa: Kendall/Hunt.

Jackson, Jay W., and Eliot R. Smith. 1999. "Conceptualizing Social Identity: A New Framework and Evidence for the Impact of Different Dimensions." *Personality and Social Psychology Bulletin* 25(1):120–135.

Kaye/Kantrowitz, Melanie. 1996. "Jews in the U.S.: The Rising Costs of Whiteness." Pp. 121–137 in *Names We Call Home: Autobiography on Racial Identity*, ed. B. Thompson and T. Sangeeta. New York: Routledge.

Keefe, Susan Emley. 1992. "Ethnic Identity: The Domain of Perceptions of and Attachment to Ethnic Groups and Cultures." *Human Organization* 51(1): 35–43.

Kim, Jean. 1981. "Processes of Asian American Identity Development: A Study of Japanese American Women's Perceptions of Their Struggle to Achieve Positive Identities." Doctoral dissertation, Department of Education, University of Massachusetts, Amherst.

Lachine, Darryl K. 1989. "Gay Identity Issues among Black Americans: Racism, Homophobia, and the Need for Validation." *Journal of Counseling and Development* 68(1):21–25.

Lewin, Kurt. 1941. "Jewish Self-Hatred." *Contemporary Jewish Record* 4:219–232.

Liebkind, Karmela. 1992. "Ethnic Identity—Challenging the Boundaries of Social Psychology." Pp. 147–185 in *Social Psychology Identity and the Self Concept*, ed. G. M. Breakwell. London: Surrey University Press.

Lipsky, S. 1977. "Internalized Oppression." *Black Re-Emergence* 2:5–10.

Lopez, David, and Yen Espiritu. [1990] 1997. "Panethnicity in the United States: A Theoretical Framework." Pp. 195–217 in *New American Destinies: A Reader in Contemporary Asian and Latino Immigration*, ed. D. Y. Hamamoto and R. D. Torres. New York: Routledge. First published in *Ethnic and Racial Studies* (1990) 13(2).

Marable, Manning. 1995. *Beyond Black and White: Transforming African-American Politics.* New York: Verso.

Marcia, James. 1966. "Development and Validation of Ego Identity Status." *Journal of Personality and Social Psychology* 3:551–558.

Marcia, James, Alan S. Waterman, David R. Matteson, Sally L. Archer, and Jacob L. Orlofsky. 1993. *Ego Identity: A Handbook of Psychosocial Research.* New York: Springer-Verlag.

McNamara, Kathleen, and Kathryn M. Rickard. 1989. "Feminist Identity Development: Implications for Feminist Therapy with Women." *Journal of Counseling and Development* 68:184–189.

Memmi, Albert. 1965. *The Colonizer and the Colonized.* Boston: Beacon Press.

Miller, Jean Baker. 1976. "Domination/Subordination." Pp. 3–12 in *Toward a New Psychology of Women.* Boston: Beacon Press.

Montagu, Ashley. 1997. *Man's Most Dangerous Myth: The Fallacy of Race.* Walnut Creek, Calif.: Altamira Press.

Nieto, Sonia. 1996. *Affirming Diversity: The Sociopolitical Context of MultiCultural Education.* 2d ed. White Plains, N.Y.: Longman.

Omi, Michael, and Howard Winant. 1986. *Racial Formation in the United States from the 1960s to the 1980s.* New York: Routledge.

Petersen, William. 1997. "Who is a Jew?" Pp. 223–242 in *Ethnicity Counts.* New Brunswick, N.J.: Transaction Publishers.

Phinney, Jean S. 1989. "Stages of Ethnic Identity Development in Minority Group Adolescents." *Journal of Early Adolescence* 9:34–49.

———. 1991. "Ethnic Identity and Self-Esteem: A Review and Integration." *Hispanic Journal of Behavioral Sciences* 13(2):198–208.

———. 1993. "A Three-Stage Model of Ethnic Identity Development in Adolescence." Pp. 61–79 in *Ethnic Identity: Formation and Transmission among Hispanics and Other Minorities,* ed. M. E. Bernal and G. P. Knight. Albany: State University of New York Press.

———. 1996a. "When We Talk about American Ethnic Groups, What Do We Mean?" *American Psychologist* 51(9):918–927.

———. 1996b. "Understanding Ethnic Diversity: The Role of Ethnic Identity." *American Behavioral Scientist* 40(2):143–152.

Phinney, Jean S., Stephanie DuPont, Carolina Espinosa, Jessica Revill, and Kay Sanders. 1994. "Ethnic Identity and American Identification among Ethnic Minority Youths." Pp. 167–183 in *Journeys into Cross-Cultural Psychology: Selected Papers from the Eleventh International Conference of the International Association for Cross-Cultural Psychology held in Liege, Belgium,* ed. A. Bouvy, F. Van de Vijver, P. Boski, and P. Schmitz. Berwyn, Pa.: Swets and Zeitlinger.

Pierce, Lori. 2000. "The Continuing Significance of Race." Pp. 221–228 in *We Are a People: Narrative and Multiplicity in Constructing Ethnic Identity*, ed. P. Spickard and W. J. Burroughs. Philadelphia: Temple University Press.

Reynolds, Amy L., and Raechele L. Pope. 1991. "The Complexities of Diversity: Exploring Multiple Oppressions." *Journal of Counseling and Development* 70:174–180.

Rivera-Santiago, Azara. 1996. "Understanding Latino Ethnic Identity Development." *New England Journal of Public Policy* 2(2):13–24.

Rodriguez, C. E. 1989. *Puerto Ricans: Born in the U.S.A.* Boston: Unwin Hyman. Quoted on pp. 197–198 in Angelo Falcón, "Puerto Ricans and the Politics of Racial Identity." Pp. 193–207 in *Racial and Ethnic Identity: Psychological Development and Creative Expression*, ed. H. W. Harris, H. C. Blue, and E. E. H. Griffith. New York: Routledge, 1995.

Roediger, David. 1991. *Wages of Whiteness: Race and the Making of the American Working Class*. New York: Verso.

Root, Maria P. P. 1997. "Multiracial Asians: Models of Ethnic Identity." *Amerasia Journal* 23(1):29–41.

———. 2000. "Rethinking Racial Identity Development." Pp. 205–220 in *We Are a People: Narrative and Multiplicity in Constructing Ethnic Identity*, ed. P. Spickard and W. J. Burroughs. Philadelphia: Temple University Press.

Russell, Glenda M. 1996. "Internalized Classism: The Role of Class in the Development of Self." *Women and Therapy* 18(3/4):59–71.

Salett, Elizabeth P., and Diane R. Koslow, eds. 1994. *Race, Ethnicity, and Self: Identity in Multicultural Perspective*. Washington, D.C.: National MultiCultural Institute.

Santos, Gonzalo. 1997. "¿Somos RUNAFRIBES? The Future of Latino Ethnicity in the Americas." Pp. 201–224 in *Latinos and Education: A Critical Reader*, ed. A. Darder, R. D. Torres, and H. Gutiérrez. New York: Routledge.

Sherif, Carolyn Wood. 1982. "Needed Concepts in the Study of Gender Identity." *Psychology of Women Quarterly* 6(4):375–398.

Sherif, Muzafer, and Carolyn W. Sherif. 1970. "Black Unrest as a Social Movement toward an Emerging Self-Identity." *Journal of Social and Behavioral Sciences* 15(3):41–52.

Smedley, Audrey. 1993. *Race in North America: Origin and Evolution of a Worldview*. Boulder, Colo.: Westview.

Sodowsky, Gargai Roysircar, Kwong-Liem Karl Kwan, and Raji Pannu. 1995. "Ethnic Identity of Asians in the United States." Pp. 123–154 in *Handbook of Multicultural Counseling*, ed. J. G. Ponterotto, J. M. Casas, L. A. Suzuki, and C. M. Alexander. Thousand Oaks, Calif.: Sage.

Sophie, J. 1985–86. "A Critical Examination of Stage Theories of Lesbian Identity Development." *Journal of Homosexuality* 12 (2):39–51.

Spickard, Paul R. 1992. "The Illogic of American Racial Categories." Pp.

12–23 in *Racially Mixed People in America*, ed. M. P. P. Root. Newbury Park, Calif.: Sage.

———. 1997. "What Must I Be? Asian Americans and the Question of Multiethnic Identity." *Amerasia Journal* 23 (1):43–60.

Spickard, Paul, and W. Jeffrey Burroughs. 2000. "We Are a People." Pp. 1–19 in *We Are a People: Narrative and Multiplicity in Constructing Ethnic Identity*, ed. P. Spickard and W. J. Burroughs. Philadelphia: Temple University Press.

Steinberg, Stephen. 1989. *The Ethnic Myth: Race, Ethnicity, and Class in America*. Boston: Beacon Press.

Sue, D. 1990. "Culture-Specific Strategies in Counseling: A Conceptual Framework." *Professional Psychology: Research and Practice* 21:424–433.

Tajfel, Henri. 1972. "Experiments in a Vacuum." In *The Context of Social Psychology: A Critical Assessment*, ed. J. Israel and H. Tajfel. London: Academic Press. Quoted in Dominic Abrams, "Processes of Social Identification." Pp. 57–99 in *Social Psychology of Identity and the Self Concept*, ed. G. M. Breakwell. London: Surrey University Press, 1992.

———, ed. 1978. *Differentiation between Social Groups: Studies in the Social Psychology of Intergroup Relations*. London: Academic Press.

———. 1981. *Human Groups and Social Categories*. Cambridge: Cambridge University Press.

———. 1982. *Social Identity and Intergroup Relations*. Cambridge: Cambridge University Press.

Tajfel, Henri, and John Turner. 1979. "An Integrative Theory of Intergroup Conflict." Pp. 33–47 in *Social Psychology of Intergroup Relations*, ed. W. G. Austin and S. Worchel. Monterey, Calif.: Brooks/Cole.

Takaki, Ronald. 1989. *Strangers from a Different Shore: A History of Asian Americans*. New York: Penguin.

———. 1993. *A Different Mirror: A History of Multicultural America*. Boston: Little, Brown.

Tatum, Beverly Daniel. 1997. "The Complexity of Identity: 'Who Am I?'" In *"Why Are All the Black Kids Sitting Together in the Cafeteria?" And Other Conversations about Race*. New York: Basic Books.

———. 1999. "Lighting Candles in the Dark: One Black Woman's Response to White Antiracist Narratives." Pp. 56–63 in *Becoming and Unbecoming White: Owning and Disowning a Racial Identity*, ed. C. Clark and J. O'Donnell. Westport, Conn.: Bergin and Garvey.

Thomas, Charles W. 1971. *Boys No More: A Black Psychologist's View of Community*. Beverly Hills, Calif.: Glencoe.

Torres, Rodolfo D., and Chor Swang Ngin. 1995. "Racialized Boundaries, Class Relations, and Cultural Politics: The Asian-American and Latino Experience." Pp. 55–69 in *Culture and Difference: Cultural Perspectives on the*

Bicultural Experience in the United States, ed. A. Darder. Westport, Conn.: Bergin and Garvey.

Turner, John C., Penelope J. Oakes, S. Alexander Haslam, and Craig McGarty. 1994. "Self and Collective: Cognition and Social Context." *Personality and Social Psychology Bulletin* 20(5):454–463.

Van den Berghe, Pierre. L. 1967. *Race and Racism: A Comparative Perspective.* New York: Wesley.

Wellman, David. 1977. *Portraits of White Racism.* Cambridge: Cambridge University Press.

Young, Iris Marion. 1990. "Five Faces of Oppression." Pp. 39–65 in *Justice and the Politics of Difference.* Princeton: Princeton University Press.

Chapter 10

Patterns of African American Identity Development

A Life Span Perspective

William E. Cross, Jr., and
Peony Fhagen-Smith

This chapter explores how mainstream and ethnic psychologists analyze Black identity development from a life span perspective, and the extent to which Nigrescence Theory can be repositioned from outside to within the mainstream developmental literature. Nigrescence is a French term that means "to become black," and originally Nigrescence Theory defined the study of adult identity *conversions* in Black Americans. Rather than remain limited to conversion experiences, we argue that, from a life span perspective, Nigrescence can be associated with three growth patterns. *Nigrescence Pattern A* refers to the ways in which a person may develop a Black identity as a consequence of her or his formative socialization experiences, from infancy through late adolescence. Pattern A probably applies to the great majority of Black people, because most reach early adulthood having achieved any one of a variety of Black *identities* (we think Blackness involves a spectrum of identity types, not just one). If Pattern A defines that which is normative, there remain a number of Black people who do not achieve a well-formed Black identity until they have gone through an identity conversion experience, generally as part of their adult development. Blackness achieved through an identity conversion, the original focus of the theory, is called *Nigrescence Pattern B*. Finally, we show that, whether Blackness is achieved through Nigrescence Pattern A (formative socialization) or Pattern B (identity conversion), during different periods of the adult life span Black identity enhancement and modification is achieved through *Nigrescence Pattern C*, or what Thomas Parham (1989) calls *Nigrescence Recycling*. Our work is grounded in the African American experience, although we will use the terms African American and Black interchangeably.

Stretching the Boundaries of Nigrescence Theory

Nigrescence Theory involves the study of Black identity development and change, especially at the adult level. There are well over ten Nigrescence models (see, for example, Cross 1971, 1991; Jackson 1976; Milliones 1973; Gerlack and Hine 1970; Toldson and Pasteur 1975) which constitute competing perceptions on how best to comprehend Black identity conversion experiences. Bailey Jackson and his students at the University of Massachusetts, Amherst, have applied the same type of thinking to a broad range of group experiences (Botkin 1988; Hardiman 1982; Kim 1981; Wijeyesinghe 1992).

In this work the model highlighted is the Cross Nigrescence Model of Adult Identity Conversion (Cross 1991), which has five stages: Stage One, *Pre-Encounter*, outlines the ongoing and stable identity that will eventually be the object of the metamorphosis; Stage Two, *Encounter*, depicts the event or series of events that challenge and destabilize the ongoing identity; Stage Three, *Immersion-Emersion*, frames the simultaneous struggle to bring to the surface and destroy the moorings of the old identity, while decoding the nature and demands of the new identity; and, given that regression or stagnation are avoided, *Internalization*, the Fourth Stage, signals the habituation, stabilization, and finalization of the new sense of self. Stage Five, *Internalization-Commitment*, describes a person who, after having achieved a strong Black identity at the *personal* level, joins with others in the community for long-term struggles to solve Black problems and to research, protect, and propagate Black history and Black culture. It cannot be overemphasized that originally all critical consciousness and conversion models, including the Cross Model, were limited to adult experiences (Cross 1971, 1978; Stokes et al. 1998), and only recently have scholars such as Beverly Tatum and Jean Phinney extended the discourse to cover a younger phase of Black identity development.

The Work of Beverly Tatum

In her recent book entitled *Why Are All the Black Kids Sitting Together in the Cafeteria?* (1997) Beverly Tatum uses Nigrescence Theory to map the evolution of Black identity from childhood through adulthood. Tatum stretches the boundaries of Nigrescence Theory by (1) reconfiguring Pre-Encounter to include developmental trends that cover childhood and preadolescence, and (2) treating as Encounter those critical childhood incidences that cause the young person to realize, for the first time, that something called racism puts a Black person's well- being at risk. Tatum opens her discussion of racial identity development by noting that:

> [At Pre-Encounter], the Black child absorbs many of the beliefs and values of the dominant White culture, including the idea that it is better to be White. The stereotypes, omissions, and distortions that reinforce notions of White superiority are breathed in by Black children as well as [by] White [children]. Simply as a function of being socialized in a Eurocentric culture, some Black children may begin to value the role models, lifestyles, and images of beauty represented by the dominant group more highly than those of their own cultural group. On the other hand, if Black children are raised by what I call race-conscious parents—that is actively seeking to encourage positive racial identity by providing their children with positive cultural images and messages about what it means to be black—the impact of the dominant society's messages are reduced. In either case, in the pre-encounter stage, the personal and social significance of one's racial group membership has not yet been realized, and racial identity is not yet under examination. At age ten [children] seem to be in the pre-encounter stage. When the environmental cues change and the world begins to reflect [one's] blackness back to [her or him] more clearly, [he or she] will probably enter the encounter stage. (Tatum 1997:55)

Tatum is clearly not discussing an adult identity. Rather, her initial emphasis is on the early negative and positive influences that shape a child's nascent ideas and attitudes about Black people and the Black experience. Tatum's objective is to explain how the majority of Black people achieve a Black identity during their formative years, and are not in need of identity conversion at adulthood. Some Black people enter adult life with a fully formed Black identity, and Tatum tries to describe how such Black identities unfold from infancy onward. What is confusing is her decision to use certain stage labels, taken from the Cross Model, without modification. In the original theory, Pre-Encounter meant a fully formed and non-Black-oriented adult identity, and Encounter was equally adult focused. One needs to replace her use of the term Pre-Encounter with *preconscious* or pre-awareness, because, in her Pre-Encounter Stage, "the personal and social significance of one's racial group membership has not yet been realized" (Tatum 1997:55). Pre-Encounter, in Tatum's hands, is not confined to early childhood but stretches forward to preadolescence, just before young people begin to exhibit the cognitive capacity necessary for critical self-reflection. According to Tatum, pubescent Black youth have not begun to actually explore the identity shaped for them by their parents and loved ones. As Tatum states, before age ten racial identity is not yet under examination.

In Tatum's schema, Encounter experiences happen as early as the seventh and eighth grade and are precipitated by an event or series of events that force the young person to acknowledge the personal impact of racism. She continues by noting that: "[With this initial] awareness of the significance of race, the individual begins to grapple with what it means to be a member of a group targeted by racism" (1997:55). Schools provide the context for much of what Tatum has to say, and she describes a long list of school-based racist events that typically act as an encounter.

During the high school years, when self-exploration is predictable, Tatum's analysis shows how the Immersion-Emersion Stage of Nigrescence and the transition phase associated with Erik Erikson's Model of Adolescent Identity Crisis (1968), overlap and are probably indistinguishable. We will have more to say about adolescence shortly, but for the time being we note that Tatum's analysis ends at early adulthood, when most Black people enter adult life with a highly developed and well-integrated sense of Blackness.

The Work of Jean Phinney

The most detailed analysis of Black identity during adolescence has been constructed by Jean Phinney (1989). Rather than view them as separate, Phinney has attempted to show how the racial-ethnic identity struggles of children of color are part and parcel of their overall ego identity development. In effect her work bridges the mainstream and the ethnic identity literature. Phinney's perspective is elegant in its simplicity: Why not view ethnicity and/or racial identity as an extension of ego identity? In this case, ethnic and racial identity development should run parallel to all other key components of ego identity development. Ego identity development generally involves the unfolding of a long list of psychological mechanisms such as, for example, impulse management skills, anger management propensities, delay of gratification mechanisms, the capacity to share and show empathy, and the like, which, for the purpose of discussion, can be labeled factors 1, 2, 3, and 4. One's ethnic or racial status stands to add still another dimension, which we can label factor z. In the case of Black people, for example, ego identity development involves factors 1, 2, 3, 4, + z, where the added dimension (the z factor) represents the Black identity component of ego identity development. Such an analysis offers a holistic picture, allowing one to map the universal ego identity trends in Black people together with the added factor (z), which captures the Black-specific ego identity component. Tracing this added dimension is revealed in Phinney's Ethnic Identity Development Model (EIDM). To better appreciate EIDM (Phinney 1992) we need to first backtrack for a moment, and summarize Erikson's perspective.

According to Erik Erikson (1968), it is during adolescence and early adulthood that the healthy integration of one's general personality and social identity becomes possible. Viewed as statuses (Marcia 1966), Erikson's model shows young people entering adolescence with ideas about themselves and the world around them that are (1) unclear and negative (diffuse ego identity status), or (2) positive, but uncritically accepting of the modeling and teachings of one's parents and significant others (foreclosed ego identity status). It is possible, in Erikson's model, for persons to move forward into adulthood with either a negative (diffuse) or positive but unexamined (foreclosed) ego identity. However, in adults such ego functioning would be associated with general immaturity.

To accomplish ownership of one's self-concept or ego identity, the young person must, according to Erikson, enter a phase of self-reflection and self-exploration that can take on crisis proportions (identity moratorium). Under the best of circumstances, the moratorium phase leads to a state of resolution, greater clarity of one's thinking, and commitment to a well-conceived and reasonably integrated sense of who I am, what I represent, and the goals and aspirations that drive

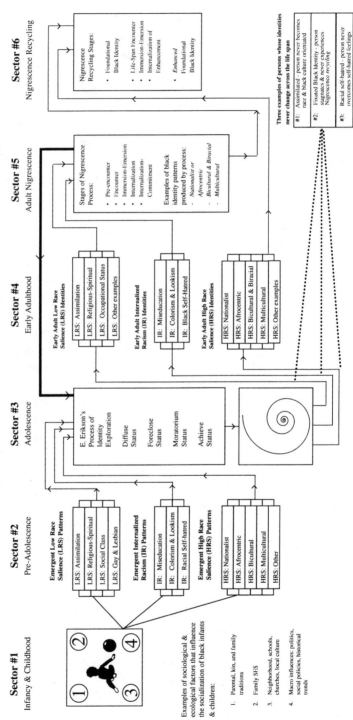

FIGURE 10.1

Descriptive Model of the Relationship between Ego Identity and Nigrescence: A Life Span Perspective

Modified from Cross and Fhagen-Smith 1996.

me. The person is said to have achieved his or her identity and the associated ego identity status is called—achieved identity. With this brief explication of Erikson's Model, let us turn to Phinney's fusion of ego identity and ethnic identity processes.

The Ethnic Identity Development Model authored by Jean Phinney (1989) assumes that the identity development experiences of different ethnic and racial groups parallel the stages of Erikson's Model. According to Phinney, ethnic and racial minorities approach adolescence with poorly developed ethnic identities (diffuse status), or with identities given to them by their parents or caregivers (foreclosed status). They may enter into an identity crisis (moratorium status), during which the challenges and conflicts associated with their minority or ethnic status are scrutinized. Should the person achieve a reasonable degree of resolution and clarity, his or her ethnic identity matures (achieved ethnicity). Phinney (1992) has developed a paper-pencil scale (Multiple Ethnic Identity Measure or MEIM) that can be administered to a broad range of ethnic groups for the purpose of empirically positioning subjects into four categories: Persons who evidence negative ethnic identity (ethnic identity diffusion); persons who evidence a developed but unexamined ethnic identity (ethnic identity foreclosure); persons in the midst of exploring their ethnicity (ethnic identity moratorium); and persons who evidence a great deal of self-criticality, self-reflection, self-acceptance, and resolution of identity conflicts (ethnic identity achieved).

When fused, the works of Tatum and Phinney make possible the mapping of Black identity development from infancy through early adulthood. Both scholars believe they have isolated *normative* trends, which means their combined schema explains how the majority of Black people develop a sense of Blackness. In anticipation of our labeling as *Nigrescence Pattern B* the attainment of a sense of Blackness as an outcome of an *adult* conversion experience, we will label the achievement of Black identity through the formative years of socialization as *Nigrescence Pattern A*.

Cross and Fhagen-Smith Life Span Model of Black Identity Development

Figure 10.1 is a schematic of African American social identity development across six sectors of the life span. It represents a vastly modified version of an earlier schematic (Cross and Fhagen-Smith 1996). It is comprehensive not only because it presents Nigrescence Patterns A (formative racial/cultural identity development across infancy, childhood, preadolescence, and adolescence), Nigrescence Pattern B (Black identity development as a conversion experience), and Nigrescence Pattern C (Black identity expansion, continued growth, or recycling across the life span), but shows as well the identity patterns made somewhat invisible in the developmental frames offered by Tatum and Phinney—the patterns of low race salience and internalized racism.

Sector One: Infancy and Childhood in Early Black Identity Development

While African Americans share to varying degrees a common nominal identity, the extent of their diverse reference group orientations has been shielded from discovery by certain myths and stereotypes. For years, and to a more limited extent today, observers have begun their discourse on Black identity as if the average Black person was psychologically damaged, if not self-hating (Gordon 1976). Part of the problem is that the life circumstances of the most desperate and vulnerable Black people are often used as the basis for generalizations about the birthing, socialization, and identity development of the average Black child. When a more objective and informed approach is considered, it becomes apparent that the human ecologies into which Black children are born show great variability with regard to a wide range of factors (Spencer 1995). Furthermore, the majority of Black ecologies are capable of producing and sustaining positive and healthy human development. As long as Black people receive a living wage or better, and have access to decent housing and schools that make a difference, the level of humanity and accomplishment they are able to effect is extraordinary (Barnes 1972; Cross 1991).

Sector #1 of Figure 10.1 highlights a select but incomplete list of the factors that, in various configurations, define the human ecologies of Black families and their children (Spencer 1995). Beyond biogenetic inclinations, the humanity of each child is shaped and molded by parental influences, kinship interactions, global family traditions and rituals, and the family's socioeconomic status. As the child moves from infancy into childhood and preadolescence, other layers of her or his ecological nest come into play, and her or his vision of the world and self are both etched and shaped by the dynamics and character of the neighborhood, community institutions, local schools, the family's church of choice, and the vitality of the economy. At the macro level, each child's life will also be touched by local and national politics, changing social policies, and historical trends. The myriad of interests, attitudes, feelings, hobbies, academic orientations, musical and artistic leanings, language patterns, and personality traits which eventually find expression in the minds and hearts of Black children, originate in the complex and diverse human ecologies embedded in the Black experience. When one breaks through the stereotypes about Black life and learns to appreciate the inherent diversity found in the human ecologies that suckle, shape, and socialize Black children, the early origins and variability of Black personality, self-concept, and group identity become self-evident. Before racism can take its toll, the dreams and self-trajectories of Black children are likely to be as diverse, whimsical, fanciful, and daring as those found among any group of American children.

One hesitates to suggest that Black children evidence stable group identity or racial preference patterns at early childhood. Scores of racial preference studies have been conducted with very young Black children (Clark and Clark 1947; Powell-Hopson and Hopson 1988; see reviews by Gordon 1976 and Cross 1991). However, there is little evidence that early childhood racial perceptions and feelings predict racial self-concepts at preadolescence or adolescence (Semaj 1980; Alejandro-Wright 1985; Spencer 1982). From our perspective, emergent identity patterns are best discussed in the context of late childhood and preadolescence.

Sector Two: Preadolescence

Whatever is the pattern of each Black child's evolving individuality (hobbies, interests, talents, and the like), we note that Black parents fall into different camps when it comes to the racial and cultural socialization of their children. Tatum (1997) has underscored that some Black parents *avoid* racial discussions because they see race as an inhibiting and negative topic. Others are more neutral, while still others are *race-conscious* in that they inject racial and cultural messages, themes, and activities into many of the child's everyday experiences. To the extent that the parent's frame of reference is complemented and reinforced by the child's experiences outside the home and in interactions with other key members of the family's kinship network, at preadolescence the young person may show signs of an emergent identity that replicates parental socialization objectives (Stevenson 1998).

LOW RACE SALIENCE

Children raised in homes that expose them to numerous experiences that stress something other than race and Black culture, are likely to show signs of an evolving self-concept that accords *minimal* significance to the fact of one's Blackness, other than in a nominal sense. That is, other than being physically Black, they accord no significance to their race—it is simply an irrelevant demographic fact. Instead of race and Black culture, the young person's emergent identity may turn on assimilationist themes, or a religious-spiritual code, or materialism and social status. Another variant might be an identity that revolves around a unique talent or competence in mathematics or the sciences, music, sports, or computer technology. In some instances, the entire notion of a group identity is rejected, and the emphasis is on one's individuality. These *Emergent Low Race Salience (LRS) Patterns* are depicted at the top of Sector #2.

HIGH RACE SALIENCE

Following a different drummer, race-conscious parents strive for a home environment and broader human ecology that steers the young person toward the building of a self-concept that gives high salience to race and Black culture. Race-conscious parents do not share the same vision of the correct or appropriate Black identity as those with low race salience. As the cluster at the bottom of Sector #2 shows, *Emergent High Race Salience (HRS) Patterns* may be either Black Nationalist or Afrocentrically focused (race as a central feature of the self-concept); biculturally framed (a self-concept that gives equal salience to one's Americanness and Blackness); or multiculturally oriented (race as one of three or four cultural anchors in one's self-concept).

The low and high race salience categories apply to all Black children, including those who are Biracial or Multiracial, as well as Black children adopted by White or mixed-race families. It is obvious that the familial contexts of such children are inherently more racially and culturally complicated than those of Black children born and raised by two Black parents. However, the identity choices are essentially the same as for any developing Black human being: Should I play down race (low race salience); should I deny part of my heritage and stress only the Black (Nationalism) or White (Eurocentrism) side; should I, as a Biracial child, embrace an openly Bicultural perspective that affirms the culture of both my parents; or should I, as a Multiracial offspring, go beyond Monoracialism and even Biculturality, to seek psychological comfort in a Multicultural frame of reference?

INTERNALIZED RACISM

Lastly, preadolescence may show the early signs of a youthful but damaged self-concept that reflects in part the internalized racism (Hardiman and Jackson 1997) found among the belief systems of their parents or significant others. In the middle of Sector #2 are the *Emergent Internalized Racism (IR) Patterns*. This cluster shows multiple expressions of internalized racism: miseducation; colorism and lookism; and self and group hatred (racial self-hatred). As a result of information picked up from inaccurate school texts, television news coverage that overreport Black crime, and historically distorted presentations at museums, and the like, it is fairly easy for *many* Black children to begin to accept as fact information about Black people that is both negative and misleading (miseducation). In other instances, society's glamorization of European physical features combined with familial preferences for certain types of physical features, can lead to the emergence of colorism and lookism (Russell, Wilson, and Hall 1992). Learning to place positive or negative value on the color of one's skin (colorism), or feeling either uncomfortable or overly proud about the shape of one's lips, buttocks, or one's hair texture—all examples of lookism—can steer a Black child toward a very vulnerable self-concept. In circumstances such as deeply troubled home environments and the larger society's open discussion of Black inferiority (for example, *The Bell Curve*), thoughts of personal self-loathing may emerge in some Black children (racial self-hatred).

Keep in mind that pubescent self-concepts and identity structures are emergent or premature, in the sense that a young girl or boy has neither the experience, cognitive skills, or capacity for self-reflection associated with adult identity operations. In the best of circumstances, the maximal development point most youth reach is the attainment of identity dynamics that have been shaped by parents and significant others. In the worse case scenario, one's emergent identity may be riddled with confusion, alienation, negativity, and lack of coherence. All the emergent identities found in Black youth require further development, and that is why *all* the identity options noted in Sector #2 are connected by lines to Sector #3—the developmental period known as adolescence.

Sector Three: Adolescence

Black children bring a wide range of identity issues to adolescence, and our discussion will highlight three identity categories: high race salience, low race salience, and internalized racism. We begin with the high salience cluster. Many Black youth move into adolescence with a positive, confused, or negative but unexplored Black identity (e.g., unexplored as in foreclosed identity status), and then enter the period of identity growth known as moratorium, during which they strive to take ownership of their self-concepts. This is depicted in Figure 10.1 by the line that connects the *Emergent High Race Salience Identity Patterns* in Sector #2, with the Eriksonian Stages of adolescence in Sector #3. If at preadolescence one is likely to take for granted the ideas, values, beliefs, and worldview which one's parents and significant others used to construct the boundaries and dynamics of one's emergent self-concepts, during the moratorium phase of adolescence every facet of the person's emergent identity is subjected to intense examination, testing, comparison, and cycles of acceptance-rejection. This tumultuous testing and sorting period allows a young person to hold up for examination the ideas about race and Black culture which she or he wants to accept or reject. In moving from an emergent or foreclosed identity status that has been shaped and constructed by others to the affirmation of a self-concept based on ideas and attributes that have been authenticated, an *achieved identity status* is accomplished.

Both Phinney and Tatum note that when the foci at adolescence are issues of race and culture, the dynamics of moratorium are very similar to those of Nigrescence, or the stages of Black identity change, something once thought to be solely an adult identity experience. The foreclosed, moratorium, and achieved identity statuses may parallel the Pre-Encounter, Immersion-Emersion, and Internalization Stages of Nigrescence. The difference is that in the adult Nigrescence experience, the person enters the Nigrescence cycle with a fully formed, nonrace-oriented identity that requires *conversion* to become focused on race and Black culture. However at adolescence, the majority of Black youth walk into moratorium with an emergent identity that is *already* Black-focused. Their struggle is not so much to be, or not to be, Black, but one of *authentication:* Of the Black ideas, values, and beliefs given to me by my parents and mentors, which shall I authenticate and make a permanent part of my self-concept?

There is one circumstance in which the dynamics of adolescent and adult Nigrescence are identical. Should the Black adolescent enter moratorium with an assimilated or color-blind emergent identity (for example, up to this point the parents and significant others have raised the child to play down race and Black culture), and then move to replace this stance with one that is more focused on race and Black culture, such a turnaround is very close to the type of identity conversion generally associated with adult Nigrescence. The same might also be true of a youth who enters adolescence having already experienced a great deal of self-hatred, and during moratorium chances upon a more positive construction and conversion of his or her racial self. As a way of representing the parallels between Nigrescence as authentication and conversion during adolescence, and Nigrescence as identity conversion during adulthood, Figure 10.1 has a bold line that starts at Sector #5 (Adult Nigrescence) and runs *back* to Sector #3 (adolescence). This shows that while identity conversion is more common among Black adults, under the circumstances just described Black youth could experience conversion toward Blackness as early as adolescence (Parham 1989).

Having shown the connection between emergent high race salient preadolescent identity structures and the dynamics of adolescence, we now make note of the fractional but significant number who are socialized into, and come to accept, various types of low race salient identities. For them, a wide range of social anchors take the place of race and Black culture. The most obvious examples are conservative youth and Black adults who operate with a self-concept that accords little significance to race and Black culture. These are not self-hating persons. Rather they are people who, though nominally Black, operate with a self-concept built upon an assimilationist-American base, a hunger for individualism, and a keenly class-oriented consciousness. In other instances, one's gay or lesbian identity, or spiritual-religious, or humanist philosophy may have greater weight than issues of race and Black culture. Recall that such identity tendencies are noted in

Sector #2 as *Emergent Low Race Salience Patterns.* Black youth who enter adolescence with such nonrace-centered self-concepts will also experience moratorium, but rather than race and Black culture *it will center on whatever nonrace issue is at the core of their emergent identity.* This connection between low race salience identity trends and the Eriksonian stages of ego identity development is reflected in the line that connects the low race salience cluster in Sector #2 with the adolescent stages in Sector #3. If the adolescent discovers he or she is gay or lesbian, the moratorium phase may be host to the struggle to take ownership of his or her sexual orientation; if the focus is on assimilation, then the focus will be on sorting through the issues of extreme versus moderate conservatism; and should the youth have a profound talent in mathematics, the sciences, or a unique sport such as fencing or world-class swimming or figure skating, his or her life will be energized by these identity building blocks instead of race and Black culture.

The final identity cluster shown in the middle of Sector #2 (Preadolescence), and connected by a line to Sector #3 (Adolescence), are the *Internalized Racism Patterns.* If a Black youth's exposure to historical and cultural distortions about Black people is not effectively refuted in and out of the classroom, the risk is high that by late adolescence such miseducation will influence, to varying degrees, her or his overall impression of Black people as a group. Likewise, if experiences with colorism have been personalized, the person may use colorism and lookism to judge her or himself, other Black people, or both. In the worst case scenario, children with emergent negative identities at preadolescence may leave adolescence with perceptions of self-hatred that are coherent and deeply ingrained in the young adult's self-concept. We do not mean to suggest that self-hatred becomes a form of achieved identity, but in a morbid sense adolescence makes it possible for the young girl or boy to become more aware and self-reflective about their negativity.

In summary, each of the identity clusters depicted as emergent trends at preadolescence (Sector #2) are subject to more elaborate development during adolescence (Sector #3). This is why all the types of identity patterns listed in Sector #2 have lines that connect to the adolescent experience or Sector #3. If things proceed in a somewhat linear fashion, persons who enter adolescence with a low salience type of identity will leave adolescence having achieved and habituated a more elaborate version of that low salience identity. This is true of the other types of identities as well. But life is seldom linear and the *spiral figure* at the base of Sector #3 is meant to indicate that the identity focus a Black youth brings to adolescence may change so that she or he exits adolescence with a *different* kind of identity focus than might have been predicted.

For example, a young boy may begin adolescence with a Black-centered self-concept, but in gaining full awareness that he is gay may shift his attention to his gay status and away from Blackness issues. In another case, a young Black girl who has been raised in a low race salience home environment may be befriended by a Black teacher who turns the young girl toward Black history and Black literature to the point that, at the end of her moratorium phase, she has developed a reference group orientation keenly focused on race and Black culture. In a reverse trend, a Black-focused preadolescent finds himself under attack for being too White in his speech and study habits; in reaction, he begins to question the entire emphasis on race and joins a Republican Youth Group. By the time he has found answers to his questions about race and society, he enters early adulthood with a strong and intelligently constructed Conservative ideology. And, as a last example, the child of a Biracial couple has been pressed by her Black father to identify as Black, while her mother stresses a color-blind perspective. Her solution might be a Multicultural identity or she might become confused, anxious, defensive, and somewhat negative and mildly self-hating.

In summary, adolescence finds many Black youth developing in a fairly linear fashion, whereby they enter and exit adolescence with the same identity content or focus. On the other hand, other Black adolescents may change the focus of their prepubescent identities, exiting adolescence with a substantially reworked self-concept. *The spiral at the bottom of Sector #3 represents the nonlinear or profound change potential of one's adolescent years.*

Sectors Four and Five: Early Adulthood and Adult Nigrescence

If the socialization, maturation, and ecological dynamics that unfold during infancy, childhood, preadolescence, and adolescence define the formative process of human development, then the wide range of reference group orientations found among young Black adults are the developmental outcomes of this process. Along with other key psychological characteristics such as one's developed intellect, anger and general emotion management, interpersonal competencies, and capacity for delay of gratification, reference group perspective takes on a *foundational* character. These factors undergird the *psychological platform* upon which will be transacted certain adult challenges, tasks, and opportunities encountered in the worlds of work; postsecondary educational settings; intimate and long-standing relationships; marriage and family interactions; property and personal effects acquisitions and management; voting, personal politics, and community service, and so on. The current discussion is limited to but one factor, the development of racial and cultural identity. However, in a more expanded analysis, we might want to trace the general personality development of different Black people in order to better understand why some Black people are shy, reserved, hesitant, and soft spoken, while others are gregarious, aggressive, outspoken, and easily distracted.

Sector #4 shows the three major clusters of Black identity types to be found among a large sample of young Black adults. Each cluster reticulates at least three or more exemplars. It is only fitting that we begin with an analysis of the early adult, high race salience identities as statistically speaking these are commonplace. By the time they reach early adulthood, the great majority of Black people have constructed a reference group orientation in which race and Black culture play a modest to highly significant role. In addition to being statistically or what we have been calling nominally Black, they are *existentially* Black in that the meaning they find in themselves and the world around them is charged with racial and Black cultural issues, perceptions, and actions. There is not one type of Black identity and we have been trying to capture its variability by making the distinction between Black Nationalists, Afrocentrists, Biculturalists, and Multiculturalists.

It stands to reason that if a young Black adult acquired a sense of Blackness as a result of his or her formative experiences from infancy through adolescence, such a person will *not* be in need of a Nigrescence conversion experience to become what he or she already is—Black-focused. Consequently, as depicted in Sector #4, there is *no* line connecting *High Race Salience* with *Adult Nigrescence* in Sector #5. Any change or modification the person may experience in his or her Black identity is likely to result from Nigrescence Recycling (Sector #6), which will be discussed shortly. There is one exception. Recall that during adolescence a person may never seriously examine his or her emergent identity. Such a person will move to early adulthood with an unexamined reference group orientation (foreclosed ego identity status), and will be in need of an adult experience that can take the place of her or his missed moratorium cycle. Let us apply this thinking to the special case of an unexamined Black identity.

Imagine a Black adolescent whom we shall name Nikka. Let us suppose that Nikka entered adolescence with an emergent bicultural identity that had strong Nationalistic themes. Her emergent identity has the potential for expansion and internalization at adulthood, and Nikka has a very positive relationship with her parents. Nikka's adolescence was essentially productive and positive; however, she never really subjected her racial and cultural ideas to critical examination. Consequently, when she reaches early adulthood, she embraces a Black identity, but having bypassed moratorium her ideas and actions reflect a foreclosed identity status.

Nikka attends Cornell University and immediately takes classes at the Africana Studies and Research Center. During that first year, she seems to go through an emotional and tumultuous identity self-examination. As she flowers, her ideas become more differentiated from those of her parents and significant others, and she affirms a more Afrocentric orientation. Her Nigrescence experience takes the place of her *skipped* moratorium cycle, and at the end she exhibits greater self-authentication. In this instance, Nigrescence did not help her to become Black for the first time; rather, it allowed her to take self-ownership of her self-concept.

The point to be made is that young Black adults who embrace a Black-oriented identity may be in need of Nigrescence to complete the identity work that is generally experienced during the formative experience. Otherwise, African Americans whose formative experience shapes a Black-oriented identity will not be in need of a Nigrescence conversion experience at early adulthood, save for identity growth, which will be handled by Nigrescence Recycling (see discussion of Sector #6).

Now let us shift attention to the second most important identity cluster found among Black adults—the low race salience cluster. A growing number of young Black adults are beginning to espouse various reference group orientations that accord little significance to race and Black culture. Their formative experiences helped them construct a vision of the world, themselves, and others with categories, processes, and a sense of history in which race and Black culture played a nonessential role. Their lives are rich, textured, vital, dynamic, and full of nuance. Thus it cannot be said that they are without an identity. On the contrary, they help to show that, with or without an emphasis on race, Black people have been ingenious in their discovery of multiple pathways to personal happiness and success.

Why, then, if such persons are living a fulfilling life, does a line connect the low race salience cluster with adult Nigrescence in Sector #5? Does not the connection suggest an inherent inadequacy or latent negativity about the low salience identities? Such persons are prime targets for Nigrescence because, should they encounter a racial cultural incident, experience, or episode which exhausts the explanatory powers of their extant, nonrace-oriented frame of reference, they might go through Nigrescence as a means of radically changing their frame of reference. As long as low race salience persons are able to find an ecological niche that supports and sustains their identities, Nigrescence will not be triggered. However, the very nature of the low race salience identity puts them at *risk* of Nigrescence because, in the face of an Encounter which requires an explanatory system that does give salience to race and Black culture, such persons essentially have no answers. The *Encounter* forces them to come to terms with the limitations of their Pre-Encounter identity, and they may slide, head first, into an identity metamorphosis. At the end of their resocialization, they will have a new or greatly modified foundational-adult, reference group orientation that is focused on race and Black culture.

The Nigrescence Process will not result in one type of Blackness. Rather, the Internalization Stage finds people fanning out into any one of the following identity pathways, each of which gives from moderate to high salience to race and Black culture: Black Nationalist, Afrocentrist, Biculturalist, or Multiculturalist. Finding Blackness through a conversion experience defines *Nigrescence Pattern B*, as contrasted with Nigrescence Pattern A, where persons achieve a sense of Black identity as a result of formative socialization processes across infancy, childhood, and adolescence. Either pattern produces the same developmental outcomes: forms of reference group orientations that give high salience to race and Black culture.

The last cluster found in Sector #4 is labeled *Early Adult Internalized Racism*. The three levels of internalized racism— miseducation, colorism and lookism, and self-hatred—have different frequencies of occurrence in young adult populations. Racism in the schools, the press, and the popular media is not as rampant as it once was. But it is more than possible for even the majority of Black adults to suffer from various degrees of miseducation about Black people as a group. The images Black people have about the Black lower class is particularly subject to miseducation. Colorism and lookism are not as prevalent as miseducation, but there are countless young Black adults who experience discomfort about their African physical features or the lightness or darkness of their skin, even though they have fairly positive attitudes about Black people as a group. An unknown but likely small percentage of Black human beings reach early adulthood with self-concepts that are damaged at both the general personality and reference group orientation levels of the self. They experience self-loathing and self-hatred, and they connect this to the fact that they are Black, which means they suffer from racial self-hatred.

Not surprisingly, Figure 10.1 shows a line that runs from the internalized racism cluster in Sector #4 to adult Nigrescence in Sector #5. This indicates that a possible corrective for internalized racism, at any level, is a Nigrescence conversion experience. The ameliorative effects of conversion on internalized racism will be discussed shortly.

BLACK PEOPLE WHO NEVER EXPERIENCE CHANGE

Not all persons who function with low salience identities, and/or suffer from internalized racism, are destined for a Nigrescence episode. In the case of those who hold low salience identities, they may find experiences, rituals, friends, networks, and both formal and informal associations that help them affirm and sustain their color-blind ideas and beliefs. Especially in the late twentieth century and beginning of the twenty-first, it is conceivable that a Black person can move through the formative years with a conservative identity at adolescence, emerge from the self-criticality of moratorium with an achieved sense of conservatism, remain steadfastly conservative through the early adult and midlife cycles, and settle into lasting conservatism at maturity and late adulthood.

Although we use conservatism in our example, that could be replaced by any number of low race salience identity frames as well. In fact, a section of Figure 10.1 offers schematic representation of *unchanged identities*. The reader's attention is guided to the *bottom* of Sectors #3 and #4. Note that just below the change symbol (spiral figure) are solid lines that connect to the three identity categories (low race salience, high race salience, and internalized racism). Note, as well, that there are *dotted lines* that run off to the right and connect with three examples of *unchanged* reference group orientations.

This part of the schema highlights the fact that some people never experience any major changes in their social outlook from early adulthood onward. Three examples are noted: (1) an assimilated Black person who never becomes more focused on race and Black culture throughout his or her life; (2) a person with a fixated Black identity, whose ideas about Blackness stagnate and are never refreshed or revitalized; and last, (3) the self-hating Black person whose damaged psyche never finds a corrective. There are countless Black people who stay the same over time and space, and this side bar represents such permanence or rigidity.

NIGRESCENCE AS IDENTITY CONVERSION

Sector #5 incorporates the Nigrescence Conversion Process itself. The first stage, *Pre-Encounter*, defines the types of identity patterns and key racial and cultural attitudes that might be serviced by conversion, and in this essay, we have stressed low race salience and internalized racism patterns. These *Pre-Encounter* identities may be disrupted by an *Encounter* that challenges the person to rethink her or his attitudes, feelings, and behavior concerning race and Black culture. The *Immersion-Emersion* Stage signals the struggle between the current and aspired to orientation. Should the metamorphosis unravel without too much negativity and disappointment, the person reaches a point where the new perspective is achieved and internalized (*Internalization*). Furthermore, should the person commit her or himself to the struggle for long-term change, *Internalization-Commitment* is achieved. Such persons will have become resocialized and their new identity patterns will now match the reference group orientations (Black Nationalist, Afrocentrist, Bicultural, and Multicultural) that most Black people achieve through their formative socialization (Nigrescence Pattern A).

Blackness achieved through *conversion* represents *Nigrescence Pattern B*. Nigrescence conversion can replace miseducation with a more balanced, accurate, and positive interpretation of the Black experience, release persons from the grip of colorism and lookism, and provide relief to persons suffering from self-hatred (Cross 1991; Helms 1990; Thompson and Carter 1997). We hesitate to suggest that a conversion experience can in and of itself cure self-hatred. However, it is conceivable that a conversion experience can help a person better understand what must be done (for example, psychotherapy, group support networks, and so on) to effectuate change in one's deep structure self-hatred. The consciousness raising that parallels the conversion experience constitutes one of the most profound developmental experiences a Black person can traverse beyond the traditional developmental period (infancy through adolescence). None other than the likes of W. E. B. Du Bois, Malcolm X, Gwendolyn Brooks, and Angela Davis, to mention but a few, have been touched by the process. The Nigrescence conversion experience may not be normative, but it is commonplace and is of historical significance (Cross 1989).

Sector Six: Nigrescence Recycling

In approaching Sector #6 of Figure 10.1—the sector dealing with *Nigrescence Recycling*—one comes face to face with the final question relevant to our developmental scheme: How does a Black individual achieve additional growth and refinement of her or his Black identity across the remainder of the adult life span? Or, stated in a slightly different fashion, how does one depict future or continued growth of Black identity beyond the formative or conversion processes? In addressing such questions we can more fully attend to a third pattern, which has been referenced in so far only a fleeting fashion.

Thomas Parham (1989) noticed that well-grounded Black people will, from time to time, go in and out of Nigrescence Stages. This recycling, as he calls it, is typically triggered by a negative or positive racial and cultural experience that partially challenges aspects of one's preexisting Black identity. Not having an answer or explanation to the triggering event or experience, the person engages the issue and processes it through to resolution. The new insight is absorbed and added to the person's preexisting Black identity. The developmental outcome is not a new identity, as happens with conversion, but a modified or enhanced extant identity. Over the course of one's life span, a person may be presented with any number of such challenges, encounters, new questions, and unanticipated insights which, if he or she is able to resolve and internalize, can lead to a state of *wisdom* about what it means to be Black. Such persons come to understand that one's Black frame of reference, at age twenty five, is not able to address, without modification, the issues, circumstances, and life events that surface at ages thirty five, forty five, and so on. It is not age per se that is the focus, but the changing phases, content, dynamics, and challenges of adult life. Being Black, single, and just out of college is different from being thirty five, married with two children, and in the middle phases of a career path. Divorce, illness, addiction, the death of one's parents or close friends, being discriminated against and fired from an attractive job, or being harassed by the police, are negative examples that can *trigger* recycling. On a more positive note, building a life with a spouse or loved one, watching and helping one's daughters and sons develop, successfully overcoming a major midlife crisis, participating in the creation and building of a new Black organization, are proactive experiences that can stimulate recycling.

In explicating what he means by recycling, Parham employs all of the stages of the original Nigrescence Model: Pre-Encounter, Encounter, Immersion-Emersion, and Internalization (for the sake of discussion, Internalization-Commitment will not be referenced). However, incorporating the Pre-Encounter Stage in an identity enhancement model is confusing, because it suggests that the person must first revert to a low salience or negative identity before he or she can progress through the stages, as a way of achieving some sense of resolution for the issues that triggered the recycling in the first place. In order to fit Parham's insights into the current developmental scheme, we have decided to modify Parham's stages.

Parham's Recycling Stages	*Modified* Recycling Stages
1. Pre-Encounter	1. Foundational Black Identity
2. Encounter	2. Life Span Encounter
3. Immersion-Emersion	3. Immersion-Emersion (unchanged)
4. Internalization	4. Internalization of Enhancement
5. (implicit change)	5. Enhanced Foundational Black Identity

Recall that one's foundational identity, or, more accurately, one's foundational Black identity, is defined as the Black reference group orientation that can be achieved through one's formative socialization experiences (Nigrescence Pattern A) or through an adult identity conversion (Nigrescence Pattern B). Regardless of whether it is achieved through Nigrescence Pattern A or B, the developmental product is an adult identity that will provide the psychological foundation upon which various adult tasks, challenges, and societal expectations will be carried out. A person with an adult, foundational, reference group orientation characterized by high race salience can in no fashion be subsumed under the category Pre-Encounter, because Pre-Encounter types are either low in race salience and/or are self-hating. Nigrescence Recycling begins with a person who is already Black-focused and ends when that person's original sense of Blackness is *enhanced*. Consequently, we suggest that the starting point of recycling is the Black adult's extant or foundational Black identity.

The recycling is triggered by an Encounter, but to distinguish between the earthshaking racial epiphany associated with a conversion experience, as well as to better capture the more limited focus of the recycling stimulus, we suggest that Encounter be changed to *Life Span Encounter*. This better communicates that the recycling encounter does not challenge the entirety of one's foundational identity, as is the case with Encounter during conversion. Instead, it is the discovery of a new question, issue, or challenge that goes beyond, but is essentially a potential extension of, one's current frame of reference.

Immersion-Emersion is an appropriate label for the transition stage, during which the person works through the life span encounter, and we suggest that the label remain unchanged. However, to more effectively capture the limited focus of the internalization phase of recycling, we suggest that Internalization be changed *to Internalization of Enhancement*. Last, Parham's conceptualization implicitly suggests that recycling results in a changed identity. In our modification we make this change more explicit by suggesting that the developmental outcome of recycling is an *Enhanced Foundational Black Identity*.

In each instance of recycling, the person begins with her or his foundational identity and if recycling is reasonably successful, enhancement is achieved. As new layers are added to the foundation, the person moves closer and closer to a state of wisdom about the complexity, relativity, depth, and multidimensionally of what it means to live a Black life. Keep in mind that we are not referring to one type of Black identity. We have stressed that being Black can mean one is a Black Nationalist, Afrocentrist, Biculturalist, or Multiculturalist. In each configuration, recycling can result in the enhancement of the type of Black identity the person brings to the recycling experience.

With these comments in mind, and making reference to Sector #6, we have modified Parham's model. From our vantage point, Nigrescence Recycling begins with an adult *Foundational Black Identity*, and in response to a *Life Span Encounter*, a person discovers a minor or major gap in his or her thinking about Blackness. Should the person take the encounter seriously, a state of *Immersion-Emersion* is entered as a way to resolve the challenges posed by the life span encounter. Following the transition phase, *Internalization of the Enhancement* becomes evident. Finally, the overall developmental outcome is an *Enhanced Foundational Black Identity*. This recycling and enhancement holds true for whatever the Black identity type (Nationalist, Afrocentrist, Biculturalist, Multiculturalist) the person brings to the recycling experience. Consequently, whether a person has achieved a Black identity through *Nigrescence Pattern A* (identity development through the formative socialization process during infancy, childhood, preadolescence, and adolescence) or *Nigrescence Pattern B* (Black identity development achieved through identity conversion), he or she will likely be subject to continued growth through *Nigrescence Pattern C* (Parham's concept of Nigrescence Recycling).

Summary

This concludes the explication of our life span model and a summary is surely in order. We have presented a descriptive model of identity development that fuses an Eriksonian or ego identity frame of reference with an understanding of the different patterns of Nigrescence. We have made occasional reference to both the general personality and reference group orientation components of the self-concept. However, for the most part our intent has been to trace the origin, evolution, and life span changes associated with the various race and nonrace-related reference group orientations found among Black people.

We began by noting the wide range of human ecologies into which Black children are born (Sector #1), and we linked early variation in Black identity development with the infinite range of social attitudes to which children are exposed through their parents, kinship network, school teachers, neighbors, and so on. We suggested that children are immersed in human ecologies that differ in the definition and significance to be accorded to race in everyday life: (1) Home environments and child-rearing strategies that suggest that race is simply a nominal category that carries very little meaning; (2) home environments and child-rearing practices that weave race and Black culture into many parent-child interactions; (3) home environments, community experiences, and parental strategies that communicate themes of racial self-hatred and within-group loathing. Growth and socialization within these ecologies can produce latent or emergent identity proclivities at preadolescence (Sector #2). Pubescent identity patterns often lack coherence, flexibility, and integration; nevertheless, we think partial signs of low or high race salience as well as early signs of self-hatred can be readily detected at preadolescence.

Our interpretation of adolescence (Sector #3) shows the great majority of Black youth examining and struggling with issues of race and Black culture. But we carefully pointed out that not every Black adolescent will use race and Black culture as primary or even secondary building blocks in the construction of her or his self-image (Sector #3). We explained that Black adolescent identity development may follow a linear as well as nonlinear course. In linear growth, the identity trajectory with which the Black youth enters adolescence predicts the type of identity patterns that emerges after adolescence. On the other hand, during adolescence some Black youth will go through an intrapsychic war, exiting with a self-image that is hardly an extension of one's pubescent sense of self. To explore this nonlinear pattern, we gave the examples of a Black youth who, in the context of adolescence, switches from a low to high race salience self-image, or vice versa. Recall that such nonlinear trends were captured by the *spiral symbol* at the base of Sector #3.

Upon leaving adolescence, young Black adults enter adult life with a spectrum of reference group orientations that tend to form three identity clusters (Sector #4). One of these focuses on practically anything but race (low salience identities); another gives high salience to race and Black culture (high race salience); and a third can entail miseducation, colorism, and racial self-hatred (internalized racism). Young Black adults whose formative experiences have resulted in a strong Black identity will not be in need of a Nigrescence Conversion experience. On the other hand, we showed how persons operating with a low race salience identity, and/or suffering from some form of internalized racism are at risk of a Nigrescence conversion experience (Sector #5). The conversion acts to resocialize the person from low to high race salience, from miseducation to better informed, and from self-hating to self-accepting. We noted that although conversions cannot heal self-hatred they can position a person to better understand what interventions are necessary to effect one's deep structure problems and racial self-loathing.

Whether a person's adult foundational Black identity is shaped and then achieved through the formative socialization process (Nigrescence Pattern A) or an identity conversion experience (Nigrescence Pattern B), both can be enhanced by successfully working through the questions and challenges that intrude at different points across the life span. Black identity enhancement is accomplished through the stages of Nigrescence Recycling, or Nigrescence Pattern C. In addition to our extended discussion of Nigrescence Recycling, we also made brief mention of the fact that some Black people become fixated at early adulthood, and never experience identity modification at any point across the adult phases of their life span.

Overall, we have tried to construct a life span perspective that (a) gives repeated recognition to Black identity variability, which has been overlooked in the past in the search for a single type of Black identity; (b) reveals both linear as well as nonlinear Black identity growth patterns across the life span; (c) presents low race salience identity patterns as nonpathological; and (d) shows internalized racism to be multidimensional.

REFERENCES

Alejandro-Wright, Marguerite. 1985. "The Child's Conception of Racial Classification: A Social Cognitive Developmental Model." Pp. 185–200 in Beginnings: The Social and Affective Development of Black Children, ed. M. B. Spencer, G. K. Brookins, and W. R. Allen. Hillsdale, N.J.: Lawrence Erlbaum.

Barnes, Edward J. 1972. "The Black Community as a Source of Positive Self-Concept for Black Children: A Theoretical Perspective." Pp. 166–192 in Black Psychology, ed. R. Jones. New York: Harper and Row.

Botkin, Steven D. 1988. "Male Gender Consciousness: A Study of Undergraduate College Men." Doctoral dissertation, University of Massachusetts, Amherst.

Clark, Kenneth, and Mamie Clark. 1947. "Racial Identification and Preference in Negro Children." Pp. 169–178 in Readings in Social Psychology, ed. T. M. Newcomb and E. L. Hartley. New York: Holt.

Cross, William E., Jr. 1971. "Negro-to-Black Conversion Experience." *Black World* 20:13–27.

———. 1978. "The Thomas and Cross Models of Psychological Nigrescence." *Journal of Black Psychology* 4(1): 13–31.

———. 1989. "Nigrescence: A Nondiaphanous Phenomenon." *Counseling Psychologist* 17(2):273–276.

———. 1991. *Shades of Black*. Philadelphia: Temple University Press.

Cross, William E., Jr., and Peony Fhagen-Smith. 1996. "Nigrescence and Ego-Identity Development." Pp. 108–123 in *Counseling across Cultures*, eds. P. Pedersen, J. Draguns, W. Lonner, and J. Trimble. Thousand Oaks, Calif.: Sage.

Erikson, Erik. 1968. *Identity: Youth, and Crisis*. New York: W. W. Norton.

Gerlack, Luther P., and Virginia Hine. 1970. *People, Power, and Change*. Indianapolis: Bobbs-Merrill.

Gordon, Vivian V. 1976. *The Self-Concept of Black Americans*. Washington, D.C.: University Press of America.

Hardiman, Rita. 1982. "White Identity Development: A Process Oriented Model for Describing the Racial Consciousness of White Americans." Doctoral dissertation, University of Massachusetts, Amherst.

Hardiman, Rita, and Bailey W. Jackson. 1997. "Conceptual Foundations for Social Justice Courses." Pp. 16–29 in *Teaching for Diversity and Social Justice*, eds. M. Adams, L. Bell, and P. Griffin. New York: Routledge.

Helms, Janet E. 1990. *Black and White Racial Identity Development*. Westport, Conn.: Greenwood Press.

Jackson, Bailey. 1976. "Black Identity Development." Pp. 158–164 in *Urban and Social Education Issues*, eds. L. Golubschick and B. Persky. Dubuque, Iowa: Kendall/Hunt.

Kim, Jean. 1981. "Processes in Asian American Identity Development." Doctoral dissertation, University of Massachusetts, Amherst.

Marcia, James E. 1966. "Development and Validation of Ego Identity Status." *Journal of Personality and Social Psychology* 3:551–558.

Milliones, Jake. 1973. "Construction of a Developmental Inventory of Black Consciousness." Doctoral dissertation, University of Pittsburgh.

Parham, Thomas A. 1989. "Cycles of Nigrescence." *Counseling Psychologist* 17(2):187–226.

Phinney, Jean. 1989. "Stages of Ethnic Identity Development in Minority Group Children." *Journal of Early Adolescence*, 9(1–2): 34–49.

———. 1992. "The Multiethnic Identity Measure." *Journal of Adolescence Research* 7(2):156–176.

Powell-Hopson, Darlene, and David S. Hopson. 1988. "Implications of Doll Color Preferences among Black Preschool Children and White Preschool Children." *Journal of Black Psychology* 14(2):57–63.

Russell, Kathy, Midge Wilson, and Ronald Hall. 1992. *The Color Complex: The Politics of Skin Color among African Americans.* New York: Harcourt, Brace and Jovanovich.

Semaj, Leakcim. 1980. "The Development of Racial Evaluation and Preference: A Cognitive Approach." *Journal of Black Psychology* 6(2):59–79.

Spencer, Margaret B. 1982. "Personal and Group Identity of Black Children: An Alternate Synthesis." *Genetic Monographs* 106:59–84.

———. 1995. "Old and New Theorizing about African American Youth: A Phenomenological Variant of Ecological Systems Theory." Pp. 37–69 in *African American Youth*, ed. R. Taylor. Westport, Conn.: Praeger.

Stevenson, Howard. 1998. "Theoretical Considerations in Measuring Racial Identity and Socialization." Pp. 217–254 in *African American Identity Development*, ed. R. Jones. Hampton, Va.: Cobb and Henry.

Stokes, Julie E., Carolyn B. Murray, David Chavez, and M. Jean Peacock. 1998. "Cross' Stage Model Revisited." Pp. 121–139, 171–181 in *African American Identity Development*, ed. R. Jones. Hampton, Va.: Cobb and Henry.

Tatum, Beverly. 1987. *Assimilation Blues.* Northampton, Mass.: Hazel-Maxwell.

———. 1997. *Why Are All the Black Kids Sitting Together in the Cafeteria?* New York: Basic Books.

Thompson, Chalmer E., and Robert T. Carter. 1997. *Racial Identity Theory: Applications to Individuals, Group, and Organizational Interventions.* Mahwah, N.J.: Lawrence Erlbaum.

Toldson, Ivory L., and Alfred B. Pasteur. 1975. "Developmental Stages of Black Self-Discovery." *Journal of Negro Education* 44:130–138.

Wijeyesinghe, Charmaine. 1992. "Towards an Understanding of the Racial Identity of Bi-Racial People: The Experience of Racial Self-Identification of African-American/Euro-American Adults and the Factors Affecting Their Choices of Racial Identity." Doctoral dissertation, University of Massachusetts, Amherst.

Contributors

Maurianne Adams, Ph.D., is Chair of the Social Justice Education Program in the School of Education, University of Massachusetts, Amherst. She teaches graduate classes on social identity development and multicultural adult development, and has written on various applications of social identity models in her *Teaching for Diversity and Social Justice: A Sourcebook* (Routledge, 1997) and *Promoting Diversity in the College Classroom* (Jossey-Bass, 1992). Most recently she has coedited *Strangers and Neighbors: Relations Between Blacks and Jews in the United States* (University of Massachusetts Press, 2000).

Suraiya Baluch works as a counselor at Barnard College Counseling Services. She also serves as a clinical supervisor for the Columbia University/Barnard College Rape Crisis/Anti-Violence Support Center. She is currently completing her doctorate in counseling psychology at Fordham University.

William E. Cross, Jr., Ph.D., is Professor in the Social Personality Program, Department of Psychology, City University of New York.

Bernardo M. Ferdman, Ph.D. (Yale, 1987), professor at the California School of Professional Psychology, consults to organizations and writes on diversity, inclusion, and Latino issues.

Peony Fhagen-Smith is a doctoral student in Developmental Psychology at Pennsylvania State University, University Park, Pa.

Plácida I. Gallegos, Ph.D. (U.C. Riverside, 1987), Vice President of The Kaleel Jamison Consulting Group and of Southwest Communication Resources, specializes in multicultural organizational development.

Rita Hardiman, Ed.D., is Vice President of New Perspectives, Inc., a training and consulting firm specializing in social diversity and social justice in organizations. She is also an adjunct faculty member in the Social Justice Education Program at the University of Massachusetts, Amherst. A pioneer in antiracism training and White racial identity development, Dr. Hardiman created one of the first models of White racial identity development in the country.

Perry G. Horse, Ph.D., is an enrolled member of the Kiowa Tribe of Oklahoma and is an alumnus of Haskell Institute, Lawrence, Kans., Harvard University, and the University of Arizona, Tucson. He currently resides in Albuquerque, New Mexico, and works as a consultant to foundations and nonprofit organizations in the fields of higher education, economic development, and organizational capacity-building.

Bailey W. Jackson III, Ed.D., is Dean of the School of Education, University of Massachusetts, Amherst. He is the founder of the school's graduate program in Social Justice Education. Dr. Jackson is the author of one of the earliest theories of Black identity development. He is also known for his work on racial and other social identity development issues in individuals and groups. In addition, Dr. Jackson is a primary architect of multicultural organization development theory and practice.

Jean Kim, Ed.D., a native of Seoul, Korea, developed her understanding of cultural diversity firsthand when she immigrated to the United States at the age of twelve. She received undergraduate and advanced degrees from the University of Massachusetts, Amherst, and had a successful twenty-five-year career in higher education administration at five universities. In addition to her work as a university administrator, Dr. Kim is a sought-after speaker and consults for a number of Fortune 500 corporations, providing leadership programs and consulting in organization development.

Amy L. Reynolds, Ph.D., is a Senior Psychologist at the Counseling Center at Buffalo State College. Previously she was a faculty member at Fordham University. Her research interests and publications emphasize multicultural counseling, training, and supervision; lesbian, gay, and bisexual issues; and feminist psychology.

Janet Rifkin, J.D., is Chair and Professor in the Legal Studies Department at the University of Massachusetts, Amherst. She was the founder of the University Mediation project, the first university-based program in the United States. She served as the University Ombudsperson for a number of years and was the cofounder of the National Association of Mediation in Education. She has published a number of articles about issues of mediation and conflict resolution, including examinations of gender, neutrality, and professionalization of practice. In addition, she has taught a number of courses on these and related topics.

Charmaine L. Wijeyesinghe, Ed.D., is a consultant and trainer who writes and lectures on Multiracial identity and the application of racial identity theory in various fields. Her professional background includes positions in higher education administration at the University of Massachusetts, Amherst, and Dean of Students at Mount Holyoke College. She was National Program Consultant for the National Conference of Community and Justice, based in New York City.

Leah Wing, M.Ed., has been a professional mediation trainer and social justice educator since 1983. She has worked with a wide variety of educational institutions and organizations, specializing in issues of racial identity and conflict. She teaches courses on diversity, conflict resolution, and education at the graduate and undergraduate levels and regularly consults with school districts on diversity and mediation program development. Ms. Wing is the Director of the Campus Mediation and Negotiation Team at the University of Massachusetts, Amherst.

Index

Abrams, Dominic, 223, 224, 233n. 10
acculturation: and American Indians, 96–98; and Latino identity, 224; and research, 159
Adams, Maurianne, 6, 209–242, 271
adolescence: and Asian American identity, 73–76; and Black identity, 246–247, 254–257, 267
African American identity development, 243–270; and Black Identity Development (BID) model, 26–27
African Americans, 8–31, 243–270; definition of, 14–15. *See also* Black, definition of
Afrocentricity, 27, 252, 258, 260
American Indians, 4–5, 91–107; and acculturation, 96–98; consciousness of, 96, 100–102; and culture, 92–95, 103; and ethnicity, 105n. 5; and European colonialism, 91; and language, 92–94, 103, 105n. 2; and Latino identity, 44–45; and music, 105–106n. 6; and racial identity research, 158–159; and racism, 104; and religion, 105n. 4; and tribal sovereignty, 102, 106n. 8
appearance: and Asian Americans, 70, 82; and Latinos, 38–40, 43–44; and Multiracial identity, 140–141, 146–147. *See also* colorism; lookism
applications: of Factor Model of Multiracial Identity, 143–145; of Latino and Latina Racial Identity Orientations, 56; of racial identity development theory, 5–6, 158–159, 163–172, 182–208
Asian American Identity Development (AAID) model, 4, 13–14, 67–90
Asian Americans, 4, 67–90; and civil rights movement, 79; and counseling, 170; and ethnicity, 158–159, 212–213,

217, 221; and immigration, 75, 84; and internalized racism, 70, 217; and political consciousness, 76–78; and racial identity research, 159; and racism, 67, 69; and Whites, 73–78
assessment: of ethnic identity, 249; of racial identity, 116, 158, 164, 165; and Racial Identity Development Theory (RIDT), 190; in supervisory relationships, 169
assimilation: and Asian Americans, 73; and Latinos, 58n. 5, 58n. 6; and Nigrescence, 255
assumptions, 1, 71–72, 131, 184
Atkinson, Donald R., 156, 227–228

Baluch, Suraiya, 5, 153–181, 271
Bennett, Sandra, 156
bicultural identity of Latinos, 46–47, 224
bilingualism, 93–94
Biracial identity, 133–137. *See also* Multiracial identity
Black, definition of, 14–15
Black children: and colorism, 253–254; and identity development, 18–19, 245–247, 250, 251, 266–267; and race salience, 252, 253
Black identity development, 8–31, 243–270; and adolescence, 246–247, 254–257, 267; context of, 213; and William E. Cross, Jr., 218–220, 243–270; diversity in, 258; and Bailey W. Jackson III, 8–31, 214–217; and Multiracial identity, 132; and race salience, 259–260; theory of, 9–14, 215
Black Identity Development (BID) model, 4, 8–31, 214–217
Black identity types, 258, 260, 262, 265

275